SCRIPTURE WITHIN SCRIPTURE

SOCIETY
OF BIBLICAL
LITERATURE

DISSERTATION SERIES

David L. Petersen, Old Testament Editor
Pheme Perkins, New Testament Editor

Number 133

SCRIPTURE WITHIN SCRIPTURE
The Interrelationship of Form and Function
in the Explicit Old Testament Citations in the Gospel of John
by
Bruce G. Schuchard

Bruce G. Schuchard

SCRIPTURE WITHIN SCRIPTURE
The Interrelationship of Form and Function in the Explicit Old Testament Citations in the Gospel of John

Scholars Press
Atlanta, Georgia

SCRIPTURE WITHIN SCRIPTURE
The Interrelationship of Form and Function
in the Explicit Old Testament Citations
in the Gospel of John

Bruce G. Schuchard

Ph.D., 1991   Advisors:
Union Seminary   Mathias Rissi

© 1992
The Society of Biblical Literature
Library of Congress Cataloging in Publication Data

Schuchard, Bruce G. (Bruce Gordon)
    Scripture within scripture : the interrelationship of form and
function in the explicit Old Testament citations in the Gospel of
John / Bruce G. Schuchard.
        p. cm. — (Dissertation series / Society of Biblical
Literature ; no. 133)
        Includes bibliographical references.
        ISBN 1-55540-711-0 (alk. paper). — ISBN 1-55540-712-9 (pbk.)
        1. Bible. N.T. John—Relation to the Old Testament. 2. Bible.
N.T. John—Criticism, interpretation, etc.   I. Title   II. Series:
Dissertation series (Society of Biblical Literature) ; no. 133.
BS2615.2.S35   1992
226.5'06—dc20   92-32117
                                                              CIP
Printed in the United States of America
on acid-free paper

Contents

Acknowledgments

A dissertation can only be written with the support and guidance of many. I would like to take this opportunity to acknowledge the following to whom I owe a debt of gratitude:

Professor Mathias Rissi, my advisor, who graciously consented to carry on in this capacity even after his retirement, whose cordial advocacy and whose scholarship have been an ever-present source of inspiration;

Professors Paul J. Achtemeier and Jack Dean Kingsbury, the other two members of my doctoral committee, who each offered numerous additional suggestions and encouraged me in my work;

The library staff of Union Theological Seminary in Richmond, Virginia, especially Mrs. B. D. Aycock, who assisted me in my research and in its form;

My family, friends, and colleagues, individuals too numerous to identify, but whose encouragement has been instrumental;

And last but not least, a recent blessing in my life, my wife Sheryl, whose love even now informs and inspires.

Abbreviations

OG	Old Greek
HTR	*Harvard Theological Review*
IIMO	Interuniversitair Instituut voor Missiologie en Oecumencia
Int	*Interpretation*
JBL	*Journal of Biblical Literature*
JETS	*Journal of the Evangelical Theological Society*
JSNT	*Journal for the Study of the New Testament*
JTS	*Journal of Theological Studies*
JTSA	*Journal of Theology for Southern Africa*
LS	*Louvain Studies*
LSJ	Liddell-Scott-Jones, *Greek-English Lexicon*
LTP	*Laval Théologique et Philosophique*
LTR	*Lutheran Theological Review*
LXX	Septuagint
MT	Masoretic Text
Neot	*Neotestamentica*
NovT	*Novum Testamentum*
NTS	*New Testament Studies*
RAT	*Revue Africaine de Théologie*
RB	*Revue biblique*
RelSRev	*Religious Studies Review*
RSR	*Recherches de science religieuse*
RTL	*Revue théologique de Louvain*
Sciences Eccl	*Sciences ecclésiastiques*
Scr	*Scripture*
SEÅ	*Svensk exegetisk årsbok*
SJT	*Scottish Journal of Theology*
SMR	*Studia Montis Regii*
ST	*Studia theologica*
StudNT Umwelt	*Studien zum Neuen Testament und seiner Umwelt*
SWJourn Theol	*Southwestern Journal of Theology*
TD	*Theology Digest*
TDNT	G. Kittel and G. Friedrich (eds.), *Theological Dictionary of the New Testament*
TZ	*Theologische Zeitschrift*
TynBul	*Tyndale Bulletin*
TZ	*Theologische Zeitschrift*
VC	*Vigiliae christianae*
ZAW	*Zeitschrift für die alttestamentliche Wissenschaft*
ZNW	*Zeitschrift für die neutestamentliche Wissenschaft*
ZST	*Zeitschrift für die systematische Theologie*

Introduction

In recent years, scholarship has exhibited great interest in the use of Scripture within Scripture. Scholars have studied (1) the use of earlier segments of the Old Testament within later segments, (2) the use of the Old Testament within the many works of the New Testament, and (3) the use of earlier New Testament passages or traditions within the New Testament. A collection of essays prepared in honor of Barnabas Lindars by Carson and Williamson provides the latest overview of many of these studies.[1] These studies both complement and are informed by the related work of those who have attempted to describe (1) the ensuing history of the Christian use of the Old Testament, (2) how the present-day church is to use and understand the Old Testament, and (3) the theological relationship between the Testaments. None of these concerns, however, constitute the primary focus of the present investigation. Instead, the goal of this investigation is to undertake the more manageable task of examining the use of the Old Testament in the Gospel of John.

For over a century, scholars have rightly recognized that John's Gospel stands apart from the other Gospels (1) in the Old Testament material it utilizes

---

[1] See Don A. Carson and H. G. M. Williamson, eds., *It is Written: Scripture Citing Scripture. Essays in Honour of Barnabas Lindars* (Cambridge: Cambridge University Press, 1988). A similar presentation of these preliminary observations appears in the introductory essay by I. Howard Marshall, "An assessment of recent developments" (pp. 1-21), who then addresses some of the more general problems which surface in the study of the use of Scripture within Scripture. The essays which follow Marshall's fail to examine the use of earlier NT passages or traditions within the NT, but do include an examination of the use of the OT in the so-called intertestamental literature.

and (2) in the manner in which it cites Old Testament passages.[2] Until relatively recently, however, few scholars have attempted to address this twofold problem in any depth, and frequently such attempts have tended only to facilitate other agendas.[3] For example, early in this century Faure maintained that one could infer from John's use of quotation formulas the existence and extent of the written sources he utilized in the creation of his Gospel.[4] Closer to the concerns of the present investigation, however, was the watershed contribution of C. H. Dodd.[5] Dodd argued that John, together with the other authors of the New Testament, (1) understood the earliest kerygma of the church in the light of the Old Testament, (2) held specific "textual fields" in the Old Testament to be of particular theological significance for his kerygma, (3) recognized in these "fields" the existence of shared themes, and therefore (4) adopted and elaborated on material derived from them, all the while with a certain respect for the original context.[6] Besides Dodd, other scholars who have contributed significantly to a better understanding of the use of the Old Testament in the Fourth Gospel include Hoskyns,[7] Barrett,[8] Braun,[9] Schnackenburg,[10] and Brown.[11]

---

[2] See, e.g., Crawford H. Toy, *Quotations in the New Testament* (New York: Scribners, 1884), xxxv.

[3] Contrast the following description of scholars' efforts with that of Don A. Carson, "John and the Johannine Epistles," in *It is Written: Scripture Citing Scripture. Essays in Honour of Barnabas Lindars*, eds. D. A. Carson and H. G. M. Williamson (Cambridge: Cambridge University Press, 1988), 245.

[4] See Alexander Faure, "Die alttestamentlichen Zitate im 4. Evangelium und die Quellenscheidungshypothese," *ZNW* 21 (1922): 99-121. Faure was opposed by F. Smend, "Die Behandlung alttestamentlicher Zitate als Ausgangspunkt der Quellenscheidung im 4. Evangelium," *ZNW* 24 (1925): 147-50.

[5] See Charles H. Dodd, *According to the Scriptures: The Substructure of New Testament Theology* (London: Nisbet, 1952).

[6] Dodd was opposed by A. C. Sundberg, "On Testimonies," *NovT* 3 (1959): 268-81.

[7] See Edwyn C. Hoskyns, *The Fourth Gospel*, 2d ed., ed. F. N. Davey (London: Faber and Faber, 1947).

[8] See esp. Charles K. Barrett, "The Old Testament in the Fourth Gospel," *JTS* 48 (1947): 155-69.

[9] See François-Marie Braun, *Jean le théologien*, tome 2, *Les grandes traditions d'Israel et l'accord des Ecritures, selon le Quatrième Évangile*, Études bibliques (Paris: Gabalda, 1964).

[10] See Rudolf Schnackenburg, *The Gospel according to St. John*, vol. 1, *Introduction and Commentary on Chapters 1-4*, trans. K. Smith (Freiburg: Herder, 1968; reprint, New York: Crossroad, 1982), vol. 2, *Commentary on Chapters 5-12*, trans. C. Hastings, F. McDonagh, D. Smith, and R. Foley (New York: Search Press, 1979; reprint, New York: Crossroad, 1987), vol. 3, *Commentary on Chapters 13-21*, trans. D. Smith and G. A. Kon (New York: Search Press, 1982; reprint New York: Crossroad, 1987); *Das Johannesevangelium*, 4. Teil, *Ergänzende Auslegungen und Exkurse*, Herders theologischer Kommentar zum Neuen Testament, Bd. 4 (Freiburg: Herder, 1984).

[11] See Raymond E. Brown, *The Gospel according to John*, vol. 1, (i-xii): *Introduction,*

While these scholars have all insisted that the Old Testament plays a key role in Johannine thought, there are others who have contended that the importance of the Old Testament in Johannine thought is minimal at best. One such scholar is Rudolf Bultmann.[12] For Bultmann, John derived the essential character of his Gospel not from the Old Testament, but from the conceptual world of gnosticism.

To grasp the situation today concerning John's use of the Old Testament, one cannot ignore the discovery of the literature of Qumran. The discovery of this literature has sparked a virtual explosion of interest not only concerning the relationship of John's Gospel to the Old Testament and Judaism but also concerning the more general issue of the hermeneutics of first-century Judaism. In addition, useful surveys have become available of the latest efforts of scholars to characterize the use John made of the Old Testament.[13] Apparent in these surveys are a variety of approaches to John's Gospel. The present investigation will address one of these approaches. Specifically, the chief goal of this investigation will be to characterize in detail the interrelationship of form and function in the explicit Old Testament citations in the Gospel of John. This is, of course, only one aspect of the overall utilization of the Old Testament in John's Gospel. Why undertake this particular task? Because previous attempts to characterize the form of John's citations have tended to overlook the issue of their function in his Gospel. Also, a careful investigation of pericopes in which John's Gospel expressly claims that it is reproducing discrete Old Testament texts (which are themselves relatively easy to identify) permits one to discern concretely exactly how John has in fact made use of Old Testament materials.

One problem associated with this investigation is that several of John's citations possess a seemingly periphrastic character. One can debate, then, how many explicit Old Testament citations are to be found in John's Gospel. It is the contention of this investigation that there are thirteen explicit Old Testament citations in John's Gospel, each of which is identified by means of a formula (1.23; 2.17; 6.31 and 45; 10.34; 12.14-15, 38, and 40; 13.18; 15.25; 19.24, 36, and 37). Excluded from this reckoning are John 7.38 and 42, 17.12, and 19.28.

Translation, and Notes, 2d ed., Anchor Bible, vol. 29 (Garden City, N.Y.: Doubleday, 1985), vol. 2, (*xiii-xxi*): *Introduction, Translation, and Notes*, Anchor Bible, vol. 29A (Garden City, N.Y.: Doubleday, 1970).

12 See Rudolf Bultmann, *The Gospel of John: A Commentary*, trans. G. R. Beasley-Murray, ed. R. W. N. Hoare and J. K. Riches, with an Introduction by W. Schmithals (Philadelphia: Westminster, 1971).

13 See esp. Carson, "John;" cf. Robert Kysar, "The Fourth Gospel. A Report on Recent Research," in *Aufstieg und Niedergang der römischen Welt: Geschichte und Kultur Roms im Spiegel der neueren Forschung*, 2. Principat, Bd. 25/3, hg. Wolfgang Haase (New York: de Gruyter, 1984), 2416-21.

The reason for excluding these passages is that although in each instance a formula plainly directs the reader's attention to the Old Testament, no discrete Old Testament passage is actually cited. Similarly excluded is John 12.13. This passage represents not a reference to the Old Testament *per se*, but simply a rendering of a popular Jewish festal greeting derived from Ps 118(117).[14]

Many scholars have attempted to characterize the form of the Old Testament citations in John's Gospel. Works of importance in this regard are those of Braun[15], Freed,[16] and Reim.[17] These works are typical of the ongoing debate over the form of John's citations. At the heart of this debate has been the attempt to establish which specific Old Testament textual tradition(s) influenced these citations (Hebrew, Greek, a particular textual recension, or some other source). But these attempts have consistently generated conflicting results.

In the last few years, however, it is especially a collection of essays authored by M. J. J. Menken which has successfully identified the principal flaw in scholars' earlier works.[18] Menken's contention is that scholars have failed to reckon adequately with John's citations as products of his editorial activity and therefore as reflecting his authorial intent. In other words, in their efforts to characterize the form of a citation, scholars have not normally asked whether John deviates intentionally from a particular textual tradition in order to adapt a citation to its eventual literary and theological context. Instead, a variety of unsatisfactory alternatives have been considered. For example, some scholars have sought to explain the form of John's citations in terms of his reliance on purely hypothetical versions of Old Testament passages.[19] Others have acknowledged that John indeed deviates from the textual tradition(s) he cites, but have preferred to describe such deviations as symptoms of John's defective memory.[20]

---

[14] This explains why John 12.13 has no introductory formula.

[15] See Braun, *Jean 2*, 3-21.

[16] See Edwin D. Freed, *Old Testament Quotations in the Gospel of John*, Supplements to Novum Testamentum, vol. 11 (Leiden: E. J. Brill, 1965).

[17] See Günter Reim, *Studien zum alttestamentlichen Hintergrund des Johannesevangeliums*, Society for New Testament Studies Monograph Series, vol. 22 (New York: Cambridge University Press, 1974), 1-96.

[18] See M. J. J. Menken, "The Quotation from Isa 40,3 in John 1,23," *Bib* 66 (1985): 190-205; "Die Form des Zitates aus Jes 6,10 in Joh 12,40," *BZ* 32 (1988): 189-209; "The Old Testament Quotation in John 6,45: Source and Redaction," *ETL* 64 (1988): 164-72; "The Provenance and Meaning of the Old Testament Quotation in John 6.31," *NovT* 30 (1988): 39-56; "Die Redaktion des Zitates aus Sach 9,9 in Joh 12,15," *ZNW* 25 (1989): 193-209; "The Translation of Psalm 41.10 in John 13.18," *JSNT* 40 (1990): 61-79.

[19] See, e.g., Georg Richter, "Die alttestamentlichen Zitate in der Rede vom Himmelsbrot Joh 6,26-51a," in *Schriftauslegung: Beiträge zur Hermeneutik des Neuen Testamentes und im Neuen Testament*, hg. Josef Ernst (München: F. Schöningh, 1972), 193-279.

[20] See, e.g., Bent Noack, *Zur johanneischen Tradition: Beiträge zur Kritik an der Literarkriti-*

But for Menken, all hypotheses of this sort overlook the most compelling solution. Recent studies of Jewish exegetical procedure around the beginning of the Christian era have shown that deviations in biblical citations and in the transmission of the biblical text are frequently the result of the conscious application of established exegetical techniques.[21] For Menken, then, John's citations are best explained in terms of his purposeful editing of extant versions of Old Testament passages. Evident in John's editorial activity is an exegetical procedure already well-established in first-century Judaism.[22]

My own efforts to characterize the citations in John's Gospel began with a premise similar to Menken's (at a time when I was still unaware of his work). Since that time, my own efforts have been significantly influenced by his. My indebtedness to Menken is especially evident in the methodological scheme I have adopted.

My investigation of each citation begins with a brief introduction to the citation in which the following matters are considered: (1) the Johannine context containing the citation; (2) the existence of parallel pericopes or parallel treatments of similar subjects in the New Testament and elsewhere; (3) the existence of parallel references to the same Old Testament passage (or of references to John's citation elsewhere); and (4) the introductory formula. Following this brief introduction is a detailed preliminary investigation of the form of the citation. This preliminary investigation considers these matters: (1) The Old Testament

---

schen Analyse des vierten Evangeliums, Teologiske Skrifter, Bd. 3 (Copenhagen: Rosenkilde og Bagger, 1954), 71-89; Charles Goodwin, "How Did John Treat His Sources?" *JBL* 73 (1954): 61-75.

21 Of chief importance among these techniques, argues Menken, is the Jewish practice of connecting analogous passages from Scripture. Two passages are "analogous" if they share at least a word or phrase, but very often such passages also share a measure of their contents as well. A portion of one passage, then, could be used as a substitute for a portion of the other, or could be appended to it. The employment of such a technique in Qumran exegesis has been established by George J. Brooke, *Exegesis at Qumran: 4QFlorilegium in Its Jewish Context*, Journal for the Study of the Old Testament Supplement Series, vol. 29 (Sheffield: JSOT Press, 1985), 166 (4QFlor), 294 (1QM 10.1-8), 297-298 (1QS 2.2-4), 306-8 (CD 7.15-19), 319 (4QTest 9-20). Its exploitation in the rendering of texts in Isa OG and in 1QIsaᵃ has been demonstrated by Jean Koenig, *L'Herméneutique analogique du Judaïsme antique d'après les témoins textuels d'Isaïe*, Supplements to Vetus Testamentum, vol. 33 (Leiden: E. J. Brill, 1982), 1-103 (Isa OG), 199-291 (1QIsaᵃ). Its use is also evident elsewhere, e.g., in Philo's *De Agricultura* and in his *De Sacrificiis* 1-10 (Brooke, pp. 22-24). It is a prevalent technique in rabbinic exegesis and is known as גזירה שוה.

22 For an extensive treatment of these procedures both in ancient Judaism and in early Christianity, see Martin Jan Mulder, ed., *Mikra: Text, Translation, Reading and Interpretation of the Hebrew Bible in Ancient Judaism and Early Christianity*, Compendia Rerum Iudaicarum ad Novum Testamentum, section 2, The Literature of the Jewish People in the Period of the Second Temple and the Talmud, vol. 1 (Philadelphia: Fortress, 1988).

passage cited; (2) the form of the citation compared with the form of the Old Testament passage in the extant textual traditions (Hebrew, Greek, the textual recensions, perhaps some other source); (3) the various hypotheses of scholars concerning the textual tradition(s) represented in the form of the citation; and (4) the hypothesis which, at this stage (i.e., without examining the function of this citation in John's Gospel), appears to have the greatest merit. My investigation of each citation concludes with a detailed investigation of the interrelationship of form and function in the citation. Describing the form of the citation as a reflection of the role that John as editor would have this citation play in the context in which he places it, I offer some final remarks concerning where and why John deviates from the textual tradition he cites.

My own investigation of John's citations parallels that of Menken. This notwithstanding, there are conspicuous and significant ways in which Menken's investigation differs from mine. The most obvious difference between us is that Menken discusses only half of the explicit citations of the Old Testament which appear in John's Gospel. But even when we both discuss the same citations, we sometimes arrive at different conclusions. We sometimes differ in defining John's intent. We differ also in defining the textual tradition(s) represented in John's citations.

I should add finally that, in suggesting that John has purposefully edited the Old Testament passages he cites, I do not intend to offer an entirely negative appraisal of the latest proposal by Achtemeier.[23] Achtemeier argues convincingly that the New Testament was produced in "a culture of high residual orality" (i.e., New Testament documents were "oral to the core, both in their creation and in their performance").[24] For this reason, and because passages in written documents were not easily accessible, "authors did not 'check references' in the way modern scholars do (or ought to do!)."[25] Instead, citations were "much more likely to be quoted from memory than to be copied from a source."[26]

My own investigation does not take issue with Achtemeier's observations. It does, however, take issue with what he subsequently infers. According to Achtemeier, because the authors of the New Testament normally cited from memory, questioning whether an author cited from a specific textual tradition or from a text not known to us or whether he offered his own rendering of an Old Testament passage "will tend to be an exercise in futility."[27] In the case of John,

---

[23] Paul J. Achtemeier, "*Omne verbum sonat*: The New Testament and the Oral Environment of Late Western Antiquity," *JBL* 109 (1990): 3-27.

[24] Achtemeier, "Oral Environment," 3, 19.

[25] Achtemeier, "Oral Environment," 27.

[26] Achtemeier, "Oral Environment," 27.

[27] Achtemeier, "Oral Environment," 27.

my own investigation will show that, even if John cited from memory, his citations do, in fact, represent precise and therefore perceptible recollections of a specific textual tradition. Indeed, there is in John's citations tangible evidence for the use of one and only one textual tradition, the OG.[28]

---

[28] Johannine scholars, of course, have heretofore preferred the use of the term "LXX." L. Greenspoon, "The Use and Abuse of the Term 'LXX' and Related Terminology in Recent Scholarship," *BIOSCS* 20 (1987); 21-29, however, identifies six different possible referents for the term "LXX" in antiquity: (1) the earliest Greek rendering of the Pentateuch; (2) the earliest Greek rendering of the entire OT; (3) Origen's Koine; (4) Origen's completed fifth column; (5) any authoritative Greek text; and (6) the entire Greek tradition (on the history of the transmission of the Septuagint, see esp. Emanuel Tov, "The Septuagint," in *Mikra: Text, Translation, Reading and Interpretation of the Hebrew Bible in Ancient Judaism and Early Christianity*, ed. Martin Jan Mulder, Compendia Rerum Iudaicarum ad Novum Testamentum, section 2, The Literature of the Jewish People in the Period of the Second Temple and the Talmud, vol. 1 [Philadelphia: Fortress, 1988], 161-88; see also Raymond E. Brown, D. W. Johnson, and Kevin G. O'Connell, "Texts and Versions," in *The New Jerome Biblical Commentary*, eds. Raymond E. Brown, Joseph A. Fitzmyer, and Roland E. Murphy, with a Foreword by Carlo Maria Cardinal Martini [Englewood Cliffs, N.J.: Prentice Hall, 1990], 1091-96). Thus, the term "LXX" "denotes both the first Greek translation of the Bible and the collection of Jewish-Greek Scripture, containing *inter alia* this translation. The latter usage is imprecise because this collection contains also late revisions of the original translation and books that were originally written in Greek" (Tov, p. 161). In order to differentiate, then, between these two usages, many scholars now prefer to reserve the term "LXX" for the entire collection of Jewish-Greek Scripture and refer to the first Greek translation of the Bible as the OG (unless otherwise indicated, references in this investigation to the OG presume either the text of *Septuaginta: Vetus Testamentum graece auctoritate Societatis Gottingensis editum* [Göttingen: Vandenhoeck & Ruprecht, 1931-] or, for those books not to be found in this edition, Alfred Rahlfs, ed., *Septuaginta: Id est Vetus Testamentum graece iuxta LXX interpretes*, 2 vols. in 1 [Stuttgart: Deutsche Bibelgesellschaft, 1979]).

Chapter 1

THE TESTIMONY OF
THE BAPTIST

Each of the Synoptics share with John's Gospel a similar specific reference to the Old Testament in their individual attempts to portray the significance of John the Baptist (cf. Matt 3.3; Mark 1.3; Luke 3.4; John 1.23). All agree that the Baptist is "the voice of one crying in the wilderness." But John's citation of this Old Testament passage, like his overall portrait of the figure of the Baptist, bears numerous features indicative of a treatment of Christian tradition thoroughly independent of the Synoptics.[1] For example, in each of the Synoptics it is always the Gospel writer who editorially refers to the Baptist as this "voice." But in John's Gospel, it is the character of the Baptist himself who, in response to the queries of a delegation from Jerusalem and its desire to know who it is that he claims to be (1.19-22), applies to himself a text from the prophet Isaiah:

ἐγὼ φωνὴ βοῶντος ἐν τῇ ἐρήμῳ·
εὐθύνατε τὴν ὁδὸν κυρίου (1.23).

John's "introductory" formula is also distinctive. First of all, John's formula appears after rather than before the citation to which it refers.[2] And second, in

---

[1] On these and related issues, see esp. the lengthy discussion by Charles H. Dodd, *Historical Tradition in the Fourth Gospel* (Cambridge: Cambridge University Press, 1963), 248-301 (see also pp. 31-46).

[2] Indeed, in the NT only Rom 2.24 offers a similar occurrence.

terms of its form, John's formula (καθὼς εἶπεν 'Ησαΐας ὁ προφήτης) is the only one of its kind in the New Testament.[3]

John's citation also appears quite independent of the extra-biblical material. That the passage John cites was the object of eschatological speculation among the Jews is now especially clear in view of the texts from the desert community of Qumran (see 1QS 8.14; cf. 9.20). John's understanding of the passage he cites, however, differs significantly from that of the residents of Qumran.[4] For John, the desert represents the preordained locus for the Baptist's eschatological summons. Those at Qumran, on the other hand, understand the desert as a place of escape and isolation from those in Jerusalem who have erred. It is a place where they are to clear the way of God through the study and observance of the Torah. The perspective at Qumran is also a decidedly eschatological one. However, unlike the Baptist this community prepares itself for holy war.[5]

John's citation, therefore, appears entirely unique and innovative. What follows will attempt to illustrate further this singularity and will attempt to determine the extent to which this can be explained on the basis of (1) extant textual traditions, and (2) the distinctive theological orientation of John.

I.

The passage John cites is Isa 40.3. But scholars have been unable to establish whether John refers to a Hebrew version of Isa 40.3, to the OG, or to some other source. This lack of unanimity can be attributed to two complicating factors: (1) In place of the two parallel lines Isa 40.3bc which occur both in the MT and in the OG, John 1.23 has only one line; and (2) while Isa 40.3b OG renders the Hebrew פנו (=MT) with ἑτοιμάσατε ("prepare") and Isa 40.3c translates the Hebrew ישרו (=MT) with εὐθείας ποιεῖτε ("make straight"), εὐθύνατε ("make straight") appears in John 1.23.

This contrasting state of affairs has prompted a number of hypotheses. Some scholars have considered the possibility that John's citation reflects the influence of a Hebrew *Vorlage*. John, therefore, either (1) translates פנו with εὐθύνατε,[6] or

---

[3] Cf., however, the somewhat similar forms in 7.38 and Rom 2.24.

[4] See esp. Schnackenburg, *St. John* 1, 291; cf. Neil S. Fujita, *A Crack in the Jar: What Ancient Jewish Documents Tell Us About the New Testament* (New York: Paulist, 1986), 118-19; J. de Waard, *A Comparative Study of the Old Testament in the Dead Sea Scrolls and in the New Testament*, Studies on the Texts of the Desert of Judah, vol. 4 (Leiden: E. J. Brill, 1965), 48-53.

[5] Cf. 1QM 1.2-3 and CD 1.15. The OT passage John cites is also interpreted in terms of messianic expectations in the rabbinic literature (see Str-B 1:96-97). Cf. *Barn.* 9.3.

[6] Cf. Krister Stendahl, *The School of St. Matthew and Its Use of the Old Testament* (Copenhagen, 1954; reprint, Philadelphia: Fortress, 1968), 52; Charles K. Barrett, *The Gospel*

(2) substitutes ישרו from the following line for פנו and offers as a translation εὐθύνατε.[7] Others, however, have pointed to the possible influence of the OG. It is argued that εὐθείας ποιεῖτε in Isa 40.3c OG triggered for John the substitution of ἑτοιμάσατε with εὐθύνατε and the condensation of the two parallel lines Isa 40.3bc into one line.[8] Finally, whether dependant upon a Hebrew or Greek *Vorlage*, it is frequently assumed that John inadvertently deviates from the Old Testament passage he recalls because he quotes from memory.[9]

Of these possibilities, the case for John's dependence upon the OG carries great weight. The following are the chief arguments for this position.

Our first (and perhaps most telling) piece of evidence begins with the observation that the OG offers an adequate translation of the Hebrew of the MT. John 1.23, with the exception of εὐθύνατε, reproduces Isa 40.3ab OG word for word. While on the surface this may not seem to be an informative detail favoring John's dependence upon the OG, it becomes one as soon as the significance of the Johannine *hapax legomenon* βοῶντος is considered. Normally, John uses the terms κράζω (1.15; 7.28, 37; 12.44) or κραυγάζω (11.43; 12.13; 18.40; 19.6, 12, 15) in order to convey the idea of "crying" or "shouting." If John were rendering of the Hebrew קורא, one would expect him to render this with either κράζω (cf. its use in the Psalms) or κραυγάζω. The *hapax* βοῶντος suggests instead John's dependence upon the OG.[10]

Another point not often discussed involves recognizing that, while the OG represents an "adequate" rendering of the Hebrew of the MT, it is not at all a

---

According to St. John: An Introduction with Commentary and Notes on the Greek Text, 2d ed. (Philadelphia: Westminster, 1978), 28-29, 173; Freed, OT Quotations, 5-6; Reim, Studien, 5, 90.

[7] Cf. Charles F. Burney, *The Aramaic Origin of the Fourth Gospel* (Oxford: Clarendon Press, 1922), 114; John H. Bernard, *A Critical and Exegetical Commentary on the Gospel According to St. John*, vol. 1, International Critical Commentary, (Edinburgh: T. & T. Clark, 1929), 38; Freed, *OT Quotations*, 4-5 (cf. p. 117).

[8] Cf. August H. Franke, *Das Alte Testament bei Johannes: Ein Beitrag zur Erklärung und Beurtheilung der johanneischen Schriften* (Göttingen: Vandenhoeck & Ruprecht, 1885), 283; Adolf Schlatter, *Der Evangelist Johannes: Wie er spricht, denkt, und glaubt. Ein Kommentar zum vierten Evangelium*, 2d ed. (Stuttgart: Calwer Verlag, 1948), 41-42; Noack, *Tradition*, 73; Braun, *Jean* 2, 10; de Waard, *Comparative Study*, 51; Bultmann, *John*, 90-91 n. 7; Barrett, *St. John* 1, 291; Brown, *John* 1, 43, 50-51; Barnabas Lindars, *The Gospel of John*, New Century Bible Commentary, (London: Marshall, Morgan, & Scott, 1972; reprint, Grand Rapids: Eerdmans, 1987), 104-5; Reim, *Studien*, 5; Menken, "John 1,23," 190-205; Roger J. Humann, "The Function and Form of the Explicit Old Testament Quotations in the Gospel of John," *LTR* 1 (1988/1989): 45.

[9] Cf. Burney, *Aramaic Origin*, 114; Bernard, *St. John*, 38; Braun, *Jean* 2, 44; Goodwin, "Sources," 61-75; Noack, *Tradition*, 71-89; Schnackenburg, *St. John* 1, 122.

[10] To my knowledge, only Menken, "John 1,23," 193, has made this key observation.

word for word rendering. Indeed, the parallelism of בַמִּדְבָּר (40.3b) and
בָעֲרָבָה (40.3c) would seem to indicate that "in the wilderness" is to be taken
with "prepare" (i.e., "prepare in the wilderness").[11] But the OG translator apparently concluded that this Hebrew parallelism is a synonymous parallelism
capable of condensation. The OG, therefore, eliminates the reference to the
"desert" in 40.3c MT.[12] Properly speaking, the resulting form of the OG is, in
terms of its punctuation, somewhat ambiguous.[13] But this move toward condensation seems to point toward a punctuation for the OG that is, I would suggest,
adopted by all four Gospel writers.[14] The absence of any reference to the MT's
עֲרָבָה in either Matt 3.3, Mark 1.3, or Luke 3.4 suggests dependence of these on
the OG. The absence of Isa 40.3c in John 1.23 complicates matters for an evalu-
ation of the John's Gospel. But John's almost certain intention that "in the
wilderness" be taken with "voice" strongly suggests that he too is working with
the OG.[15]

Finally, it is noteworthy that John's Gospel also seems to betray a knowledge
of the larger context of Isa 40.[16] And among the many interesting features of Isa
40 reflected in John's Gospel is this. The prophecy of the announcement of God's
impending salvation which (according to Isa 40.1-2) is to be communicated
specifically to Jerusalem finds its fulfillment in John's portrayal of the Baptist's
encounter with the Jewish delegation from the capital city (1.19-28).[17] It is these
Jews who complete the prophecy when they later return to Jerusalem with their
report of what they have heard the Baptist say (1.22!).[18] Why is this significant?
Because within John 1.19-28, John's specific reference to the "priests and

---

[11] Cf. also the parallelism of the introductory lines in Isa 40.3 MT ("A voice cries, . . .")
and 40.6 ("A voice says, 'Cry!'").

[12] The parallelism of "in the wilderness . . . in the desert" is maintained by 1QIsa[a] and
1QS 8.14.

[13] See B. F. Westcott, *The Gospel according to St. John: The Authorized Version with
Introduction and Notes* (London, 1880; reprint, Grand Rapids: Eerdmans, 1981), 18; John J.
O'Rourke, "Explicit Old Testament Citations in the Gospels," *SMR* 7 (1964): 39 (who also
notes the ambiguity of the MT and the Gospels).

[14] Cf. de Waard, *Comparative Study*, 50-51.

[15] Cf. Stendahl, *St. Matthew*, 48; Freed, *OT Quotations*, 3; Brown, *John* 1, 43.

[16] See Dodd, *Scriptures*, 37-9; Reim, *Studien*, 5. Cf., e.g., v. 11 with John 10.1-18; v. 5
with John 1.14; v. 25 with John 6.69. Other points of convergence will be developed further
below.

[17] This scene does not appear in any of the other Gospels.

[18] I owe this insight to a series of lectures on the Fourth Gospel conducted by Professor
Mathias Rissi which I attended in the Spring of 1987 at Union Theological Seminary in
Richmond, Virginia.

Levites" (1.19)[19] who make up this delegation fulfills nicely the prophecy of Isa 40.2 OG which indicates that it is the temple "priests" who will convey this message of God's salvation to Jerusalem. The OG alone mentions these priests! Once again, therefore, the OG appears to have served as John's source.[20]

This brings us to the problem of the enigmatic appearance of εὐθύνατε.[21] Is it conceivable that John has rendered the Hebrew פנו with εὐθύνατε? (see above). This is not likely. In the OG and in the other Greek versions of the Old Testament, one finds the following renderings where the MT reads פנה pi'el: ἀποσκευάζω (OG Lev 14.36; Aq. Isa 40.3; 57.14; 62.10; Mal 3.1; Symm. Ps 79.10; Isa 62.10; Theod. Isa 40.3; 62.10); ἑτοιμάζω (OG Gen 24.31; Isa 40.3; Theod. Mal 3.1); εὐτρεπίζω (Symm. Isa 40.3;); ὁδοποιέω (OG Ps 79.10; Isa 62.10); σκευάζω (Theod. Isa 57.14; 62.10); and σχολάζω (Symm. Mal 3.1; Isa 57.14).[22] Neither εὐθύνω nor any of its compounds occur as translations of פנה pi'el. Indeed, in the OG, neither εὐθύνω nor even words derived from the same stem ever translate פנה. There is simply no agreement in meaning between the two.

Εὐθύνω, however, and words derived from its stem are frequently found as translations of ישר in its various forms.[23] Is it possible, then, that John substituted ישרו (Isa 40.3c) for פנו (Isa 40.3b) and rendered this εὐθύνατε? This possibility cannot be denied outright. But there are other alternatives as well.

One must reckon, for example, with those who have argued that John regarded εὐθύνατε as an expression synonymous with εὐθείας ποιεῖτε and that

---

[19] Only here does John refer to either priests or Levites. The distinction is one which reaches back to the Old Testament (see esp. Ezekiel and the Priestly Code) and is maintained in rabbinic literature where the Levites form an intermediate class between the priests and the Jewish people (Hor. 3.8) and function both as musicians and as temple police (see, e.g., Tamid 7; Mid. 1-2).

[20] The scene is full of irony. The priests and Levites are the primary functionaries in the temple cultus. Experts in ritual purification, they fail to recognize the "friend" (3.29) of (and eventually also) the person who will replace their temple (see below my discussion of 2.17). They have been sent (cf. 5.33) by those who will function in the rest of John's Gospel as the major protagonists of Jesus, i.e., the "Jews," (here, the Jewish leadership), especially the Pharisees (cf. 1.19 and 1.24). The reaction of the doctors of the Law to the teaching of Jesus will be representative of the reaction of the nation as a whole which refuses to receive him (cf. 1.11).

[21] For what follows, Freed, OT Quotations, 4-6, and Menken, "John 1,23," 193-95, have been particularly influential.

[22] In Mal 3.1, the OG translator has apparently read פנה qal and has translated it with ἐπιβλέψεται In Zeph 3.15, he seems to read פדה rather than פנה and has rendered this λελύτρωται.

[23] In fact, εὐθύνω apparently translates only ישר and נטה.

he simply substituted one for the other.[24] There is also Aquila's translation which (according to ms. 86) renders יֹשֶׁר with εὐθύ<νατε>. It is conceivable, therefore, that εὐθύνατε appeared in the tradition prior to Aquila.[25] This, in turn, raises the possibility that εὐθύνατε appeared in John's *Vorlage* as well. This latest possibility is an especially tantalizing one. It should be noted, however, that Aquila's translation of Isa 40.3a does not correspond to what appears in John.[26]

Thus far, the evidence presented is less than conclusive. The influence of the OG is apparent. But one question remains. How is one to explain the presence of εὐθύνατε in John 1.23?

What one observes in John's Gospel represents the culmination of a rather interesting textual evolution. The OG apparently condensed the synonymous parallelism of its Hebrew *Vorlage* by dropping its reference to the "desert" in Isa 40.3c. John has, in turn, condensed this parallelism even further. Many in the past have attributed this Johannine development to the fact that he quotes from a faulty memory. Is it possible, instead, to detect and characterize in this his conscious intentionality?

II.

What might have prompted John to offer his citation of Isa 40.3 in this way? Why might he be interested in condensing Isa 40.3bc and suppressing ἑτοιμάσατε in 40.3b?

Few in the past have ventured to offer a solution to this problem as I have posed it. The recent work of M. J. J. Menken, however, has broken with the past. Menken suggests that the precise form of John's citation can be attributed to the conscious intentionality of John and that it has resulted from the following factors.[27]

---

[24] Cf. Isa 40.3c OG where יֹשֶׁר pi'el (with מְסִלָּה as its direct object) is rendered with εὐθύ ποιέω; Isa 45.13b Symm. where יֹשֶׁר pi'el (with דְּרָכָם as its direct object) is rendered with εὐθύνω; and OG 2 Chron 32.30; Prov 9.15; and 15.21 where κατευθύνω appears as a translation of יֹשֶׁר pi'el.

[25] Menken, "John 1,23," 194-95, stresses the likelihood of this (cf. de Waard, *Comparative Study*, 51). Consult Dominique Barthélemy, *Les devanciers d'Aquila: Première publication intégrale du texte des fragments du Dodécaprophéton*, Supplements to Vetus Testamentum, vol. 10 (Leiden: E. J. Brill, 1963).

[26] Specifically, in place of φωνὴ βοῶντος in John 1.23 we find in Aquila φωνὴ καλοῦντος. Cf. Freed, *OT Quotations*, 6.

[27] Menken, "John 1,23," 195-205. Because Menken is one of the very few who have attempted to offer a solution to this problem, and because I have found his contribution very similar to what I myself hope to accomplish in this chapter, much of what follows will represent both a reproduction of and a reaction to his effort.

According to Menken, the verb ἐτοιμάζω when accompanied by an explicit or implicit indirect object frequently conveys an understood sequence of ideas: (1) Something is "prepared" by a subject A for an indirect object B. (2) Only when this has been prepared, however, can B come to where A is and use that which has been prepared, partake of it, etc. (3) This implies that A always precedes B temporally and that A always completes the task of preparation prior to the arrival of B.[28]

Ἐτοιμάζω, argues Menken, could not be used by John because its meaning would stand in conflict with the portrait of the Baptist which John wished to construct. In other words, John chooses another verb because he purposes to offer a portrait of the Baptist quite distinct from that of the Synoptics.

The Synoptics assert that the preparation of the way of the Lord is accomplished by those who submit to the baptism of John and repent of their sin (cf. Matt 3.1-2, 4-12; Mark 1.4-8; Luke 3.1-3, 7-18) The Baptist himself, therefore, through his baptizing and preaching also "prepares the way" (cf. Mark 1.2, Matt 11.10, and Luke 7.27 with Luke 1.76). In John's Gospel, however, the Baptist alone is held responsible for the work of preparation. In John 1.19-37, nothing is said of a preaching of "baptism of repentance for the forgiveness of sins" (Mark 1.4; Luke 3.3). And only indirectly do people come to the Baptist in order to be baptized (1.25, 26, 28, 31, 33; cf. 3.23-30; 10.40-42). It is the Baptist alone, therefore, who "makes straight" when he testifies to the identity of Jesus.[29]

If John had retained the use of ἐτοιμάσατε in his citation, concludes Menken, then the phrase "prepare the way of the Lord" would have suggested that the Baptist was to complete his testifying to Jesus before Jesus would arrive on the scene. In other words, only when the Baptist had completed his preparation of the "way" (in non-figurative terms: his testimony) could Jesus make use of that which had been prepared and come. This seems to be precisely how the Synoptics understand Jesus' temporal relationship to the Baptist (cf. Matt 3.13-17; Mark 1.9-11; Matt 4.12; Mark 1.14a; Luke 3.19-22; see also Acts 13.24-25; 19.4). But John's Gospel describes a decidedly different state of affairs. In John's account, when the Baptist appears Jesus does also (cf. the three days narrated in 1.19-28, 29-34, and 35-37). Even later, after a period of considerable activity on the part of Jesus, the Baptist is still testifying concerning Jesus (3.27-30). For John, Jesus and the Baptist are contemporaries who work alongside one another.

---

[28] Menken, "John 1,23," 196-98, refers to numerous examples of this from the non-canonical Greek literature, from the OG, the NT, and other early Christian literature.

[29] Cf. Robert T. Fortna, *The Fourth Gospel and Its Predecessor: From Narrative Source to Present Gospel* (Philadelphia: Fortress, 1988), 18. This interpretation, it is claimed, dispenses with the suggestion of Schnackenburg, *St. John* 1, 291, and Reim, *Studien*, 5, that the second line of John's quotation receives no "inhaltliche Ausdeutung" in the Fourth Gospel.

The Baptist is not so much the forerunner or precursor of Jesus as he is a witness whose activity is contemporaneous with that of Jesus.[30] Certainly, John acknowledges the historical priority of the Baptist. But John also relativizes this priority by underlining the Baptist's meta-historical inferiority (cf. the Prologue, esp. 1.1, 6, 15; and 1.30; 3.31-36, esp. 3.21, 32).[31]

The substitution of εὐθύνατε for ἑτοιμάσατε by John, therefore, was motivated by his desire to portray the Baptist as this contemporaneous witness. That this was John's motive is confirmed by a somewhat unexpected detail in this context, i.e., the Baptist's explicit refusal to be identified with Elijah (cf. 1.21 and 25). Scholars have suggested that the Baptist says "no" when asked whether he is the Christ, Elijah, or the Prophet (1.19-21) because Jesus is to be regarded as all of these.[32] But these same scholars fail to explain why Jesus then is never called "Elijah" in John's Gospel. John has the Baptist refuse any identification with Elijah because John, like the other Gospel writers, understands Elijah to be not the expected contemporary of the Messiah, but the prophesied precursor of the

---

[30] Significant for this point are Martin Dibelius, *Die urchristliche Überlieferung von Johannes dem Taüfer*, Forschungen zur Religion und Literatur des Alten und Neuen Testaments, Bd. 15 (Göttingen: Vandenhoeck & Ruprecht, 1911), 102-13; Walter Wink, *John the Baptist in the Gospel Tradition*, Society for New Testament Studies Monograph Series, vol. 7 (London: Cambridge University Press, 1968), 89-95; C. H. H. Scobie, *John the Baptist* (London: SCM Press, 1964), 143-45; Ernst Bammel, "The Baptist in Early Christian Tradition," *NTS* 18 (1971/1972): 95-128, esp. 126; G. Gaeta, "Battesimo come testimonianza. Le pericopi sul Battista nell'evangelo di Giovanni," *Cristianesimo nella storia* 1 (1980): 279-314, esp. 302 (cf. Fortna, *Fourth Gospel*, 16, 18, 22-24, 230). As an example of one who has too easily applied the designation "precursor" to John the Baptist, see Georg Richter, "'Bist du Elias?' (Joh 1,21)," *BZ*, n.F. 6 (1962): 79-92, 238-56, and 7 (1963): 63-80.

[31] Menken observes that the possibility of a conflict between a Baptist sect and the Johannine community defended by Wilhelm Baldensperger, *Der Prolog des vierten Evangeliums: Sein polemisch-apologetischer Zweck* (Tübingen: Mohr-Siebeck, 1898), continues to generate interest. See, e.g., Dibelius, *Johannes der Taüfer*, 119-23; Wink, *John the Baptist*, 98-105; Oscar Cullmann, "'Ο 'ΟΠΙΣΩ ΜΟΥ 'ΕΡΧΟΜΕΝΟΣ," in *In honorem Antonii Fridrichsen sexagenarii*, Coniectanea Neotestamentica, vol. 11 (Lund: C. W. K. Gleerup, 1947), 26-32. In favor of the possibility that the overlapping of the ministries of Jesus and the Baptist may have some historical basis are Maurice Goguel, *Au seuil de l'évangile: Jean Baptiste* (Paris: C. Payot, 1928), 235-74; Dodd, *Historical Tradition*, 279-301; Scobie, *John the Baptist*, 153-56.

[32] Significant for this point are John A. T. Robinson, "Elijah, John and Jesus. An Essay in Detection," *NTS* 4 (1957/1958): 263-81, esp. 270; Richter, "Bist du Elias?" According to James L. Martyn, *The Gospel of John in Christian History: Essays for Interpreters*, Theological Inquiries: Studies in Contemporary Biblical and Theological Problems (New York: Paulist, 1979), 9-54, this parallelism has been derived from John's source (cf. Fortna, *Fourth Gospel*, 17, 30, 37-38, 41, 226, 228-30, 232).

Messiah (cf. Mal 3.1, 23; Matt 11.10 and Luke 7.27; Matt 11.14; Mark 1.2; Matt 17.10-13 and Mark 9.11-13).[33]

In essence, it is the job of Elijah as forerunner to "prepare" the way for the Messiah. The refusal of the Baptist to be regarded as Elijah complements nicely, therefore, John's substitution of εὐθύνατε for ἑτοιμάσατε in his citation of Isa 40.3.[34] Both Johannine innovations, according to Menken, participate in the same scheme. John desires to rule out any notion that the Baptist's work was completed prior to the initiation of Jesus' public ministry.

The contribution of Menken is noteworthy in many respects. But it also carries with it a number of serious flaws. I am fully in agreement with him that John's primary assertion concerning the Baptist (i.e., that he is a contemporary of Jesus whose principal function is to testify[35] concerning him) is quite distinct from the claim of the Synoptics (that the Baptist is the precursor or forerunner Elijah).[36] Hence, John has the Baptist refuse this identification.[37] I also agree that

---

[33] Evidence for this appears in Tg. Ps.-J. Num 25.12; the rabbinic material in Str-B 4:791; Ferdinand Hahn, *Christologische Hoheitstitel: Ihre Geschichte im frühen Christentum*, Forschungen zur Religion und Literatur des Alten und Neuen Testaments, Bd. 83 (Göttingen: Vandenhoeck & Ruprecht, 1963), 375-80.

[34] Cf. Fortna, *Fourth Gospel*, 18. Menken notes that there may have been other motives as well for John's refusal to identify the Baptist with Elijah. E.g., Marinus de Jonge, "Jewish Expectations about the 'Messiah' according to the Fourth Gospel," *NTS* 19 (1972/1973): 246-70, esp. 252-56, has called attention to the messianic expectations of the Jews evident in Justin's *Dial.* 8.3; 49.1; 110.1. According to these expectations, the Messiah, a mere man, would not be cognizant of his own identity and mission until Elijah anoints and reveals him. John, de Jonge asserts, knew of these conceptions (cf. 1.25, 31) and dismisses them. For John, Jesus is at all times fully aware of his mission and does not depend upon Elijah for being revealed to his own. For this reason, John has the Baptist refuse any identification with Elijah.

[35] On the subject of "witness" in John's Gospel, see esp. J. C. Hindley, "Witness in the Fourth Gospel," *SJT* 18 (1965): 319-37; James M. Boice, *Witness and Revelation in the Gospel of John* (Grand Rapids: Zondervan, 1970); J. Beutler, *Martyria: Traditionsgeschichtliche Untersuchungen zum Zeugnisthema bei Johannes*, Frankfurter Theologische Studien, Bd. 10 (Frankfurt am Main: J. Knecht, 1972); Severino Pancaro, *The Law in the Fourth Gospel: The Torah and the Gospel, Moses and Jesus, Judaism and Christianity according to John*, Supplements to Novum Testamentum, vol. 42 (Leiden: E. J. Brill, 1975), 194-208; see also the survey by M. Walton, *Witness in Biblical Scholarship: A Survey of Recent Studies 1956-1980*, Interuniversitair Instituut voor Missiologie en Oecumenica, Bd. 15 (Leiden: IIMO, 1986).

[36] Still, scholars continue to posit the primary influence of Elijah and also Elisha traditions on either the Christology of the Gospel or its portrait of the Baptist. Cf., e.g., Reim, *Studien*, 156-58; Ernst Haenchen, *John 1: A Commentary on the Gospel of John Chapters 1-6*, trans. R. W. Funk, Hermeneia (Philadelphia: Fortress, 1984), 147-48; Louis T. Brodie, "Jesus as the New Elisha: Cracking the Code," *ExpTim* 93 (1981): 39-42; Ingo Broer, "Noch einmal: Zur religionsgeschichtlichen 'Ableitung' von Jo 2,1-11," *StudNTUmwelt* 8 (1983): 103-23; Wolfgang Roth, "Scriptural Coding in the Fourth Gospel," *BR* 32 (1987): 7, 22-24, 26-28; A. Mayer, "Elijah and Elisha in John's Sign Source," *ExpTim* 99 (1988): 171-73. See also the contribution of Dieter Zeller, "Elijah und Elischa im Frühjudentum," *BK* 41 (1986): 154-60.

the substitution of εὐθύνατε for ἑτοιμάσατε in John 1.23 is entirely consistent with this unique portrait of the Baptist. Because it is especially Elijah who is understood as that figure who will specifically "prepare"[38] the way, John deletes the idea of "preparation" from the Baptist's quotation of Isa 40.3.

However, it simply does not follow that ἑτοιμάζω carries with it the significance in the Synoptics which Menken stresses. The mere retention of ἑτοιμάσατε in the Baptist's quotation of Isa 40.3 in John 1.23 would in no way necessitate the termination of the activity of the Baptist with the beginning of Jesus' public ministry (as in the Synoptics). There are a number of problems here.

First, in the Synoptics the Baptist's work of preparation ends with the arrival of Jesus only because the Baptist is understood in the Synoptics to be the precursor of Jesus. As such, the Baptist's task is complete once Jesus has arrived. The use of ἑτοιμάζω has nothing to do with this. The meaning of this verb in Matt 3.3, Mark 1.3, or Luke 3.4 does not require, as Menken asserts, that Jesus' coming depend upon the completion of the task of preparation (*none* of the Gospel writers would suggest this). Jesus will come whether the way is prepared or not. Neither does the use of this verb require that, when Jesus arrives, what remains of his journey cannot yet be "prepared" by someone other than the Baptist. John has not dropped ἑτοιμάσατε because it carries with it this purported significance. Instead, he has done this because its use in this context would recall expectations concerning Elijah which John wishes to avoid.

Moreover, for John more than the Baptist's testimony alone "makes straight" the way of the Lord. Menken has curiously overlooked the fact that εὐθύνατε is a second person plural imperative![39] Those who heed the exhortation of the Baptist are also those who make straight the way. Those who go with Jesus,

---

For a recent attempt to characterize the influence of Malachi upon the whole New Testament, see J. A. Brooks, "The Influence of Malachi Upon the New Testament," *SWJournTheol* 30 (1987): 28-31.

[37] Opting in favor of de Jonge's proposal (see above) are Leon Morris, *Reflections on the Gospel of John*, vol. 1, *The Word Was Made Flesh: John 1-5* (Grand Rapids: Baker, 1986), 28-29; George R. Beasley-Murray, *John*, Word Biblical Commentary, vol. 36 (Waco, Tx.: Word Books, 1987), 24.

[38] It is intriguing to note once more, however, that Mal 3.1 OG has rendered פנה with ἐπιβλέπω and not ἑτοιμάζω. The Synoptics read κατασκευάζω (cf. Aq.: ἀποσκευάζω; Symm.: σχολάζω; Theod.: ἑτοιμάζω). Cf. Luke 1.76: ἑτοιμάζω.

[39] In addition, it is John's concerted effort to purge his portrait of the Baptist of Elijah-like traits (and to concentrate on his function as witness) that has resulted in the absence of any calling to a baptism of repentance for the forgiveness of sins (Mark 1.4; Luke 3.3). Cf. Mal 3, esp. 3.7: "Return to me!" Note also the exhortation to remember the Law in 3.22 (see also Sir 48.1-11). Unlike Elijah, who turns the hearts of the people (3.23), the Baptist in John's Gospel simply testifies and no more.

therefore, will have this opportunity. Menken really doesn't seem to recognize that, for John, the "way of Jesus" is a path that returns him ultimately to the Father (John 14.1-7). The possibility of making that journey straight exists up until the moment of its completion.[40] Those who go with Jesus, facilitate his journey, and help him in accomplishing his purposes along the way "make straight the way of the Lord."

Overall, while Menken has made numerous key observations, his attempt to furnish a solution founders. Most significantly, he has failed to provide a satisfactory explanation for John's selection of the verb εὐθύνατε. We have already noted that elsewhere in his citation John recalls the OG. Why, then, does he not select the OG's εὐθείας ποιεῖτε?

It is my conviction that those few who have pointed to the probable influence of the sapiential traditions on John 1.23 have provided the final piece to this puzzle.[41] In substituting εὐθύνατε, John recalls the use of (κατ)ευθύνω with ὁδός in the wisdom literature.[42] By inserting εὐθύνατε into John 1.23, he suggests, in effect, that the identity and the message of the Baptist is also to be understood from a sapiential standpoint.

Scholars have amassed an impressive amount of evidence which suggests that the Logos of John's Prologue is to be understood in terms of the Wisdom of God.[43] It should be no surprise, then, that the quintessential witness to the

---

[40] In fact, up to now, aside from John's desire to avoid portraying the Baptist as Elijah, nothing else would preclude the use of ἐτοιμάζω in John 1.23.

[41] Freed, OT Quotations, 5, 116, 123; Barrett, St. John, 173 (cf. Humann, "OT Quotations," 45 n. 49). Menken, "John 1,23," 195 n. 15, admits only that these traditions may have provided a "secondary inducement."

[42] See, e.g., Prov 4.25-26; 9.15; 13.13; 29.27 [cf. 20.24]; see also Sir 2.6 [cf. 2.2; 6.17]; 37.15 [cf. 38.10]; 49.9; contrast T. Sim. 5.2. It is highly significant that, within the wisdom literature, the combination of εὐθείας ποιέω with ὁδός never occurs. The verb ἑτοιμάζω occurs with ὁδός only in Job (see 28.1-28, esp. 27; similarly, 38.25; cf. 38.36-37), where the exclusive agency of God in his creating of the world, his "preparing" it and ordering it according to Wisdom is described (cf. Isa 40.12-27). In John's Gospel, the use of ἑτοιμάζω is reserved for Jesus' "preparation" of a place for his disciples in the Father's house (14.2,3; cf. Wisdom's building of a "house" and her "preparation" of a feast for those that she summons in Prov 9.1-6). What one observes seems to be a consistent effort to establish a kinship with the sapiential Weltanschauung.

[43] See esp. Brown, John 1, 33, 521-23; Braun, Jean 2, 137; Andre Feuillet, Le prologue du quatrième évangile (Paris: Brouwer, 1968), 224-25, 239-42; H. R. Moeller, "Wisdom Motifs and John's Gospel," BETS 6 (1963): 93-98; Basil de Pinto, "Word and Wisdom in St. John," Scr 19 (1967): 19-27. Cf. also Ceslaus Spicq, "Le Siracide et la structure littéraire du Prologue de saint Jean," in Memorial Lagrange: Cinquantenaire de l'école biblique et archéologique française de Jérusalem (15 novembre 1890 - 15 novembre 1940) (Paris: Gabalda, 1940), 183-95; Charles H. Dodd, The Interpretation of the Fourth Gospel (Cambridge: Cambridge University Press, 1953), 274-77; Rudolf Bultmann, "Der Religionsgeschichtliche Hintergrund des Prologs zum

Logos (1.6-8, 15; cf. 10.41!) speaks in a manner reminiscent of a disciple of Wisdom. Indeed, the language of John 1.23 seems to suggest that all those who heed the exhortation of the Baptist will also become, like the Baptist, disciples of Wisdom.[44]

It is conspicuous and striking how much it is that Jesus and the Baptist share in common. Both Jesus and the Baptist are called "Rabbi" (cf., e.g., 1.38, 49, and 3.26); both baptize" (1.33); both have disciples (cf. 3.22 and 3.25); both testify (cf. 1.6-9 and 3.11); both are "sent" (cf. 1.6 and 3.17); both bring "light" (cf. 1.4-5 and 5.33-36); both actively seek out others and cry out to them (cf. 1.23 and 5.14; 7.28, 37; 9.35; 12.44); both even speak in characteristic first person discourse.[45] What differs, however, between Jesus and the Baptist is equally

---

Johannesevangelium," in *Exegetica: Aufsätze zur Erforschung des Neuen Testaments*, hg. Erich Dinkler (Tübingen: Mohr-Siebeck, 1967), 10-35; Barrett, *John*, 153, 165-66; Schnackenburg, *St. John* 1, 124, 231, 269; Mathias Rissi, "Die Logoslieder im Prolog des vierten Evangeliums," *TZ* 31 (1975): 321-36; Haenchen, *John 1*, 135-40; Hartmut Gese, *Essays on Biblical Theology*, trans. K. Crim (Minneapolis: Augsburg, 1981), 190-99; John Painter, "Christology and the Fourth Gospel. A Study of the Prologue," *AusBR* 31 (1983): 45-62; idem, "Christology and the History of the Johannine Community in the Prologue of the Fourth Gospel," *NTS* 30 (1984): 460-74; J. Ashton, "The Transformation of Wisdom. A Study of the Prologue of John's Gospel," *NTS* 32 (1986): 161-86; Walter Grundmann, *Der Zeuge der Weisheit: Grundzüge der Christologie des Johannesevangeliums*, mit einer Einfuhrung hg. von W. Wiefel (Berlin: Evang. Verlaganstalt, 1985), 16-29; Michael E. Willett, "Wisdom Christology in the Fourth Gospel" (Ph.D. diss., Southern Baptist Theological Seminary, 1985), 63-113; P. Schoonenberg, "A Sapiential Reading of John's Prologue: Some Reflections on Views of Reginald Fuller and James Dunn," *TD* 33 (1986): 403-21.

44 On discipleship in wisdom, see Braun, *Jean* 2, 123-25; Andre Feuillet, *Johannine Studies*, trans. Thomas E. Crane (Staten Island, N.Y.: Alba House, 1965), 89-91; Willett, "Wisdom," 194-206. Rissi, "Logoslieder," 335-36 n. 72, however, rightly remarks: "Die seit Baldensperger oft geaüsserte Vermutung, die Taüfereinschube im Prolog richteten sich gegen Taüfersekten, ist unwarscheinlich. Dass die poetischen Teile des Prologs aus Taüfertraditionen stammen, ist nicht zu halten." Rather than engaging in polemics, this material seeks to demonstrate that the Baptist was "von Anfang an der Prototyp des christlichen Jungers und Zeugen." Most today have given up the opposing viewpoint represented by Barrett, *St. John*, 172; Schnackenburg, *St. John*, 129-30, 288; Brown, *John* 1, 46-47; Lindars, *John*, 102; Fortna, *Fourth Gospel*, 23-24. Cf. the surveys of scholarship by Robert Kysar, *The Fourth Evangelist and His Gospel: An Examination of Contemporary Scholarship* (Minneapolis: Augsburg, 1975), 159 n. 30; idem, "Recent Research," 2429 n. 155.

45 Contrast Edwin D. Freed, "*Egō Eimi* in John 1:20 and 4:25," *CBQ* 41 (1979): 288-91. Cf. with this also the portrait of Wisdom who teaches her own of the things that are above (Job 11.6-7; Wis 9.16-18), collects disciples (Prov 8.32-33; Sir 4.11; Wis 6.17-19), utters the truth (Prov 8.7; Wis 6.22), is "sent" (Wis 9.10), gives light (Wis 7.26; Sir 1.29), seeks others and cries out to them (Prov 1.20-21; 8.1-4; Wis 6.16), and also speaks in characteristic first person discourse (Prov 8.3-36; Sir 24). With reference to the Johannine "I am" sayings, Mathias Rissi, "Voll grosser Fische, hundertdreiundfünfzig, Joh. 21,1-14," *TZ* 35 (1979): 77 n. 19, writes, "Formal entsprechen die johanneischen Formulierungen weisheitlichen Spruchen."

striking. As the Creator is different from the creature (cf. 1.3 and 1.6), Jesus the primordial light (1.9) is different from the Baptist, the enlightened one (1.8). The Baptist has been sent by God (1.6) in order to live as the "voice" of God. His is a life that both parallels and thus points to the coming of a greater voice[46] who will be like the Baptist, yet so ultimately unlike him. The Baptist comes in order to point to the coming of Jesus and, in doing so, to challenge those who hear his testimony to make straight Jesus' way.[47]

In summary, the Baptist's exhortation to "make straight the way of the Lord" reaches back, recalls, and capitalizes upon two independent yet, from the standpoint of John, complementary Old Testament traditions. To respond to this exhortation involves first recognizing that the coming of Jesus is the coming of God and his salvation in fulfillment of Isaiah's prophecy. Isaiah's prophecy envisioned a salvation for Israel after the pattern of the "way" which God had made for the Jews as they marched out of Egypt.[48] And second, to "make straight the

---

John's use of ἐγώ in John 1.23 seems, therefore, to function as part of a larger scheme which purposes to portray the Baptist as the consummate disciple of Wisdom (=Jesus).

[46] Φωνή in John's Gospel is consistently used with reference to the revelatory voice of God (cf. 1.23; 3.8; 3.29; 5.25, 28; 5.37; 10.3, 4, 5, 16, 17; 11.43; 12.28, 30; 18.37). Cf. Prov 1.20-21; 8.1. There is no doubt that the Baptist is to be understood as the voice of God (cf. Isa 40.3, 6). Barrett, St. John, 170-71, makes the significant observation that "whereas in the synoptic account of the baptism a voice from heaven declares that Jesus is the Son of God, in John this assertion is made by the Baptist himself." Conversely, Augustine (Sermons 293.3) reminds us that John the Baptist was a voice for a brief time (John 5.35), but Christ is the eternal Word from the beginning (cf. the absence of ἰσχυρότερος [Matt 3.11; Mark 1.7; Luke 3.16] in John with its preference for references to Jesus' preexistence).

[47] John is careful, however, not to suggest that the Baptist is in any way divine. Everything about the Baptist, then, points to the identity of Jesus, even John's baptism (1.31). Reminiscent of the purification rites of the Jews (cf. καθαρισμος in 2.6 and 3.25), John's Baptism functions for the sake of testimony (see Dodd, Historical Traditions, 280). His baptism points to that which is incapable of achieving, i.e., eschatological cleansing and the giving of eschatological life (see Barrett, St. John, 171). The Jews were confused (1.25), presumably because their traditions had not informed them of an eschatological figure who would baptize (see Haenchen, John 1, 145-46; de Jonge, "Expectations," 255 n. 5). Yet what was happening before them reeked with unmistakable eschatological significance. The Baptist tells them that his baptism is a sign, a preparation, a foil, prefiguring and pointing away from the Baptist to Jesus the giver of Spirit baptism (Dodd, Historical Traditions, 269, 289; Schnackenburg, St. John 1, 294). Indeed, this may explain why John makes no reference to Jesus' baptism. The Baptist's job is to testify. His baptism of the Jews participates in his function as witness. To include the baptism of Jesus, however, would introduce the competing testimony of the voice of the Father (Matt 3.16-17; Mark 1.10-11; Luke 3.22). In place of Jesus' baptism is apparently his designation as the "Lamb" (1.29, 36).

[48] See in particular Isa 43.14-21, esp. the reference to Exod 14.21-22 (though ὁδός does not appear here) in 43.16 (cf. also 51.10 and 11.16). Cf. W. Michaelis, "ὁδός," TDNT 5:42-96; Thomas Wieser, "The Way of Life," EcumR 34 (1982): 221-27. In the OT, "the way" is a concept constitutive for Israel as a people (see esp. Deut). The salvific way that God has

way of the Lord" is to see in Jesus the way of Wisdom as well, to be conformed
to Wisdom, to become a disciple of Wisdom, and to find in the way of Wisdom
the way to salvation.[49]

John's selection of εὐθύνατε, we have seen, plays the pivotal role in relating
these two separate streams of Old Testament tradition. Now because John selects
εὐθύνατε in order to recall the use of the same term in the wisdom literature,
there is no need to resort to hypotheses concerning his dependence upon a
Hebrew or alternate Greek version of Isa 40.3c. Instead, it is likely that John
recalls only one version of Isa 40.3, the OG. As it stands, John's citation repre-

---

chosen for his people is "perfect" (Ps 18.30). To be led by God presupposes that one no longer
follows one's own "evil ways" (cf., e.g., Zech 1.4). The just seek the way of Yahweh rather than
their own way (Isa 56.11). The former is the way of life, the latter death (Jer 21.8-9), for the
ways of God are "higher" than our own (Isa 55.7-9). Preeminently, the way of the Lord is the
Exodus (cf. Deut 26; Ps 105 and 106), the way to life, for in this event Israel is "born" (Ps
100.3). And finally, crucial to being "on the way" is the function of the Torah, Israel's charter,
its guidelines for maintaining the right way. Those who walk in this way "delight" in the Law
of the Lord (Ps 1.2). For John, through traversing the way himself Jesus becomes our new and
living way to the Father (John 14.4-6; cf. Heb 10.20). Thus, Christianity came to be known as
"the Way" (Acts 9.2; 18.25-26; 19.9, 23; 22.4; 24.14, 22). Also, bear in mind that in the OT a
way blocked or walled up (Josh 2.8; Lam 3.9) appears as an apt metaphor for God's punitive
actions as well complementing his promise to make a salvific way in the desert (Isa 43.19) or
to make mountains into ways (Isa 49.11; cf. 35.8-9; 57.14; 62.10).

[49] In the sapiential writings as well, the "way" is constitutive. Here too, we encounter a
juxtaposition of the way(s) of the evil (e.g., Prov 2.12) with that of the good (e.g., Prov 2.20).
The former is the way of life (Prov 6.23; 12,28; 16.17), the latter, death (Prov 7.27). But here
the way of the Lord (Prov 10.29; Wis 5.7) is the "way of Wisdom" (cf. Prov 3.17; 4.11; Job
28.13, 23; Sir 6.26; 14.21-22). Baruch in particular helps us to understand the sapiential
world-view. The way of wisdom (3.29-31, esp. 3.23), the way of knowledge (3.20, 27, 36),
finds its ultimate expression in the "book of the commandments of God and the Law that
endures forever" (4.1). Those who walk in the "light" of it will live. But those who leave it shall
die (4.1-2). Note that Baruch, like Isaiah, makes reference to Israel's exile and the possibility of
an "Exodus" (3.8-15; 4.4-59). Israel stands in exile because it has "forsaken the fountain of
Wisdom" (3.12). If Israel will heed the commandments of life, seek Wisdom (3.9), and walk
in the "way of God" (3.13), this will result in its salvation (3.13-15; cf. 4.4-8). Cf. with this the
reference to Israel's "way" out of the Red Sea in Wis 19.7 (cf. 14.3?). Cf. also Sirach's view of
Israel's Exodus in Gerald T. Sheppard, *Wisdom as a Hermeneutical Construct: A Study in the
Sapientializing of the Old Testament*, Beiheft zur Zeitschrift für die alttestamentliche
Wissenschaft, Bd. 151 (New York: de Gruyter, 1980), 29-30, 38-43, 81-82, 106. It is clear
from these few examples that John's attempt to interrelate the "way of the Lord" with both the
Exodus traditions and the way of Wisdom is not at all unique. Indeed, what Isaiah itself says
in Isa 40 in referring to the "way of the Lord" (40.3), the "way of understanding" (40.14), and
the way of foolish Israel (40.27) seems itself to interrelate Exodus motifs with themes common
to Wisdom (cf., e.g., Isa 40.12-14 and Job 28.12-20; and Isa 40.22, Prov 8.27, Job 22.14, and
Sir 24.5).

sents a condensed version of Isa 40.3 OG in which εὐθύνατε appears not as a substitute for ἑτοιμάσατε, but as the equivalent of εὐθείας ποιεῖτε.

III.

In conclusion, the Baptist's reference in John 1.23 to Isa 40.3 has in all likelihood been taken from the OG. John's citation differs from his source. But this can be attributed to John's conscious desire to highlight the Baptist's identity as the quintessential disciple of and witness to Wisdom.

Chapter 2

JESUS AND THE TEMPLE

Accounts relating an incident in which Jesus clears the temple grounds in Jerusalem during a Passover festival appear in each of the canonical Gospels (cf. Matt 21.12-13, Mark 11.15-17, Luke 19.45-46, and John 2.13-17).[1] The Synoptics offer three slightly differing portraits of the same event. But it is not immediately evident that John too offers nothing more than another portrait of the event appearing in Matthew, Mark, and Luke.[2] A close examination of some of the similarities and differences between John and the Synoptics yields interesting and informative results.

Certainly the most conspicuous difference between John's account and that of the Synoptics has to do with the question of chronology. In John's Gospel, the clearing of the temple occurs at the very beginning of Jesus' public ministry. In each of the Synoptics, Jesus' action takes place just prior to his arrest, trial, and crucifixion (and as such, plays a key role in the final outrage of the Jews).

John's Gospel also differs from the Synoptics in (1) its reference to such objects as sheep and oxen (2.14),[3] a whip made out of cords (2.15),[4] and the coins (2.15) of the money-changers and (2) its reference to such activities as

---

[1] On the Passover, cf. Exod 12.14-20, 43-49; Lev 23.4-8; Deut 16.1-8.

[2] Dodd, *Interpretation*, 300, writes, "(John's account) is given here with little substantial difference from the Marcan version, though with no great measure of verbal agreement."

[3] These together with the pigeons were available for the purpose of sacrifice. Thus, travelers who had come from a long distance were able to acquire suitable animals in the market. The complicated system of purchase is described in *Seqal.* 5.3-5.

[4] *Ber.* 9.5 outlaws the carrying of a staff (מקל) in the temple. Some scholars have offered this as an explanation for Jesus' resorting to an improvised whip.

"finding" (2.14), "sitting" (2.14; although the "seats" of those who are selling pigeons are noted), "pouring out" (2.15), and "taking away" (2.15). All of these features are absent in the Synoptics. John's explicit reference to the presence of the disciples (2.17) is also unique to John. So too is his indication that, there in the temple,[5] while witnessing the character and intensity of Jesus' actions, "his disciples remembered that it was written,[6]

ὁ ζῆλος τοῦ οἴκου σου καταφάγεταί με " (2.17).[7]

John's Gospel is reminiscent of the Synoptics and yet also distinct from them at these points: (1) when John refers to the money-changers as τοὺς κερματιστάς (cf. 2.14 with Matt 21.13 and Mark 11.15: "the tables τῶν κολλυβιστῶν");[8] (2) when Jesus "turns over" (cf. ἀνέτρεψεν in John 2.15 with κατέστρεψεν in Matt 21.12 and Mark 11.15) tables; and (3) when Jesus protests concerning the "house of my Father" and the so-called "house of trade" (contrast "my house" and

---

[5] Scholars are somewhat divided over the question of whether the disciples recalled a passage from the OT immediately in this scene or only after the resurrection of Jesus. In favor of an immediate recollection are Bernard, St. John, 91-92; Dodd, Historical Tradition, 158; Schnackenburg, St. John 1, 347; Barrett, St. John, 198, Haenchen, John 1, 184; Jürgen Becker, Das Evangelium des Johannes, Bd. 1, Kapitel 1-10, 2. Aufl., Ökumenischer Taschenbuchkommentar zum Neuen Testament, Bd. 4/1 (Gütersloh: Gerd Mohn, 1985), 124; Fortna, Fourth Gospel, 125-26. In favor of a post-resurrection recollection are Bultmann, John, 124; Reim, Studien, 10; O'Rourke, "Citations," 55; Birger Olsson, Structure and Meaning in the Fourth Gospel: A Text-Linguistic Analysis of John 2:1-11 and 4:1-42, trans. Jean Gray, Coniectanea Biblica: New Testament Series, vol. 6, (Lund: C. W. K. Gleerup, 1974), 265; Anthony T. Hanson, The New Testament Interpretation of Scripture (London: SPCK, 1980), 115; Robert Kysar, John, Augsburg Commentary on the New Testament (Minneapolis: Augsburg, 1986), 49; Kenneth A Mathews, "John, Jesus and the Essenes: Trouble at the Temple," CTR 3 (1988): 117. John does not in any way indicate that the "remembering" in v. 17 is to be taken temporally with the same in v. 22. Therefore, the natural sense of v. 17 is that the disciples recalled a passage from the OT in the temple. John's purpose is to contrast their understanding and believing here with the same after the resurrection. The contrast between them and "the Jews" is also of interest to John. See further below.

[6] The expression γεγραμμένον ἐστίν is a common participial formula in John's Gospel (see 6.31, 45; 10,34; 12.14; cf. 12.16), but does not occur in the New Testament outside of his Gospel. Paul and the Synoptists prefer γέγραπται (cf. John 8.17). The differing forms, however, do not result in any real difference in meaning, and both correspond to the common rabbinic formula כתוב(ן) (cf. Bultmann, John, 124 n. 3; Freed, OT Quotations, 8 n. 1). On the use of formulas in the Mishna, see Bruce M. Metzger, "The Formulas Introducing Quotations of Scripture in the NT and the Mishna," JBL 70 (1951): 297-307.

[7] John is, in fact, the only NT writer who refers to this OT passage.

[8] The term John uses for the money-changers in John 2.14 is a hapax legomenon in the New Testament (and is absent in the OG). The genitive τῶν κολλυβιστῶν appears in John 2.15, but here modifies "coins" rather than "tables"). Bultmann, John, 123 n. 8, suggests that the use of two different terms for the money-changers by John may represent an attempt to avoid the "clash" τῶν κερματιστῶν...τά κέρματα in v. 15.

σπήλαιον ληστῶν in Matt 21.13, Mark 11.17, and Luke 19.46 with John 2.16; cf. 10.1, 8, 10; 12.6; 18.40).[9]

Unique to the Synoptics are the following details: (1) Jesus' "entering" (Matt 21.12; Mark 11.15; Luke 19.45); (2) those who come to "buy" in the temple (Matt 21.12 and Mark 11.15); (3) the "seats" of those who are selling pigeons which are also "turned over" (Matt 21.12 and Mark 11.15); (4) Jesus' insistence that the temple be called a "house of prayer" (Matt 21.13; Mark 11.17; Luke 19.46);[10] (5) Jesus' insistence that no one carry a vessel through the temple (Mark 11.16); and (6) Jesus' "teaching" that the temple was to be a house of prayer "for all the nations" (11.17).

John's Gospel, therefore, only shares with the Synoptics a simple sketch of a clearing of the temple grounds with the following shared terminology: "Jerusalem," "temple," "selling," "money-changers," "tables," "pigeons,"[11] and "driving out." Still, for most scholars such a revolutionary act could hardly have been repeated.

From this, many scholars have gone on to argue the merits of either Synoptic chronology[12] or Johannine chronology.[13] Others have debated whether John's scene is historically probable or not.[14] What I wish to emphasize in making these

---

[9] Dodd, Historical Tradition, 158, observes a significant difference in pace as well.

[10] In the Synoptics, Jesus quotes Isa 56.7 and Jer 7.11. In John's Gospel, Jesus does not cite an Old Testament text.

[11] Pigeons served as the offering of the poor (cf. Lev 5.7; 12.8).

[12] See, e.g., Barnabas Lindars, New Testament Apologetic: The Doctrinal Significance of the Old Testament Quotations (Philadelphia: Westminster, 1961), 105; Reim, Studien, 11; Schnackenburg, St. John 1, 353-55; Barrett, St. John, 195 (who suggests dependency on Mark); F. F. Bruce, The Gospel of John: Introduction, Exposition and Notes (Grand Rapids: Eerdmans, 1983), 77. Recently, Roth, "Coding," 6-29, has attempted to explain the differing chronologies by suggesting that, while Mark represents a "veiled, selective and non-inverting rewriting of the Elijah-Elisha Narrative," John has produced a selective inverting narrative rewriting of the Law and the Prophets. Roth's proposal, however, lacks credibility. Cf. Andre Lacocque, "The Narrative Code of the Fourth Gospel: Response to Wolfgang Roth's Paper," BR 32 (1987): 30-41.

[13] See, e.g., William Temple, Readings in St. John's Gospel (London: Macmillan, 1939), 175-77; Dorothy L. Sayers, The Man Born to be King (New York: Harper, 1943), 35 n. 1; Ivor Buse, "The Cleansing of the Temple in the Synoptics and in John," ExpTim 70 (1958/1959): 24; François-Marie Braun, "L'expulsion des vendeurs du Temple (Mt. xxi,12-17, 23-27; Mc. xi,15-19, 27-33; Lc. xix,45-xx,8; Jo. ii,13-22)," RB 38 (1929): 178-200; John A. T. Robinson, The Priority of John, ed. J. F. Coakley (London: SCM Press, 1985), 127-31. Marie-Joseph Lagrange, L'évangile selon saint Jean, 7 éd., Études bibliques (Paris: Gabalda, 1948), 65, argues that the temple cleansing was early and that Jesus' confrontation with the Jews occurred just prior to the passion. Brown, John 1, 117-18, attempts precisely the opposite.

[14] Haenchen, John 1, 187-90, has overemphasized some of the historical difficulties. Cf. Becker, Johannes, 123-24; Siegfried Mendner, "Die Tempelreinigung," ZNW 47 (1956): 104; Victor Eppstein, "The Historicity of the Gospel Account of the Cleansing of the Temple," ZNW

observations, however, is this. John's account represents such an independent portrayal[15] that the Synoptics offer little as an aid in understanding his intention in constructing this pericope (except, of course, by way of contrast).[16] Such is especially the case as regards John's source for and his intent in citing the Old Testament.

I.

The Old Testament passage to which John refers is Ps 69(68).10a.[17] There is some question, however, whether the influence of a specific textual tradition is evident in this citation. Consider the following: (1) There is significant textual support for a reading for the OG which represents an exact rendering of what one observes in the MT. (2) John's citation differs from this reading only in that it has the future "will consume" rather than the aorist "has consumed." (3) Two

---

55 (1964): 42-58; Joachim Jeremias, "Zwei Miszellen: 1. Antik-jüdische Munzdeutungen. 2. Zur Geschichtlichkeit der Tempelreinigung," NTS 23 (1976/1977): 179-80; R. J. Campbell, "Evidence for the Historicity of the Fourth Gospel in John 2:13-22," in Studia Evangelica, vol. 7, Papers Presented to the Fifth International Congress on Biblical Studies Held at Oxford, 1973, ed. E. A. Livingstone, Texte und Untersuchungen zur Geschichte der altchristlichen Literatur, Bd. 112 (Berlin: Akademie-Verlag, 1982), 101-20.

15 Dodd, Historical Tradition, 157, 161, in particular has convincingly argued for the independence of the two traditions represented in the Synoptics and in John's Gospel. Dodd exaggerates unnecessarily, however, when he writes, "The suggestion that the temple was twice cleansed is the last resort of a desperate determination to harmonize Mark and John at all costs" (p. 157 n. 2). Cf. Westcott, St. John, 44; Leon Morris, The Gospel according to John: The English Text with Introduction, Exposition and Notes, the New International Commentary on the New Testament (Grand Rapids: Eerdmans, 1971), 189-91; Douglas J. Moo, The Old Testament in the Gospel Passion Narratives (Sheffield: Almond Press, 1983), 233 n. 1.

16 This is true also of the relationship between John 2.18-22 and the Synoptics (see further below). The texts of Qumran also offer little help. Here, "temple" functions as a metaphor for the end-time desert community (cf. 1QH 6.25-28; 7.7-9; 1QS 5.5-6; 8.7-10; 4QpPs 37 2.16). POxy 840.2 is similarly distant from the theological concerns of John.

17 John, we have noted, is alone among New Testament writers in citing Ps. 69(68).10a. V. 10b, however, is quoted by Paul in Rom 15.3. Indeed, the frequent appearance of references to this psalm in the New Testament (cf. v. 5 with John 15.25 [?], v. 22 with Matt 27.34, v. 22b with Mark 15.36 and John 19.28, and v. 26 with Acts 1.20) has led many to suggest that both John and Paul were guided by a common early tradition in which the whole of Ps 69(68) was referred to Jesus. See Dodd, Scriptures, 57-58; E. Earle Ellis, Paul's Use of the Old Testament (Grand Rapids: Baker, 1957), 97 n. 4; Bultmann, John, 124 n. 5; Schnackenburg, St. John 1, 347; Bruce, John, 75; Becker, Johannes, 124; Kysar, John, 49. Lindars, NT Apologetic, 105, claims that almost every line of vv. 23-29 is quoted or alluded to in the New Testament. Against a general acceptance of the psalm and its messianic utilization is Freed, OT Quotations, 9.

important OG witnesses (B and ℵ), however, offer a reading which agrees with John 2.17.[18]

Most scholars have responded to this evidence with one of two different hypotheses. Some have asserted that John 2.17 comes without change from "the OG."[19] Others have claimed that John's citation is, again, from the OG, but that John has changed the aorist of the OG to a future in order to adapt his citation to the context in which he places it.[20]

There is an obvious problem with these arguments. On the one hand, advocates of the former solution rarely say something about the appearance of the aorist κατέφαγε in OG manuscripts other than B or ℵ.[21] On the other hand, advocates of the latter generally claim that B and ℵ have been influenced by John without explaining why this may or may not be probable.[22]

A well-argued case must begin with the following observations. First, a Hebrew perfect is, at times, rendered in the OG with the future.[23] It is questionable, however, that this has taken place in this instance. The evidence suggests otherwise: (1) The Hebrew verbs in both Ps 69.10a and 10b are perfects. The

---

[18] While there exists some ms. evidence for the reading κατέφαγε in John, the external evidence is overwhelmingly in favor of the future (καταφάγεται is supported by P66 P75 ℵ B Θ W sa Or; κατέφαγε by Φ it vg sys syp bo Eus). Barrett, St. John, 199, writes, "the aorist in the predominantly Western texts may have been due . . . to the retroversion into Syriac, where naturally the Semitic perfect was resumed."

[19] I.e., OG Bℵ. Cf., e.g., Dodd, Scriptures, 57; Braun, Jean 2, 14; Burney, Aramaic Origin, 116; Bultmann, John, 124; Humann, "OT Quotations," 42.

[20] Cf., e.g., Franke, Alte Testament, 283; Schnackenburg, St. John 1, 347; Reim, Studien, 10, 91, 94-95, 224-25; Lindars, NT Apologetic, 104, 107, 266; Richard W. Longenecker, Biblical Exegesis in the Apostolic Period (Grand Rapids: Eerdmans, 1975), 137; Moo, Passion Narratives, 233; Kysar, John, 49; Menken, "John 1,23," 193. Those scholars who have resorted to speculating about the accuracy of John's memory (e.g., Goodwin, "Sources," 62), however, are surprisingly few in number. According to Mathews, "Temple," 117, John's citation represents an adaptation of a Hebrew Vorlage.

[21] A welcome exception is Braun, Jean 2, 14, who writes, "Jean prend à son compte la leçon καταφάγεται ('dévore' ou 'dévorere') des grands onciaux, contrairement à l'hébreu 'akālatnī ('m'a dévoré'), qui semble avoir influencé la variante κατέφαγεν (Bb Sinc et nombreux mss.)." See further below.

[22] Suggesting the possible influence of John are Schnackenburg, St. John 1, 347; Barrett, St. John, 199; Freed, OT Quotations, 9-10, 117; Menken, "John 1,23," 193; Humann, "OT Quotations," 42 n. 37. To my knowledge, only Freed has offered a satisfactory explanation for John's probable influence on the OG. What follows closely approximates his argument (cf. Fortna, Fourth Gospel, 268 n. 76).

[23] So Barrett, St. John, 28; Gleason L. Archer and Gregory Chirichigno, Old Testament Quotations in the New Testament: A Complete Survey (Chicago: Moody, 1983), 73; Humann, "OT Quotations," 42 n. 37; cf. Ronald J. Williams, Hebrew Syntax: An Outline, 2d ed. (Toronto: Univ. of Toronto Press, 1976), 29-30.

OG renders the second of these perfects with an aorist.[24] (2) The aorist appears in Paul's citation of v. 10b as well (for which there are no significant textual variants for either the OG or Rom 15.3). (3) Symmachus utilizes a different verb (κατηνάλωσε), but he too renders the Hebrew perfect with an aorist. (4) Κατέφαγε also appears in Origen's translation.[25]

It seems likely, then, that the OG renders אכלתני with κατέφαγε rather than καταφάγεται. And in this case, the reading of OG Bℵ probably reflects the Christian influence of John's Gospel.

This brings us to a final observation. If, in fact, the OG and the MT are equivalent to one another, then it is not possible to establish whether John derived his citation from one or the other.[26] The evidence is ambiguous.[27] John's reference(s) to the same psalm elsewhere in his Gospel[28] are similarly difficult to characterize.

For the moment, the issue remains unresolved. It remains, then, to turn to John and his apparent intention in having the disciples cite the psalm in this manner in this context.

II.

An additional difficulty, however, immediately presents itself. The significance of the event portrayed in John 2.13-16 has been the subject of consider-

---

[24] The OG normally renders the Hebrew perfect with an aorist. Cf. Richard R. Ottley, *The Book of Isaiah according to the Septuagint*, vol. 1, *Introduction and Translation with a Parallel Version from the Hebrew* (London: C. J. Clay, 1904), 43; for examples of this, cf. idem., *A Handbook to the Septuagint* (New York: E. P. Dutton, 1919), 120-25.

[25] Cf. the similar expression in Ps 119.139 where the OG also renders the Hebrew with an aorist.

[26] Among the very few scholars who have exercised due caution in this regard are Barrett, *St. John*, 28, 198-99; and Freed, *OT Quotations*, 9-10, 117-18, 126.

[27] Reim, *Studien*, 10, errs conspicuously when he (1) notes the equivalency of the OG and the MT, then (2) asserts that, "Die Sprache des Zitates ist die der LXX," without indicating why the OG is a likely source, and then (3) concludes later that "Da Johannes in 2,17 LXX Ps 68 zitiert, wird man mit grosser Warscheinlichkeit auch die anderen beiden Zitate (i.e., 15.25 and 19.28) aus der LXX herleiten können" (p. 94).

[28] Cf. my remarks above. Lindars, *NT Apologetic*, 104, has claimed that the "whole plot of the psalm is brought into play" when the evangelist has the disciples "remember" Ps 69(68).10a in the context of the temple incident (cf. Reim, *Studien*, 11, 91; Braun, *Jean* 2, 14; Brown, *John*, 124; Hanson, *NT Interpretation*, 115). It is not always clear, however, how much of this context John knows or how much of it he alludes to in his construction of this scene (see below).

able recent debate.[29] The more traditional interpretation of this event (a viewpoint that continues to predominate) is reflected in the title this pericope normally receives in the modern synopses: the *cleansing* of the temple. "This implies a prior profanation or contamination, and the profanation has been readily found in the conducting of trade in or around the temple precincts."[30] Jesus' intent, then, was to purify the temple of this defiling presence.

In the last few years, however, this traditional viewpoint has been challenged. The services provided by this market place, it is pointed out, were necessary ones, essential to the proper functioning of the sacrificial cultus. The temple was the divinely appointed place for sacrifice. And sacrifices could not be carried out without the provision of appropriate animals. Furthermore, it is self-evident that pilgrims from diverse lands would bring with them various coinages. Thus, "In the view of Jesus and his contemporaries, the requirement to sacrifice must always have involved the supply of sacrificial animals, their inspection, and the changing of money."[31] All of these services would naturally involve a fee. Additionally, "the money changers were probably those who changed the money in the possession of pilgrims into the coinage accepted by the temple in payment of the half-shekel tax levied on all Jews."[32]

The market place in the temple was necessary, therefore, if the commandments given by God were to be followed. But an assault on what is compulsory cannot be regarded as an attack on current practice. How is one, then, to understand this attack? In this case, there can be only one other way of interpreting the event: symbolically. Specifically, one recent proposal attracting considerable attention concludes from Jesus' overturning the tables of the money-changers "that Jesus publicly predicted or threatened the destruction of the temple, that the statement was shaped by his expectation of the arrival of the eschaton, (and)

---

[29] See esp. the contribution of E. P. Sanders, "Jesus and the Temple," in his *Jesus and Judaism* (Philadelphia: Fortress, 1985), 61-76. Cf. Anthony J. Saldarini, *Jesus and Passover* (New York: Paulist, 1984), 73. See further below.

[30] Sanders, *Jesus*, 61 (his excellent overview and critique of those who have espoused this viewpoint appears on pp. 61-69). For the debate over what occurred within the temple grounds and what was limited to the area outside, see p. 365 n. 6 and 367 n. 45. The precise location of this market cannot be determined with certainty, but many assume that the trade was only permitted in the court of the Gentiles (on this as an expression of the exclusivism of the Jews, see Mathews, "Temple," 124).

[31] Sanders, *Jesus*, 63.

[32] Sanders, *Jesus*, 64 (he adds, "The desire of the authorities to receive the money in a standard coinage which did not have on it the image of an emperor or king is reasonable, and no one ever seems to have protested this;" contrast, however, Morris, *Reflections*, 80). For information on the priesthood, the temple service, the taxes, and the coinage accepted by the temple, see p. 366 nn. 26-31.

that he probably also expected a new temple . . . ."[33] Jesus' act prophetically heralded these future events.

This recent trend toward a symbolic appreciation of Jesus' actions is a positive one. However, it simply does not follow that the clarity and the force of the point Jesus makes becomes obscured or confused if one continues to regard Jesus' actions as a critique of what he finds in the temple.[34] Indeed, in the Old or New Testament God is never said to act with such violence for the sake of mere symbolism (neither does he destroy) without immediate and concrete provocation.

What has provoked Jesus? The answer to this is the traditional one stated unmistakably in John 2.16 ("you shall not make my Father's house a house of trade"). The conducting of business in this holy place is specifically rejected. "The concept was that from anything which exists for the purpose of fulfilling divine commandments one must derive no secular profit."[35] This is evident, for example, in the law for the synagogue which prohibits even its use as a thoroughfare.[36] Jesus' response recalls the zealous fervor of Nehemiah in Neh 13.15-22.[37]

Indeed, the narrative itself seems to be constructed in order to recall various Old Testament prophecies containing complementary themes.[38] In Mal 3.1b-5,[39] for example, Malachi prophesies that with the emergence of the eschaton the Lord will suddenly come to his temple. At that time, the Lord "will sit as a refiner

---

[33] Sanders, *Jesus*, 75.

[34] Cf. esp. Craig A. Evans, "Jesus' Action in the Temple: Cleansing or Portent of Destruction?" *CBQ* 51 (1989): 237-70. esp. 269; see also idem, "Jesus' Action in the Temple and Evidence of Corruption in the First-Century Temple," in *Society of Biblical Literature 1989 Seminar Papers*, ed. David J. Lull, Society of Biblical Literature Seminar Papers Series, nr. 28 (Atlanta: Scholars Press, 1989), 522-39.

[35] J. Duncan M. Derrett, "The Zeal of the House and the Cleansing of the Temple," *DR* 95 (1977): 82; cf. Morris, *Reflections*, 79-81. The market itself is necessary, but its presence in the temple is not. Jesus' critique addresses this presence. There are no charges of greed, corruption, extortion, or insurrection. There is no threat, here or elsewhere, to destroy (note the absence of any reference to the σπήλαιον λῃστῶν in Jer 7.11 [Matt 21.13; Mark 11.17; Luke 19.46] or the threat of destruction in Jer 7.14 [and 26.6,9; cf. Matt 24.1-2; Mark 13.1-2; Luke 21. 5-6]). See further below.

[36] See *m. Meg.* 3.3 (even within the ruined remains of a synagogue, these prohibitions apply).

[37] Derrett, "Zeal," 82, 92-93. In this text, Nehemiah will not even allow the merchants to enter the city!

[38] Cf. Evans, "Temple," 248-56; Mathews, "Temple," 102-4.

[39] Note how Malachi's Elijah figure (Mal 3.1a, 23-24) is passed over by John (see chapter one) in favor of the "Lord," i.e., the "messenger of the covenant" (3.1bc; cf. 3.2 with Rev 6.17) who comes as a judge/witness (3.5) against those who "rob" God in their tithes and offerings (3.8).

and purifier of silver, and he will purify the sons of Levi and refine them like gold and silver till they present right offerings to the Lord."[40]

Many scholars rightly see in John 2.16 ("you shall not make my Father's house a house of trade [οἶκον ἐμπορίου]") a reference to Zech 14.21 ("And there shall no longer be a כְּנַעֲנִי [OG: χαναναῖος] in the house of the Lord of hosts on that day").[41] John has apparently opted against understanding Zechariah's prophecy as a reference to the Gentiles.[42] Instead, he has taken it correctly[43] as a reference to "traders" and their mercantile activity in the temple.[44] For this reason, John conspicuously emphasizes the role of the merchants in this narrative. Nothing, in turn, is said in vv. 14-17 of others who were in the temple.[45]

Ezekiel as well exhibits a similar zeal for a purified temple. And this too appears significant for John.[46] The prophet is transported in a vision to the temple in Jerusalem and views there the abominations that Israel has committed (8.1-18). Judgment is decreed (8.18; cf. 22.23-31, esp. v. 26) and the Judge is commissioned (9.1-2) to go to Jerusalem *beginning* with the sanctuary (9.6). He does so *beginning* "with the elder men who were within in the house" (9.6 OG).[47] Ezekiel's prophecy appears to have guided not only John's portrait of the charac-

---

40 Cf. Mal 3.3 OG "he shall pour them" and John's "he poured out the coins" (Derrett, "Zeal," 90). Contrast Rev 16.1, 2, 3, 4, 6, 8, 10, 12, 17.

41 For the two prevalent interpretations of this passage which are presented below, see Cecil Roth, "The Cleansing of the Temple and Zechariah xiv 21," *NovT* 4 (1960); 178-80. Cf. Lynn A. Losie, "The Cleansing of the Temple: A History of a Gospel Tradition in Light of Its Background in the Old Testament and in Early Judaism" (Ph.D. diss., Fuller Theological Seminary, 1984), 244-45 n. 77.

42 This interpretation is reflected in the Jewish exclusivism appearing in, e.g., Josephus, *Wars*, 5.193-98; 6.124-26; *Ant.* 15.417; an inscription discovered in Jerusalem; the Zealot movement in 66 C.E.; and Qumran (4QFlor 1.1-7). Lindars, *NT Apologetic*, 108 n. 3 (idem, *John*, 139) and Losie, "Cleansing," 223, conclude from the reading of the OG that John was working with a Hebrew text. But χαναναῖος is equally capable of being taken as a reference to "traders" (LSJ, 1976; see below). Cf. Zeph 1.11.

43 Most scholars agree. See esp. Dodd, *Interpretation*, 300.

44 See the Targum (תַּגָּרָא עָבִישׁ); Aquila (μετάβολος [followed by Jerome: "mercator"]); and the Syriac (*mybln'*). Cf. *b. Pesah.* 50a.

45 Matt 21.12 and Mark 11.15 mention both those who sold and those who bought. Luke 19.45 mentions only the venders. Cf. πωλέω in Rev 13.17 (cf. Ezek 7.12-13; Zech 11.5) with the woe against Babylon and her merchants in Rev 18 (note ἔμπορος in vv. 3, 11, 15, 23; cf. the woe against the merchant city Tyre in Ezek 27-28). Contrast with this the feast of the Lamb in Rev 19.

46 C. Hassell Bullock, "Ezekiel: Bridge between the Testaments," *JETS* 25 (1982): 29-30; cf. Evans, "Temple," 251.

47 The MT reads, "with the elders who were *before* the house." Note that Ezek 40-43 anticipates the establishment of a new temple, cleansed (43.20), purified (43.26), and holy (42.13-14).

ter of Jesus' encounter with the Jews but also his placement of this pericope at the *beginning* of Jesus' public ministry.

In terminating the activity of the market place,[48] therefore, Jesus performs actions characteristic of his eschatological identity as both Savior and Judge in fulfillment of several Old Testament prophecies.[49] John thereby underlines the present reality of the final age.[50] To see Jesus' actions in temple, then, as a mere critique is to miss their greatest significance. Jesus' actions are, instead, indicative not only of a present eschatological reality but also of its eminent consummation. That one is to look to the future as well is confirmed both by the "incompleteness" of what Jesus accomplishes in clearing the temple and by his ensuing dialogue with the Jews.[51]

---

[48] Most interpreters correctly see πάντας as a reference to all the merchants. Some are apparently uneasy with the suggestion that Jesus may have used his whip on these people and therefore seek another referent for πάντας (cf. Dodd, *Historical Tradition*, 157 n. 3 [idem, *Interpretation*, 300-1]; Haenchen, *John 1*, 183; Etienne Trocme, "L'expulsion des marchands du Temple [Mt 21:12-17]," *NTS* 15 (1968/1969): 9. These efforts, however, clearly detract from a proper understanding of the scene. Concerning ἐκβάλλω, cf. Hos 9.15 (see also *Pss. Sol.* 17.26-46, esp. vv. 35 and 36). Jesus will never drive his followers away from himself (John 6.37). This is reserved for his enemies and, of course, for Satan himself (12.31). It is striking, however, that what is for Jesus' enemies an expression of his displeasure (ἐκβάλλω, 2.15) becomes for the followers of Jesus a means for blessing (ἐκβάλλω, 10.4: the redeemed [cf. 5.24-25] leave the temple at the direction of Jesus [cf. 9.34, 35]). Cf. Wis 11.5-8; 18.6-9.

[49] Recently, Losie, "Cleansing," has suggested that the earliest tradition concerning Jesus' cleansing of the temple interpreted it as an eschatological act in preparation for the advent of God's kingdom based upon Isa 52.7-12. Only later, Losie claims, was Jesus' act interpreted as a negative critique in which Jesus functioned as the messianic judge of the Jews. Losie fails, however, to adequately demonstrate any initial connection of this tradition with Isa 52. Cf. Bultmann, *John*, 128-29.

[50] See the brief but instructive description of John's portrait of the final judgment as a present reality in Jack Dean Kingsbury, "The Gospel in Four Editions," *Int* 33 (1979): 374. Cf. the various attempts of others surveyed by Kysar, *Fourth Evangelist*, 207-14 (cf. idem, "Recent Research," 2449-51).

[51] Keep in mind that, even though the merchants only appear in vv. 14-16, and the Jews only in vv. 18-20, John's narrative portrays the activity of the merchants as an extension of the activity of "the Jews." Actively or passively, the presence of the merchants has been authorized by the Jewish leadership. Therefore, Jesus' indictment of the temple does not distinguish between these two groups (neither does it distinguish between the money-changers and the other merchants).

"The Jews"[52] waste no time in challenging Jesus' authority: "What sign have you to show us for doing this?" (2.18).[53] Jesus' response is not what they expect: "Destroy this temple,[54] and in three days I will raise it up" (2.19; cf. 5.21; 6.39-40). Jesus refuses to grant their demand for a sign that will validate his authority. Because they understand neither his immediate actions nor the true function of his signs, Jesus points to that which both anticipate.[55] Rather than playing into

---

[52] As was the case in John 1.29, "the Jews" probably refers to the Jewish leadership functioning in a representative fashion. The varying attempts to characterize the role of the Jews in John are surveyed by Kysar, "Recent Research," 2426-28 (cf. idem, *Fourth Evangelist*, 149-56); Urban c. von Wahlde, "The Johannine 'Jews:' A Critical Survey," *NTS* 28 (1982): 33-60.

[53] Most scholars rightly recognize that the Jews here demand that Jesus perform an authenticating miracle as proof of the authority he has claimed for himself in clearing the temple grounds. Reim, *Studien*, 106, 143, sees in this a "warscheinliche Anspielung" to Exod 4.1-5 (see further in the following chapter). Such questions are typical of the Jews in the first ten chapters of John's Gospel and serve only to "challenge, generate confrontation, and eventually demonstrate that the Jews cannot accept the answers they are given" (R. Alan Culpepper, *Anatomy of the Fourth Gospel: A Study in Literary Design*, with a Foreword by Frank Kermode, Foundations and Facets: New Testament [Philadelphia: Fortress, 1983], 127).

[54] The construction is neither a concessive clause (cf. BDF, 195 [387.2]) nor a condition (cf. Dodd, *Interpretation*, 302 n. 1; Barrett, *St. John*, 199; Schnackenburg, *St. John*, 350, n.27; Lindars, *John*, 142-43; Mathews, "Temple," 120 n. 55). It is, instead, a prophetic imperative (cf. Bultmann, *John*, 125; Barrett, *St. John*, 199; Brown, *John* 1, 115; Beasley-Murray, *John*, 40; Fortna, *Fourth Gospel*, 123 n. 277) which should be accorded full force. Jesus has come as the Lamb so that he might die. He instructs (cf. 13.27) the Jews to do precisely what he would have them do. See Lloyd Gaston, *No Stone on Another: Studies in the Significance of the Fall of Jerusalem in the Synoptic Gospels*, Supplements to Novum Testamentum, vol. 23 (Leiden: E. J. Brill, 1970), 207, who favors the translation "You will destroy." Cf. Lucius Nereparampil, *Destroy This Temple* (Bangalore: Dharmaram, 1978), 84: "The ironic imperative of this first part of the *Temple-Logion* implies that the Jews have already been destroying the temple . . . and are still continuing to do so." Jesus does not threaten to destroy. He suggests, instead, that they have already done this and, true to their character, they will destroy again.

[55] The Jews misunderstand Jesus' signs as mere proofs of his divine power and authority and fail to recognize that Jesus' signs point beyond themselves in anticipation of the climactic revelation of his glory on the cross. Cf. Rissi, "Hochzeit," 90: "Das Wesentliche am Semeiabegriff tritt nicht ins licht, wenn man die unmittelbare Beziehung der Zeichen zu Leiden, Kreuz und Auferstehung Jesu nicht erkennt (in Joh 12,33; 18,32 wird auch das Verbum σημαίνειν auf den Tod Jesu bezogen [damit wird auch zusammenhangen 21,19, wo das Verbum auf den Tod des Petrus anspielt, der ein 'Verherrlichen' Gottes genannt wird!]). Es geht im Zeichen, das eine Wirklichkeit zur Erscheinung bringt, die grosser ist als das Zeichen selbst, die sich in ihm anzeigt, aber in ihm nicht aufgeht, nicht nur um die Offenbarung des 'Sohn-seins' oder 'Gott-seins,' überhaupt nicht um ein Sein, sondern um ein Werk, nämlich das im Tode Jesu vollzogene Erlösungswerk Gottes." For the many proposals concerning the nature of faith in the Fourth Gospel and its relationship to Jesus' signs, see Kysar, *Fourth Evangelist*, 225-33 (cf. idem, "Recent Research," 2441-42, 2453-56; idem, "The Gospel of John in Current Research," *RelSRev* 9 [1983]: 320).

their thirst for the miraculous and their inability to perceive its function, Jesus instead verbalizes that which his signs non-verbally signify.[56] If the Jews truly desire to know who Jesus is, what authority he has, and what his actions and words mean, they must begin by seeing in his death and resurrection after "three days" the final testimony[57] to his eschatological identity and purpose.

Jesus' statement suggests that his purification of the temple (the center of the sacrificial cultus) in the context of a Passover feast is to be understood as the inauguration of that which will culminate in the perfect sacrifice of the final eschatological Passover. His advent in the temple, therefore, envisions his going to prepare a place (14.2),[58] his death as the true Lamb of God.[59] His death will

---

[56] Cf. D. K. Clark, "Signs and Wisdom in John," *CBQ* 45 (1983): 201-9; Willett, "Wisdom," 208-14; and Wolfgang J. Bittner, *Jesu Zeichen im Johannesevangelium: Die Messias-Erkenntnis im Johannesevangelium vor ihrem jüdischen Hintergrund*, Wissenschaftliche Untersuchungen zum Neuen Testament, 2. Reihe, Bd. 26 (Tübingen: Mohr-Siebeck, 1987), 28, who notes of signs in apocalyptic intertestamental literature that "Sie gelten . . . als 'Vorzeichen,' in denen sich die kommende Zeit ankündigt."

[57] Rissi, "Hochzeit," 90, writes, "Hier liegt der Grund, warum der Evangelist Tod und Auferstehung selbst nicht 'Zeichen' nennen kann. Die Wunder und der Hingang zum Vater verhalten sich zueinander wie Zeichen und Wirklichkeit." This "Wirklichkeit" constitutes God's final fulfillment of his promises for which the resurrection offers a threefold "witness" to its significance. Other threefold testimonies in the Fourth Gospel include the following: (1) the Baptist's threefold testimony (1.19-21; his testimony also spans a period of three days [cf. vv. 19-28, 29-34, 35-36; cf. Jesus' testimony in vv. 29-34, 35-42, 43-51]); (2) Peter's threefold denial (cf. 13.38; 18.17, 25-27 [contrast his threefold confession, 21.15-19]); (3) Jesus' three-fold testimony on the cross (19.26-27, 28, 30). This is enough to demonstrate a pattern based upon the idea contained in Deut 19.15 (cf. 17.6). Cf. John 8.17; 1 John 5.7-8. See also Matt 18.15-20; 2 Cor 13.1; Heb 10.28.

[58] Cf. the recent attempt to find significant temple imagery in this text in James McCaffrey, *The House with Many Rooms: The Temple Theme of Jn. 14,2-3*, Analecta Biblica, vol. 114 (Rome: Editrice Pontificio Istituto Biblico, 1988). See also Günter Fischer, *Die himmlischen Wohnungen: Untersuchungen zu Joh 14,2f*, Europäische Hochschulschriften, 23. Reihe, Theologie, Bd. 38 (Bern: H. Lang, 1975).

[59] G. L. Carey, "Lamb of God and Atonement Theories," *TynBul* 32 (1981): 97-122, concludes that Old Testament traditions concerning the Paschal Lamb and Suffering Servant probably lie in the background of John 1.29. The likelihood of this synthesis, however, is frequently challenged. Cf. Isa 53.7 ("like a lamb that is led to the slaughter"). Offering an exposition of John's Gospel with particular emphasis on Jesus as the Lamb of God is Ray Summers, *Behold the Lamb: An Exposition of the Theological Themes in the Gospel of John* (Nashville: Broadman, 1979). Cf. the other approaches to this question discussed by Kysar, *Fourth Evangelist*, 137-38; Carson, "John," 253; Peter Whale, "The Lamb of John: Some Myths About the Vocabulary of the Johannine Literature," *JBL* 106 (1987): 289-95; Morris, *Reflections*, 35-42. To object to a traditional understanding of this event (see above) because it "obscures" or "confuses" (Sanders, *Jesus*, 70, 368 n. 60) the intended symbolism is to fail to see in it more than a reference to Jesus' role on the cross as Savior. Jesus will also judge (12.31) and be judged (Derrett, "Zeal," 91).

mean the passing away of the sacrificial cultus[60] and the beginning of Jesus' eschatological reign as God's true temple, the new place where God and his children meet.[61]

It is appropriate now to return to John's citation of Ps 69(68). What role does the disciples' remembering of the psalm play in this context? The reader is to understand it as an additional complementary "interpretation" of what Jesus has done and said in John 2.13-16.

The problem is that the disciples do not seem to immediately understand it this way. They have seen in Jesus the "Lamb of God" (1.29, 35) who "was" before John (1.30). He is the Son of God (1.34, 49), the Messiah (1.41; cf. 1.32-33), the one about whom Moses and the prophets wrote (1.45), the King of Israel (1.49), and the Son of Man (1.51). They have seen his "glory" and "believed in him"

---

[60] Edwin C. Hoskyns, *The Fourth Gospel*, 2d ed., ed. F. N. Davey (London: Faber, 1947), 194; J. K. Howard, "Passover and Eucharist in the Fourth Gospel," *SJT* 20 (1967): 332-33 (who quotes Tasker); cf Barrett, *St. John*, 197-98; Derrett, "Zeal," 90; Beasley-Murray, *John*, 40; Mathews, "Temple," 125. It is also possible that Jesus purposes to strike out against the market place in another way. It may be that Jesus also attacks the Jewish idea that, by offering sacrifices, the Jews purchase for themselves atonement and expiation for sin. On this point, see Jacob Neusner, "Money-Changers in the Temple: The Mishnah's Explanation," *NTS* 35 (1989): 287-90, who illustrates from the Mishnah (see *m. Seqal.* 1.3; cf. *t. Seqal.* 1.6) that it was especially the money-changers in the temple who facilitated this "purchase" by collecting the half-shekel tax. These monies served throughout the coming year to provide the daily whole offerings for the nation (cf. Exod 30.16). Neusner's points are largely well taken. I would not, however, confine Jesus' critique, as Neusner does, to the whole offering. Nor do I regard Jesus' critique as a "rejection" (p. 290) of the offering. His attack is, instead, on their understanding of this (they give in order to receive; Jesus gives in order that they might receive). And finally, the cross is envisioned, not the Eucharist (p. 290).

[61] This is not the first time in John's Gospel that Jesus has been portrayed in terms of tabernacle/temple imagery. See, e.g., John 1.14 where "tabernacle imagery is uniquely able to portray the person of Jesus as the locus of God's Word and glory among humankind" (Craig R. Koester, *The Dwelling of God: The Tabernacle in the Old Testament, Intertestamental Jewish Literature, and the New Testament*, The Catholic Biblical Quarterly Monograph Series, vol. 22 [Washington, D.C.: Catholic Biblical Association, 1989], 102; cf. McCaffrey, *House*, 222-24). Similarly, John 1.51 (cf. Gen 28.12) seems to imply that Jesus is to be understood as "Bethel," i.e., "the House of God" (cf. the survey of the interpretations that have been offered in Brown, *John 1*, 88-91; see also Hanson, *NT Interpretation*, 113; Gaston, *No Stone*, 210; Carson, "John," 255; McCaffrey, *House*, 225-27; Gary M. Burge, *The Anointed Community: The Holy Spirit in the Johannine Tradition* [Grand Rapids: Eerdmans, 1987], 86-87). For Schnackenburg, *St. John 1*, 352, John 2.21 "makes Jesus the 'place' where God is to be adored, the true 'house of God' (cf. 1:51). With him and in him the time of the worship 'in spirit and truth' (4:23) has dawned." John's shifting from the use of ἱερόν (2.14, 15) to ναός (2.19, 20, 21) is both conspicuous and consistent with his intent to identify Jesus' "body" (cf. the only other uses of this term in 19.31, 38, 40; 20.12) with the temple sanctuary itself and not the surrounding courtyards (cf. Rev 11.2; 21.22-23).

(2.11).[62] In spite of this, they characteristically fail to comprehend the way (cf. 13.36; 14.5). They do not recognize the necessity of Jesus' death (cf. 18.10-11).[63] Neither do they know "the Scripture, that he must rise from the dead" (20.9).[64]

Indeed, what the disciples do understand is notoriously difficult to quantify. Perhaps one is to infer that they simply saw Jesus' zeal for the temple, heard him speak of the "house," and then recalled a psalm in which similar motifs occur.[65] Perhaps they are familiar with the larger context of the psalm and know that it refers to a pious individual's sufferings at the hands of his own brethren.[66] Perhaps they see in the psalm only a prediction of Jesus' consuming anger.[67]

---

[62] The significance of the purposeful contrasting of the believing of the disciples with the lack thereof in "the Jews" is rightly recognized by Schnackenburg, *St. John* 3, 206-9; Culpepper, *Anatomy*, 135.

[63] Culpepper, *Anatomy*, 115, rightly remarks, "They are marked especially by their recognition of Jesus and belief in his claims. Yet, they are not exemplars of perfect faith, but of positive responses and typical misunderstandings." He adds (pp. 117-19), "This misunderstanding is part of a pattern. The disciples do not understand Jesus' words about his body as a temple (2:21-22); they do not understand what sustains Jesus (4:32-33); they do not understand the relationship between sin and suffering (9:2); they do not understand the experience of death (11:11-15); and they do not understand the significance of the entry into Jerusalem (12:16)." Even as Jesus prepares to return to the Father, "they have grasped very little of what Jesus has revealed to them. They do not know where he is going (13:36; 14:5). They do not know the way to the Father or that they have seen Him in Jesus (14:5-11) . . . . They do not understand what Jesus says about a 'little while' (16:17-18). Even at the end of the discourse, when the disciples think they have got it, they can only parrot proudly what Jesus has just said (cf. 16:27, 29)." Only later will they understand what Jesus has revealed to them.

[64] Cf. Culpepper, *Anatomy*, 116-17. The crux of the matter, however, is not "understanding," but "abiding." "This is the true test of the disciple: 'If you continue in my word [λόγος], you are truly my disciples' (8.31)" (p. 117). Indeed, this seems to be the very problem Jesus encounters in general in 2.23-25 and in specific with Nicodemus (as a character representative [cf. "we," 1.22; 3.2] of those in 2.23-25). Jesus refuses to entrust himself to those who believe in him as a worker of signs come from God (cf. 2.23; 3.2), but when confronted later will not accept his testimony (3.11; cf. "we," 1.14, 16, 41, 45; 3.11).

[65] R. C. H. Lenski, *The Interpretation of St. John's Gospel* (Minneapolis: Augsburg, 1943), 210.

[66] If this is case, "they here contemplate with foreboding the reckless action of their Master in a situation of manifest tension" (Dodd, *Historical Tradition*, 158) expecting estrangement, conflict, and reviling (Ps 69[68].10b). What they expect, then, commences immediately (John 2.18). The disciples do not, however, anticipate that this is only the beginning. And whether or not they comprehend the thrust of καταφάγεται is not clear.

[67] Many have argued otherwise, but the general significance of אכלתני/κατέφαγε utilized in this context (in which the "consumption" of the zealous one stands in parallel with the abuse he suffers in v. 11) makes a reference to destruction as a result of one's own zeal a natural way to understand this passage. Similarly, Hanson, *NT Interpretation*, 116; Moo, *Passion Narratives*, 233-34 n. 4 (who refers to A. A. Anderson, *The Book of Psalms*, vol. 1, New

John offers no answers to these questions. Because he proceeds quickly to other issues, the reader probably should do so as well, noting at least that in seeing Jesus' zeal and "remembering" the disciples understand little and probably think only of the immediate present.

What John is intent on establishing is this. Only after Jesus' resurrection (2.22) do his disciples again "remember" (cf. 12.16; 14.25-26; 15.20, 26; 16.4) his words and *with understanding* (14.20; 16.13; cf. 7.39) believe both his utterance concerning the temple of his body and the content of Ps 69(68).[68] Only after the psalm's fulfillment in Jesus' passion, then, do they finally understand. The psalm they had previously recalled spoke not of the temple scene, but of Jesus' zeal which would lead to his consumption on the cross at the hands of the Jews.[69]

In summary, this investigation of John's intent in citing Ps 69(68) has failed to provide any additional information concerning John's *Vorlage*. Whether he recalls a specific textual tradition remains uncertain.[70]

Century Bible [London: Oliphants, 1972], 502); Carson, "John," 249; Lars Hartman, "'He Spoke of the Temple of His Body' (Jn 2:13-22)," *SEÅ* 54 (1989): 76.

[68] John 2.22's reference to "the Scripture and the word which Jesus had spoken" parallels nicely the two most significant foci of this pericope: vv. 17 and 19 (cf. Dodd, *Interpretation*, 302; Braun, *Jean 2*, 14-15; Lindars, *NT Apologetic*, 106; Olsson, *Structure*, 265; Hanson, *NT Interpretation*, 116; Beasley-Murray, *John*, 41). Vv. 17 and 19 anticipate the same eventuality. The Jews will kill Jesus. Note how Jesus' "word" bears an authority for the post-resurrection community equivalent to that of the Scripture (contrast 18.9 and 32 where the word of Jesus is "fulfilled;" cf. Haenchen, *John 1*, 185; Gerald Sloyan, *John*, Interpretation: A Bible Commentary for Teaching and Preaching [Atlanta: John Knox, 1988], 41; Morris, *Reflections*, 84; Adele Reinhartz, "Jesus as Prophet: Predictive Prolepses in the Fourth Gospel," *JSNT* 36 [1989]: 3-16, esp. p. 10; Fortna, *Fourth Gospel*, 126).

[69] The majority of scholars see in καταφάγεται a reference to Jesus' passion. Exceptions to this include Westcott, *St. John*, 42; Bernard, *St. John*, 92; S. L. Edgar, "Respect for Context in Quotations from the Old Testament," *NTS* 9 (1962/1963): 58; Barrett, *St. John*, 199; Morris, *Reflections*, 196.

[70] Unlike John 1.23, the influence of the sapiential traditions has not been detected in this citation. Indeed, considering John's portrait of the disciples and their lack of understanding it is not likely that he would have them allude to such traditions in their "remembering" the content of the psalm. However, aspects of John 2.13-22 do bear features recalling or possessing a kinship with wisdom themes. This is particularly true of Jesus' identity as the temple. For the sapiential understanding of the tabernacle/temple and its affinities with the Fourth Gospel, see Koester, *Dwelling*, 24-26, 58-59, 63-65, 73-75, 108-12, 114-15, who concludes (p. 114), "John's prologue is the earliest extant work to apply the wisdom tradition's tabernacle imagery to Christ." Cf. Leo G. Perdue, *Wisdom and Cult: A Critical Analysis of the Views of Cult in the Wisdom Literatures of Israel and the Ancient Near East*, Society of Biblical Literature Dissertation Series, vol. 30 (Missoula: Scholars Press, 1977). See esp. the parallel imagery in Prov 9-10 where God "thwarts" (ἀνατρέπω 10,3; cf. John 2.15) the wicked who have set themselves up in opposition to the "house" (οἶκος, 9.1; cf. John 2.16) which Wisdom

III.

In conclusion, the disciples' reference to the Old Testament in John 2.17 recalls Ps 69(68).10a. This investigation, however, has failed to establish whether the influence of a specific textual tradition is evident in this citation. John's citation itself (especially his use of the καταφάγεται) appears to serve a twofold function in his Gospel. First, John's citation suggests that initially the disciples mistakenly supposed that this psalm passage found its fulfillment in Jesus' first appearance in the Jerusalem temple. At the same time, however, John's citation represents to those who view it from a post-resurrection perspective a prophecy concerning Jesus' crucifixion.

---

has "built" (οἰκοδομέω, 9.1; cf. John 2.20) and the "table" (τράπεζα, 9.2; cf. John 2.15) which she has prepared by slaughtering an animal for the feast (9.2; cf. the animals in John 2.14). John's selection of the rather unusual verb ἀνατρέπω seems specifically designed to recall this complementary sapiential context.

Chapter 3

BREAD FROM HEAVEN (1)

Each of the canonical Gospels make reference to at least one occasion in which Jesus miraculously multiplies a meager supply of bread and fish sufficient for an enormous throng (cf. Matt 14.15-21; 15.32-39; Mark 6.35-44; 8.1-10; Luke 9.12-17; and John 6.1-15). Three Gospels make reference to an episode in which Jesus walks on water (cf. Matt 14.22-34; Mark 6.45-53; and John 6.16-24). But only John's Gospel relates Jesus' encounter with a crowd of Jews (cf. 6.41) in which he speaks of the bread of life (6.25-59).[1] The focus of the next two chapters will be John's unparalleled citations of the Old Testament in John 6.31 and 6.45.

John's first citation of the Old Testament in John 6 takes place in the context of a dialogue between Jesus and a Jewish crowd which has followed him to a synagogue in Capernaum (cf. 6.59). Again, they demand a sign from Jesus (cf. 2.18). In this instance, however, their demand takes the unique form of an explicit citation of the Old Testament (cf. 7.42; 12.34): "So they said to him, 'Then what sign do you do, . . . ? Our fathers ate the manna in the wilderness; as it is written,

ἄρτον ἐκ τοῦ οὐρανοῦ ἔδωκεν αὐτοῖς φαγεῖν " (6.30-31).

---

[1] The requests of the Jews for a sign in Matt 12.38 and Luke 11.16 hardly serve as parallels to what one observes in John 6.30. Mark 8.11, while in a somewhat more similar context, also fails to offer a true parallel.

The miraculous provision of manna in the wilderness was a topic of considerable interest to the Jews.[2] With the exception of John's Gospel, however, explicit references to these traditions are rare in the New Testament (cf. 1 Cor 10.3; Heb 9.4; Rev 2.17). The rarity of such references has complicated scholars' efforts to establish the relationship of these traditions to John's Gospel. Scholars have especially struggled in their efforts to establish whether one or more passages is recalled in John 6.31.

The formula John uses in his citation, however, provides an important initial indication how one is to regard this citation. The participial phrase καθώς ἐστιν γεγραμμένον is likely to be John's own creation. The phrase appears only here and in John 12.14 in the New Testament (cf., however, Luke 4.17).[3] Initially, then, it appears that little can be inferred from John's use of this unique formula concerning the character of his citation.[4] Yet in every other instance in which ἐστίν is used with γεγραμμένον to introduce a citation in John's Gospel (2.17; 6.45; 10.34; 12.14; cf. 12.16), only one passage is cited!

This pattern suggests already that only one passage is recalled in John 6.31. What follows will, in fact, confirm this initial hypothesis.

I.

In their efforts to establish which Old Testament passage(s) John 6.31 recalls, scholars have directed most of their attention to four possibilities: Exod 16.4, 15; Neh 9.15 (2 Esdr 19.15); and Ps 78(77).24. The problem is that each of these passages is only somewhat similar to John 6.31. None of them correspond precisely to what one observes in John's Gospel.

The differences between John 6.31 and each of these passages can be summarized as follows:[5] (1) Exod 16.4 exhibits a differing word order, verb, (explicit) subject, tense, and indirect object; it also lacks the infinitive "to eat" (the imperative "behold" in Exodus is absent in John, but this is of questionable

---

[2] These traditions appear in the rabbinic literature as well (Str-B 2:481-82). Cf. Philo in Freed, OT Quotations, 12-13; Schnackenburg, St. John 2, 449 n. 106. See also Josephus, Ant. 3.30.

[3] Cf. Schnackenburg, St. John 2, 449 n. 107: "This and similar formulas probably all derive from the one Hebrew original לאשר כתיב which can now also be found in the Qumran texts." See also my remarks on the formula in John 2.17. Cf. Joseph A. Fitzmyer, "The Use of Explicit Old Testament Quotations in Qumran Literature and in the New Testament," NTS 7 (1960/1961): 297-333, esp. 300; Richter, "Zitate," 196 n. 14; Fujita, Crack, 126.

[4] Contrast, however, Menken, "John 6:31," 40.

[5] Cf. Menken, "John 6:31," 41-44.

significance).[6] (2) Exod 16.15 exhibits a differing sentence structure ("this is the bread which . . . "), (explicit) subject, indirect object, and it lacks the prepositional phrase "from heaven."[7] (3) Neh 9.15 exhibits a differing subject, lacks the article τοῦ, and apparently also lacks the infinitive "to eat."[8] (4) Ps 78(77).24, lacks ἐκ τοῦ and the infinitive "to eat."[9]

Over the years, scholars have responded to this perplexing textual state of affairs in a number of different ways.[10] Recently, however, most scholars have directed their attention to Ps 78(77).24.[11] Some have identified the psalm as John's primary source while arguing also for the secondary influence of one or more of the other passages identified above (usually Exod 16.4, 16.15, or

---

[6] In all four of the passages under consideration, the OG does not deviate from the Hebrew of the MT, with one exception. In Exod 16.4, the OG has in place of the singular direct object לחם the plural ἄρτους. Variant readings exist in which the singular ἄρτον (F[b?]) and forms of the verb δίδωμι (<76[a?]> Eus) appear, but these are probably to be attributed to the influence of John's Gospel (cf. Menken, "John 6:31," 42 n. 9).

[7] Even a conflation of Exod 16.4 and 16.15 would exhibit a differing (explicit) subject and indirect object (and probably a differing word order as well).

[8] Menken, "John 6:31," 43, offers several provocative suggestions. John's use of φαγεῖν may be a variant of the similar expression εἰς σιτοδοτείαν αὐτῶν (2 Esdr 19.15 B). The rendering εἰς σιτοδείαν αὐτῶν (Ralphs), in turn, may represent an adaptation of the OG to a Hebrew Vorlage (cf. Aquila's translation of רעב in Ps 37(36).19 with σιτοδεία). Even in this case, however, the lack of correspondence between John 6.31 and Neh 9.15 remains significant (on John's omission of καί, cf. John 2.17 and 19.37; contrast 6.45).

[9] Again, the absence of καί in John is insignificant.

[10] Richter's survey of 1972 ("Zitate," 197-208) does a nice job of presenting a detailed sketch of the many proposals that have been made concerning John 6.31. For more recent efforts, see below.

[11] Exceptions to this include Schnackenburg, St. John 2, 40-41, who finds it impossible to say whether the citation is a composite or altered single passage; Reim, Studien, 13-15, 90, 96, et. al., who sees the citation as a combination of MT Exod 16.4 and 16.15, improperly cited and incorrectly exegeted; Becker, Johannes, 204, who finds John 6.31 to be a "freie Anspielung" to Ps 78.24; Exod 16.4.15; Neh 9.15; and Wis 16.20; Beasley-Murray, John, 91, who suggests that it has come from "Exod 16:15, modified by Neh 9:15 and Ps 78:24;" and Richter, "Zitate," 208-31, who argues that the Gospel's citation was not derived from the Old Testament at all, but was originally part of a Jewish haggadic tradition concerning the manna in which Moses was understood as the giver of the bread from heaven (cf. Joel B. Green, The Death of Jesus: Tradition and Interpretation in the Passion Narrative, Wissenschaftliche Untersuchungen zum Neuen Testament, 2. Reihe, Bd. 33 [Tübingen: Mohr-Siebeck, 1988], 118). Richter may well be correct in identifying John 6.30-31 as representative of a Jewish haggadah (see below). Even in this case, however, an Old Testament text is quoted (which Richter himself recognizes, pp. 248-50). And the fact that it is John who has made this fragment a part of his narrative must still be reckoned with. "Apparently, his (Richter's) solution via the Jewish haggadah only put the problem elsewhere " (Menken, "John 6:31," 40; cf. my remarks in the following chapter).

both).[12] Others have attempted to demonstrate the solitary use of the psalm.[13] Only a few have suggested that the influence of a specific textual tradition is evident in John's citation.[14]

Indeed, these scholars' efforts to demonstrate that the psalm is John's primary referent move in the right direction. There is, in fact, no need to look elsewhere in order identify John's source for all of the seemingly anomalous aspects of his citation.

Φαγεῖν is perhaps the easiest of these anomalies to explain. The same infinitive occurs elsewhere in the same verse of the psalm that John cites, in v. 24a: "and he rained down upon them manna to eat." Now lines 24a and 24b together represent another example of synonymous parallelism.[15] This suggests persuasively that the infinitive in John's citation has come from v. 24a.[16] John 6.31, then, represents either (1) a citation of 24b in which the infinitive from the synonymous parallel 24a has simply been transferred to 24b (in order to supply the verbal idea which is understood with both lines of the psalm appearing next to one another, but would be lost if only 24b were cited)[17] or (2) a condensation

---

12 For Lindars, *John*, 256-57, an abbreviated form of the psalm has been combined with a conscious reminiscence of Exod 16. Similarly, Karl-Gustav Sandelin, *Wisdom as Nourisher: A Study of an Old Testament Theme, Its Development within Early Judaism and Its Impact on Early Christianity*, Acta Academiae Aboensis, Ser. A, Humaniora, vol. 64, nr. 3 (Åbo: Åbo Akademi, 1987), 183, points to a conflation of Exod 16.4, 16.15 and Ps 78.24 (see also Pancaro, *Law*, 329; Humann, "OT Quotations," 33, 40 n. 26, 47). Cf. Haenchen, *John 1*, 290, who speaks of a combination of an abbreviated and contracted form of the psalm with Exod 16.4 OG and Ps 104.40 OG. Finally, for Jean-Noël Aletti, "Le discours sur le pain de vie (Jean 6): Problèmes de composition et fonction des citations de l'Ancien Testament," *RSR* 62 (1974): 190-91, the primary sources are Exod 16 and Ps 78.24. However, it is also Aletti's claim that John 6.31 "appelle toutes les autres lectures de l'événement en question" (i.e., Deut 8.3-16; Num 11.6-9; Josh 5.12; Neh 9.15-20; Ps 105.40; Prov 9.5; Wis 16.20).

13 See Morris, *John*, 363; Pancaro, *Law*, 461 n. 29 (Pancaro does not, however, rule out either Neh 9.15 or Exod 16.15 as possibilities); Rissi, "Fische," 77 (for John, however, the psalm is "eine Stelle, die sich ihm mit Ex. 16.15 verwob"); Hanson, *NT Interpretation*, 159-60; Craig A. Evans, "On the Quotations Formulas in the Fourth Gospel," *BZ* 26 (1982): 80; Bruce, *John*, 151-52; Georg Geiger, "Aufruf an Ruckkehrende: Zum Sinn des Zitats von Ps 78, 24b in Joh 6,31," *Bib* 65 (1984): 449-64; Menken, "John 6:31," 39-56; Carson, "John," 246. Cf. Kysar, *John*, 99, who finds it difficult to decide whether John 6.31 is a paraphrase of Ps 78.24 or a combination of the psalm with Exod 16.4 or Neh 9.15.

14 And these scholars have unanimously identified the OG as John's source. Cf. Rissi, "Fische," 77; Haenchen, *John 1*, 290; Menken, "John 6:31," 39-56, esp. 44-46, 54-56.

15 See my remarks in chapter one.

16 Similarly, Braun, *Jean 2*, 10; Freed, *OT Quotations*, 15, Schnackenburg, *St. John 1*, 122; Archer/Chirichigno, *OT Quotations*, 75; Humann, "OT Quotations," 47.

17 Menken, "John 6:31," 44, compares this with the procedure described in the twenty-second of the thirty-two exegetical rules of R. Eliezer b. Jose ha-Gelili. John capitalizes upon established exegetical practice when he supplies the infinitive from line 24a. Cf. Geiger, "Joh

of lines 24a and 24b in which virtually all of 24b is preserved together with the infinitive from 24a (with the essential thrust of both lines preserved).[18]

The appearance of ἐκ τοῦ in John's citation is a somewhat more difficult anomaly to explain. Sufficient parallels exist in Exod 16.4 and Neh 9.15. A better solution, however, is to see in ἐκ τοῦ the influence of v. 26 of the psalm ("he caused an east wind to blow in the heavens" [MT]; ἀπῆρεν νότον ἐξ οὐρανου [OG]) as well as v. 27 ("he rained flesh [OG: σάρκας] upon them like dust, winged birds like the sand of the seas."[19] The parallelism between vv. 24 and 27 is conspicuous. It seems likely, then, that John's knowledge of these verses and of the declaration in v. 23 ("he commanded the skies above, and opened the doors of heaven") provided sufficient contextual impetus for rendering the phrase "bread of heaven" in v. 24b ἄρτον ἐκ τοῦ οὐρανοῦ.[20]

Two conclusions, therefore, are in order: (1) Ps 78(77).24 is closer to what one finds in John 6.31 than any of the other possible sources that have been considered by scholars. (2) Every feature of John's citation can be traced to this passage and to its immediate context.[21] It is also possible to identify the textual tradition that is mostly likely represented in John's citation. The OG version of this passage from the psalm represents an "adequate" rendering of the Hebrew of the MT. But it is also unique in that it is apparently the only instance in the OG where ἄρτος appears as a rendering of דגן (which is normally translated σίτος). That John's citation of the psalm corresponds at this point with the OG argues significantly, therefore, for his use of the OG.[22] Also, if v. 26a has been influential, then this too favors the OG as John's source for his citation (OG: ἐξ οὐρανοῦ; MT: בשׁמים; cf. v. 16a OG: ἐκ πέτρας).[23]

6,31," 449 n. 2: "Joh muss das Wort φαγεῖν von Ps 78, 24a zitieren, weil V.24b eine Ellipse ist!"

[18] See Noack, *Tradition*, 73-74.

[19] Cf. Menken, "John 6:31," 44.

[20] For Menken,"John 6:31," 45, John's use of the preposition "only makes explicit what the psalm verse implicitly says."

[21] According to Freed, *OT Quotations*, 15, the presence of the words "manna" and "bread" in both John 6.31 and v. 24 of the psalm also indicates that John had the psalm in mind (cf. Menken, "John 6:31," 45). John 6.30-31 shares with the larger context of the psalm the following additional expressions/vocabulary: (1) "our fathers" (see vv. 3, 5); (2) "in the wilderness" (see vv. 15, 19); (3) "sign" (see v. 43); (4) "to believe" (see v. 22); and (5) "to work" (cf. v. 7: "the works of God" [cf. John 6.28]). That this is the result of the conscious intent of John, however, is difficult to demonstrate. Geiger, "Joh 6,31," esp. 459-64, has attempted to demonstrate the pervasive influence of the whole psalm on John 6 (v. 2 is quoted in Matt 13.35). But Geiger fails to show why the features which he finds in both the psalm and John 6 could not just as easily have come from, e.g., Exod 16.

[22] Cf. Freed, *OT Quotations*, 15; Menken, "John 6:31," 45.

[23] Cf. Menken, "John 6:31," 45-46. The use of ἐκ τοῦ rather than ἐξ will be explained below.

That the form of John's citation can be traced in this manner back to the OG version of the psalm suggests persuasively that it is not to be regarded as the symptom of John's faulty memory.[24] It is, instead, the product of his conscious intent. What follows will attempt to discern and characterize this intent.

II.

The key to a proper understanding of John's purpose in having this crowd quote the Old Testament is the recognition that John 6 represents "an extended exegesis, by accepted methods, of Ps. 78.24."[25] This is especially evident in John 6.25-59. In these verses, the crowd's citation of the psalm in v. 31 prompts Jesus to enter into an explicit dialogue with them on the proper significance of this reference to the Old Testament.[26] That this dialogue functions as an explication of v. 31 is confirmed poignantly by the fact that each of its three chief parts (beginning with vv. 32, 41, and 52) corresponds to the three chief parts of v. 31.[27] A careful examination of vv. 25-59, therefore, is in order.

---

[24] See the overview and critique of Richter, "Zitate," 205-8.

[25] Barrett, St. John, 284. On this, see esp. Peder Borgen, Bread from Heaven: An Exegetical Study of the Writings of Philo, Supplements to Novum Testamentum, vol. 10 (Leiden: E. J. Brill, 1965). Cf. Aileen Guilding, The Fourth Gospel and Jewish Worship: A Study of the Relation of St. John's Gospel to the Ancient Jewish Lectionary System (Oxford: Clarendon Press, 1960), 58-68; Bertil Gärtner, John 6 and the Jewish Passover, Coniectanea neotestamentica, vol. 17 (Lund: C. W. K. Gleerup, 1959). Borgen has recently responded to his critics in "Bread From Heaven: Aspects of Debates on Expository Method and Form," in his Philo, John and Paul: New Perspectives on Judaism and Early Christianity, Brown Judaic Studies, nr. 131 (Atlanta: Scholars Press, 1987), 131-44.

[26] It is especially Borgen, Bread, who has attempted to show that the citation in v. 31 has been expounded by means of a detailed analysis which proceeds according to a Jewish-Hellenistic homiletic scheme and extends through the dialogue to v. 58. Cf. the contribution of Abraham Finkel, The Pharisees and the Teacher of Nazareth: A Study of their Background, their Halachic and Midrashic Teachings, the Similarities and Differences, Arbeiten zur Geschichte des antiken Judentums und des Urchristentums, Bd. 4 (Leiden: E. J. Brill, 1964), 149-59. While it cannot be maintained that John's dialogue corresponds exactly with the structure of the homilies that are known to us, it does seem to show a "recognizable family likeness" (Lindars, John, 252). It must be maintained, however, that John's text is now thoroughly adapted to its present context and is typically Johannine. Even if John knew what it was to offer a homily in the synagogue according to appropriate methods, this "must be stated in such a way as to make due allowance for other influences upon John's method" (Barrett, St. John, 284). Cf. Menken, "John 6:31," 42-43; Humann, "OT Quotations," 35, 47.

[27] See esp. Rissi, "Fische," 79-80. Cf. the numerous approaches to this text outlined in the survey by Michel Roberge, "La composition de Jean 6,22-59 dans l'exégèse récente," LTP 40 (1984): 91-123.

In John 6.25, this crowd finds Jesus in a synagogue in Capernaum (cf. 6.59). They had witnessed Jesus' sign of the previous day (6.1-13) and had followed Jesus to the other side of the sea of Galilee. Jesus, however, sees beyond their opening inquiry (6.25: "Rabbi, when did you come here?") to what ultimately has motivated them to come so far: "Truly, truly, I say to you, you seek me, not because you saw signs, but because you ate your fill of the loaves" (6.26).

Jesus indicts them for their failure to recognize that his sign was no mere self-authenticating deed of power. It was, again, an act pointing beyond itself in anticipation of his death and resurrection.[28] But they see only the miraculous. They see only the man, the miracle-worker, and his power to feed them with mere mortal food.[29] They are *blind* to the true significance of Jesus and his signs (12.40).[30]

Jesus refuses their hunger for the miraculous and attempts to redirect the focus of their expectations (cf. 3.1-3): "Do not labor (ἐργάζεσθε) for the food which perishes, but for the food which endures . . . " (6.27; cf. 4.13-14; 6.55).[31] But again they misunderstand, apparently perceiving Jesus to mean that they should forget about the food they received on the previous day and should now

---

[28] Cf. my remarks on Jesus' signs and the Jewish understanding of signs in chapter two. Jesus' death, then, is for John God's once-and-for-all giving of the bread of life for the life of the world (see further below) and the inauguration of the eschatological banquet. Feuillet, *Studies*, 53-128, esp. 66-80, has shown convincingly that the Old Testament's portrait of the messianic banquet (Isa 25.6-8; 49.9-10; 55.1-3; 65.13) and that of the banquet of Wisdom (Prov 9.1-6; Sir 24.19-22 [cf. 6.19; 15.3]) are featured in a prominent and creative synthesis in John 6. Cf. esp. the recent contribution of Sandelin, *Wisdom*, 177-85. Numerous opportunities to illustrate this will present themselves below (see also Brown, *John* 1, 272-74; Schnackenburg, *St. John* 2, 44-45; Borgen, *Bread*, 154-58; Willett, "Wisdom," 172-75; Marie-Émile Boismard, *Moïse ou Jesus: Essai de christologie johannique*, Bibliotheca Ephemeridum Theologicarum Lovaniensium, vol. 84 [Leuven: University Press, 1988], 81-84; and the numerous other approaches to this question outlined in the survey by Michel Roberge, "Le discours sur le pain de vie [Jean 6,22-59]: Problèmes d'interprétation," *LTP* 38 [1982]: 265-99).

[29] Cf. M. J. J. Menken, "Some Remarks on the Course of the Dialogue: John 6,25-34," *Bijdragen* 48 (1987): 140 and 147 n. 8. John uses ὁράω to convey both the idea of mere physical perception (e.g., 1.39; 4.45; 6.24; 11.31) and the idea of perceiving heavenly realities (e.g., 1.34; 12.41; 20.8). Cf. esp. John 6.36 and 14.9 (cf. θεωρέω in 6.19 and 12.45). Jesus repeats in John 6.36 what he stated in John 6.26. The crowd sees, but does not see. I.e., in "seeing" him (cf. 6.2) they have failed to perceive the heavenly realities Jesus would have them see.

[30] In this case, Westcott, *St. John*, 100, may well be right in suggesting that χορτάζω in John 6.26 (cf. 6.12) is intended as a pejorative ("as animals with fodder"). Cf. Morris, *John*, 358 n. 6; and Rev 19.21.

[31] Lindar's claim (*John*, 254-55) that John's allusion to Isa 55.2 must depend here on a Hebrew *Vorlage* does not seem well-founded. Cf. the invitation of Wisdom (Prov 9.5-6; Sir 24.19-20) and John 6.63. The bread that "abides" (cf. 6.56) does not itself perish (cf. the manna in Exod 16) and also preserves the believer from "perishing" (cf. 3.16; 6.12, 39; 10.10, 28; 11.50; 12.25; 17.12; 18.9).

work for and earn a better food that he will give them today. This misunderstanding is evident in their response: "What must we do,[32] ἵνα ἐργαζώμεθα τὰ ἔργα τοῦ θεοῦ.[33] Jesus again perceives their intent and once more attempts to lead them in a different direction. There is only one work for them to do: "This is the work (ἔργον) of God, that you believe in him whom he has sent" (6.29; cf. 1.7, 12; 6.35, 36, 40, 47, 69; 20.31).[34]

The reader is now in a position to discern the essential content of Jesus' first exhortation (6.27). In essence, he has said, "Do not come to me thinking that I am a mere man, a mere performer of miracles. Do not come to me hoping to receive mere mortal food on the basis of your mistaken notions about what it means to deserve this through your performance of the works that God requires. Instead, come to me, the one whom God has sent,[35] for an eschatological banquet. Come to me and thereby receive eschatological life which is yours if you do one and only one work, i.e., believe in me."

Why, then, does Jesus in John 6.26-27 begin in such a cryptic way? John would have the reader understand that, from the very beginning, Jesus knew both what his audience wanted and on what basis they hoped to acquire it.

---

[32] "The question is not mere carping. They understand that they must please God, if they are to have the food" (Bernard, St. John, 192).

[33] On doing the "work(s) of God" in the Old Testament and in the extra-biblical literature of Judaism, see Pancaro, Law, 380-84.

[34] In spite of the objections of Urban C. von Wahlde, "Faith and Works in Jn VI 28-29. Exegesis or Eisegesis?" NovT 22 (1980): 304-15, the transition from "works" (6.28) to "work" (6.29) is highly significant. Jesus' observation in John 8.39 concerning the "works of Abraham" is simply another cryptic way of challenging the Jews to do the work of God (6.29) and not to rely on the "works of the Law" (6.28). Jesus clarifies the matter in John 6.37 and especially in John 6.44 (see the following chapter). The work that they are to do is not possible unless the Father "gives" (cf. 1.12; 3.16, 27; 4.10; 6.31, 32, 37, 39, 65; 10.29; 17.2, 6, 9, 24; 18.9; cf. also Prov 2.6) or "draws" (6.44). This work, then, is fundamentally something that the Father alone "works" (cf. 3.21; 9.4; 1 John 3.23). Cf. the "work" that Jesus does in John 4.34 (cf. 4.32; 5.17). For Jesus as well, "to work" means to do "the will" of the Father (cf. 1.13; 5.30; 6.38, 39, 40). In Jesus' case, however, this means "to accomplish" the task laid before him (cf. 8.55; 15.10; see further below).

[35] On the "envoy christology" in John, see the survey of scholars' efforts to characterize this by Kysar, "Recent Research," 2417-18, 2447. Cf. the recent contributions of Jürgen Becker, "Ich bin die Auferstehung und das Leben. Eine Skizze der johanneischen Christologie," TZ 39 (1983): 138-51; Otto Michel, "Der aufsteigende und herabsteigende Gesandte," in The New Testament Age: Essays in Honor of Bo Reicke, vol. 2, ed. William C. Weinrich (Macon, Ga.: Mercer, 1984), 335-61; Schnackenburg, Johannes 4, 60-66 (pp. 58-72 appeared originally as "Der Missionsgedanke des Johannesevangeliums in heutigen Horizont," in ". . . denn Ich bin bei Euch" (Mt 28,20): Perspektiven christlichen Missionsbewusstsein heute. Festgabe für Josef Glazik und Bernhard Willeke zum 65. Geburtstag, hg., H. Waldenfels [Einsiedeln: Benziger Verlag, 1978], 53-65); Willett, "Wisdom," 127-34; Boismard, Moïse, 62-71; Burge, Community, 199-204.

Jesus, in turn, instigates a dialogue in which he purposes to systematically address both aspects of their misunderstanding.[36]

The crowd recognizes that, in his challenging them to believe in him (6.29), Jesus has summarily dismissed their presumption concerning the works of God. But from their standpoint, Jesus must prove to them that he is worthy of any honor at all through the performance of a sign. Indeed, they have a specific and appropriate sign in mind for the present circumstances (which again demonstrates that it is their desire to be fed [6.26] that motivates them).[37] As Moses proved himself to Israel in the desert,[38] so too must Jesus prove himself to them now (cf. 2.18): "Then what sign do you do, that we may see, and believe you? Τί ἐργάζῃ? Our fathers ate the manna in the wilderness; as it is written, 'He gave[39] them bread from heaven to eat'" (6.30-31; cf. 6.49, 58).

The reader is again in a position to discern in greater detail the essential content of another of Jesus' prior statements, John 6.26 ("you seek me . . . because you ate your fill of the loaves"). On the previous day, they had concluded from Jesus' feeding miracle (6.1-13) that Jesus must be the prophet like Moses (6.14; cf. Deut 18.15, 18)[40] and should therefore be made king (6.15).[41] However, this appears to have meant to them only that God's prophetic

---

36 Cf. Pancaro, Law, 460; Schnackenburg, St. John 2, 35-36: "[The imperative in v. 27] is used deliberately here to provoke a typically Jewish misunderstanding (28), which provides an opportunity to emphasize that only 'work' God wants, faith (29)."

37 Cf. Bernard, St. John, 193; Barrett, St. John, 282; Becker, Johannes, 204.

38 On faith in Moses and in Moses' signs in the Old Testament (esp. Exod 4), see Pancaro, Law, 259-60. See also Schnackenburg, St. John 2, 39-40.

39 Note the secondary assimilation of the aorist in v. 31 to the perfect in v. 32 in ℵ Θ f13 pc, and the reverse in v. 32 in B D L al Clement (the perfect and the aorist are interchanged in W).

40 This is acknowledged by most scholars. Cf. the references to Deut 18 in early Christian tradition (Acts 3.22; 7.37), Qumran (4QTestim 5-8), and the literature of the Samaritans (John Macdonald, The Theology of the Samaritans, New Testament Library [London: SCM Press, 1965], 160, 197-98, 359-71; Wayne A. Meeks, The Prophet-King: Moses Traditions and the Johannine Christology, Supplements to Novum Testamentum, vol. 14 [Leiden: E. J. Brill, 1967], 250-54; Boismard, Moïse, 4-5). On the presence of Mosaic motifs in John's Gospel, see esp. Meeks, Prophet-King; T. Francis Glasson, Moses in the Fourth Gospel, Studies in Biblical Theology, vol. 40 (Naperville: Allenson, 1963); Aelred Lacomara, "Deuteronomy and the Farewell Discourse (Jn 13:31-16:33)," CBQ 36 (1974): 65-84; Tadashi Saito, Die Mosevorstellung im Neuen Testament, Europäische Hochschulschriften, 23. Reihe, Theologie, Bd. 100 (Bern: Peter Lang, 1977), 109-21; Boismard, Moïse. John's references to the "prophet" in 1.21 and 1.25 are discussed in chapter one. Cf. 7.40 (and 7.52?). I am also inclined to see similar references to the prophet in 4.19 and 9.17. Cf. also Deut 18.18-19 and John 3.34; 7.16; 8.28, 40; 12.49-50; 14.10, 24; 17.8 (Reim, Studien, 125-26; Menken, "John 6,25-34," 139).

41 Meeks, Prophet-King (cf. idem, "Moses as God and King," in Religions in Antiquity: Essays in Memory of E. R. Goodenough, ed. J. Neusner, Studies in the History of Religion, vol. 14 [Leiden: E. J. Brill, 1968], 354-71). Note as well the recent attempt to analyze in detail the

deliverer, when he came, would be for Israel a second Moses (not a prophet greater than Moses),[42] and that he, as such, would repeat the glorious deeds of Moses. Among these deeds, the repetition of the manna miracle was for them, it seems, a special focus of their expectations.[43]

Thus, in John 6.26 Jesus indicates that he knows why they have come. Their hope is that Jesus, like the first Moses, will feed them now with "bread from heaven" (6.26).[44] Only in John 6.30-31, however, are these desires finally made explicit.[45]

There are, however, from Jesus' standpoint a number of problems both with their expectations and with their use of the psalm in support of them. John, therefore, has Jesus address their lack of understanding in the form of a three-part dialogue on the proper significance of the passage they have just cited. His three-part explication of the psalm derives its own structure from the structure of their citation and proceeds as follows.

Beginning in John 6.32, and focusing first on the word ἔδωκεν in their citation, Jesus commences with a critique of their use of the psalm. The crowd has suggested to Jesus that he should perform in a manner equivalent to the Moses of the past (as evidenced by the psalm) and give to them manna from

---

various accounts of miraculous feedings in the Gospels in Ludger Schenke, *Die wunderbare Brotvermehrung: Die neutestamentlichen Erzählungen und ihre Bedeutung* (Würzburg: Echter Verlag, 1983).

[42] See Westcott, *St. John*, 101; Dodd, *Interpretation*, 344; Pancaro, *Law*, 461-62; Rissi, "Fische," 77; Bruce, *John*, 151-52; Leon Morris, *Reflections on the Gospel of John*, vol. 2, *The Bread of Life: John 6-10* (Grand Rapids: Baker, 1987), 224-25; Beasley-Murray, *John*, 91. Contrast Saito, *Mosevorstellung*, 110-11. Cf. 4.12; 8.53.

[43] Cf. esp. 2 *Apoc. Bar.* 29.8; *Sib. Or.* 7.148-49; *Sib. Frag.* 3.46-49; *Midr. Qoh.* 1.9. The expectation developed that the deliverer would come during the Passover (cf. 6.4), and that the manna would fall again at this time (Gärtner, *John 6*, 19). Jesus refuses their attempt to make him king (6.15) because their purposes and his are in utter conflict.

[44] Why do they require a second sign? The event in John 6.1-13 was evidently "insufficient" for them because it was either (1) sufficiently reminiscent of Moses' provision of manna in the wilderness for them to conclude that Jesus was the prophet, but no more (i.e., now they expect *real* manna, not ordinary bread) or (2) regarded by them as only the first in a necessarily constant offering of bread (cf. "always," 6.34). Cf. the other attempts to answer this question outlined in Menken, "John 6,25-34," 140-42 (see also the proposal by Menken, pp. 142-46). In either case, they will not believe unless Jesus performs a sign (cf. 4.48). Indeed, there was no mention of them "believing" in John 6.14 either.

[45] Bernard, *St. John*, cxi, 191, is probably correct in suggesting that, beginning with v. 27, the crowd has consistently believed that Jesus was referring (1) to the manna when he spoke of the "food that endures" (but Jesus was actually referring to himself) and (2) to the bread they had already eaten when he spoke of the "perishable food" (but Jesus was actually referring to the manna). Cf. Dodd, *Interpretation*, 336; Sandelin, *Wisdom*, 182. Again, there is great irony here. They circumvent Jesus' challenge to believe and thereby receive by demanding to receive in order that they might believe.

heaven.[46] However, "Neither in Ps 78(77).24 nor elsewhere in the O.T. is Moses considered to be the performer of the manna miracle; it is God who gives the manna."[47] Since, therefore, it was not Moses who in previous times gave the bread, they should not expect that a second Moses would do so now: "Truly, truly, I say to you, it was not Moses who gave you the bread from heaven;[48](therefore, it is not Moses who now gives,) but my Father gives you the true bread from heaven"[49] (6.32). The true[50] bread (cf. 1.9; 15.1) is unlike the former perishable (cf. 6.27) bread from heaven. The true bread is the imperishable eschatological "bread of God"[51] (cf. Rev 2.19) which/who[52] "comes down from heaven and gives (eschatological) life[53] to the world" (6.33; cf. Num 11.9).

Once more, however, and again without understanding, the crowd is quick to infer that there is mere food for them to eat: "Lord give us this bread always" (6.34).[54] The irony of their misunderstanding provides Jesus with yet another

---

[46] Admittedly, in the Jewish literature that is known to us there are apparently no references to Moses as the performer of the manna miracle prior to the close of the third century. See, however, Menken, "John 6.31," 46-54, who convincingly argues for the currency of this point of view among the Jews of the first century (cf. B. J. Malina, *The Palestinian Manna Tradition: The Manna Tradition in the Palestinian Targums and Its Relationship to the New Testament Writings*, Arbeiten zur Geschichte des späteren Judentums und des Urchristentums, vol. 7 [Leiden: E. J. Brill, 1968], 87-88). See also Richter, "Zitate," 209; Schnackenburg, *St. John* 2, 41-42; Reim, *Studien*, 13-14; Rissi, "Fische," 78; Carson, "John," 246, 260 n. 5; Humann, "OT Quotations," 34-35, 47.

[47] Menken, "John 6:31," 46. See also his critique (p. 54 n. 50) of Borgen's suggestion (*Bread*, 173) that the substitution of subjects can be explained on the basis of a combination of the manna event with the giving of the Torah at Sinai (cf. Pancaro, *Law*, 469-71; Sandelin, *Wisdom*, 183-84).

[48] I.e., the OT bread was not given by Moses, but God.

[49] I.e., the OT bread was indeed bread from heaven, but it was not the "true bread" (see below).

[50] The adjective "true" denotes here the fulfillment of that which the manna in the wilderness promised. Cf. Schnackenburg, *St. John* 2, 42; Feuillet, *Studies*, 63; Lindars, *John*, 249-50; Barrett, *St. John*, 290; Brown, *John* 1, 266; Kysar, *John*, 99. Note how both the manna (and, therefore, Ps 78[77].24) and Jesus' "breads" (observe the plural in 6.5, 7, 9, 11, 13, 26) in 6.1-13 (which themselves recall the manna) anticipate the same event: the giving of the eschatological bread. Cf. Deut 8.3 (see also Deut 8.16; Neh 9.20; Wis 16.26). Very early on, it was understood that the manna was given in order to show that "man does not live by bread alone, but . . . by everything that proceeds out of the mouth of God." In Jesus, this saying is fulfilled (cf. ῥῆμα in Deut 8.3 OG and John 6.63).

[51] Cf. the showbread in Lev 21.6, 8, 17, 21, 22; 22.25.

[52] On the intentional ambiguity of this construction, see Pancaro, *Law*, 463-64.

[53] See 1.4; 3.15-16; 6.27, 33, 35, 40, 47, 48, 51, 53, 54, 57, 58, 63, 68; 20.31 (cf. also Prov 8.35; 9.6, 11).

[54] See Schnackenburg, *St. John* 2, 43, 449 n. 113 (cf. Chrysostom, *Hom.* 45.1). Morris, *John*, 365, calls attention to the similar motives of the Samaritan woman in 4.15. Again, it is

opportunity to explain further.[55] He has already identified the "giver" (6.32). Now he identifies himself as the "given," the ἄρτον. Jesus thus rules out any hope in him as a second Moses: "I am[56] the bread of life" (6.35).[57] Jesus is the gift of God for all those who believe in (= to come to)[58] him (6.35-39; cf. 5.24). This they cannot bear to hear.

The second stage of this dialogue begins with the objection of the Jews in John 6.41-42 (cf. the "murmuring" in Exod 16.2). All attention now shifts to Jesus' assertion that he, as the gift of God, has come ἐκ τοῦ οὐρανοῦ.[59] Only one

---

likely that the crowd is still thinking only of the manna (Bernard, St. John, cxi; Beasley-Murray, John, 92).

[55] Rissi, "Fische," 79-80, convincingly identifies this as one of two perceptible "wesentliche Strukturelemente" in vv. 34-59: "Einmal ist zu beobachten, dass ein je neues Thema aufgrund eines Jesuswortes immer durch eine verständnislose Bitte oder Frage der Juden eingeleitet wird (6,34. 41. 52) . . . . Und zweitens haben wir gesehen, dass jeder der drei Abschnitte einen zusammenfassenden Abschluss aufweist, der jeweils mit demselben Wortlaut beginnt: toûtó (bzw. hoûtós estin . . . [6,39. 50. 58]). Die Gliederung der drei Teile wird unterstrichen durch die die neuen Abschnitte eröffnenden, erzählerischen Bemerkungen in 6.41 und 52 (egóngyzon oûn . . . und emâchonto oûn . . .). V. 59 closes the whole dialogue. Cf. Aletti's suggestion ("Jean 6," 195-97) that the use of καθώς at the end of this dialogue (cf. 6.57, 58) recalls and summarizes what began in v. 31.

[56] The Johannine "I am" sayings recall the self-presentation of God in the OT theophany formulas (Rissi, "Fische," 77 n. 19; cf. the overview of scholarship by Kysar, "Recent Research," 2418-19, 2421). Schnackenburg, St. John 2, 43-44, has concluded that the closest parallel to the Fourth Gospel's "bread of life" is to be found in the Jewish romance Joseph and Aseneth (cf. idem, Johannes 4, 119-31). The parallel, while intriguing, probably demonstrates no more than a shared dependence on similar Jewish traditions (cf. Sandelin, Wisdom, 152-59, 179-80; Randall D. Chesnutt, "Bread of Life in Joseph and Aseneth and in John 6," in Johannine Studies: Essays in Honor of Frank Pack, ed. James E. Priest [Malibu, Ca.: Pepperdine University Press, 1989], 1-16).

[57] Barnabas Lindars, Behind the Fourth Gospel (London: SPCK, 1971), 72 (idem, John, 250, 259), argues convincingly that both here and elsewhere the "I am" sayings of John's Gospel, like the Prologue, reflect the influence of the sapiential traditions (cf. 6.35 with esp. Prov 9.5 and Sir 24.21). See also Feuillet, Studies, 68, 83-88; Bruce, John, 167-68 n. 15; Sandelin, Wisdom, 177-85; Barrett, St. John, 292-93, who makes the significant observation, "It is . . . important that the image of thirst and drinking is included; this does not arise first in vv. 51-58, and there is no need to regard this latter paragraph as a later insertion designed to introduce a sacramental note otherwise entirely wanting" (cf. 4.13, 14, 15; 7.37; 19.28; Sir 24.21; Rev 7.16; Isa 49.10); Willett, "Wisdom," 167-70.

[58] See esp. the parallelism of "he who comes . . . he who believes . . ." in John 6.35; cf. 6.37, 44, 45, 65 (contrast 7.37-38). Cf. Prov 9.5-6 (Sandelin, Wisdom, 178; Borgen, Bread, 155). The work of Jesus is also "to come" (1.9, 11, 15). Cf. the "sending" of Wisdom in Wis 9.10, 17; 16.20.

[59] On this point, see esp. Menken, "John 6:31," 44-45. John frequently refers to Jesus' coming ἐκ/ἀπὸ τοῦ οὐρανοῦ or ἐξ οὐρανοῦ (see below). Similar expressions include ἄνωθεν (3.31) and ἐκ τῶν ἄνω (8.23). Also related are statements in which Jesus is said to be "from God" (3.2; 6.46; 8.42, 47; 9.16, 33; 13.3; 16.27, 30), "from the Father" (1.14; 16.28), or sent

whose origins are also "heavenly" (i.e., only one who is "taught by God," 6.45), says Jesus, can embrace Jesus' heavenly origins and come to him (the following chapter will discuss in detail this second section).

The final stage of this dialogue begins with the incredulous exclamation of Jesus' audience in John 6.52 (cf. the "disputing" in Exod 17.2 and Num 20.3, 13). All attention is now directed to the "eating" (φαγεῖν) of the true bread. Jesus is eschatological food (and drink) and, therefore, life for those who believe in him (6.53-57).[60] The Jews do not belong to Jesus, neither do they possess this life, because they do not believe (= to eat and drink the flesh and blood of the Son of Man).[61]

This brief sketch of the function of this citation in its narrative context now makes it possible to answer the questions posed above. Why is the psalm cited rather than Exod 16 or Neh 9? And why does it appear in this unique form?

The psalm is cited because v. 24 "lends itself best to the crowd's desire to attribute the giving of the manna to Moses."[62] In all four of the possible Old Testament sources that have been considered, God is understood as the giver of the manna. But only in the psalm is God the non-specified subject of a third person singular verb. Indeed, it is only a knowledge of the larger context of the

---

by the Father (cf. 3.17; 4.34; 6.38, 39, 44). "For John, who considers Jesus as the true manna, it is apparently not enough that Jesus is ἄρτος οὐρανοῦ, 'heavenly bread;' he is ἄρτος ἐκ τοῦ οὐρανοῦ, 'bread from heaven,' 6.31-33. The former expression could be misread as only saying that he belongs to the heavenly sphere; the second one unmistakably indicates that he was with God in heaven and has come down from there to the world" (p. 45).

[60] Again, the blending of exodus motifs (where "eating" and "drinking" already appear together) with sapiential themes is evident. Rissi, "Fische," 77-78, has made the significant observation that sacrificial themes as well are evident: "Fleisch und Blut ist Umschreibung der Person, darüber hinaus aber in Anlehnung an alttestamentlich-jüdische Opferterminologie Hinweis auf Jesu Opfer" (p. 77). The giving of the Lamb/Bread of God (= the cross), therefore, makes it possible for those who "come" to "eat and drink" (again, note that the occasion is a Passover festival [6.4]).

[61] Cf. esp. Prov 9.5; Sir 6.19; 24.21 (the language of discipleship). Contrast the irony of John 18.28. It cannot be stressed enough that all of vv. 25-59 and not merely vv. 52-59 wrestle with what it means for Jesus' audience to "labor" for and receive *now* the food which endures to eternal life (6.27). In each of the complementary stages of this dialogue, Jesus offers only one answer ("This is the work of God, that you believe" [6.29]). Various synonymous expressions, then, serve in Jesus' effort to elaborate on this point. One receives the bread given by God (6.23) which itself gives eschatological life (6.33) by "believing" (6.35, 47), i.e., by "coming" (see above) or by "eating and drinking" (6.53-58; cf. the equivalence of the statements made in 6.47 and 6.50; note esp. 6.35 where "coming" and "believing" are substituted for "eating" and "drinking"!). V. 29, therefore, has served as a short form for all of Jesus' ensuing exhortations (Becker, *Johannes*, 201; see further below).

[62] Cf. Menken, "John 6:31," 54-56.

psalm that makes the identity of the subject apparent.[63] The crowd's substitution of Moses for God as the subject of v. 24 of the psalm may, in fact, recall vv. 15-16 and 20 (where it is said that God struck the rock in the desert and water flowed out of it; cf. Exod 17.1-7 and Num 20.2-13 where Moses is the subject!).[64] The psalm, therefore, best suits the crowd's purposes.

As for the unusual form of this citation, one need only look to John's use of ἐκ τοῦ οὐρανοῦ in John 6.41-51 (cf. 6.41, 42, 50, 51; cf. 3.13, 31; contrast 6.32, 33, 38, 58)[65] or to φαγεῖν in John 6.52-59 (cf. 6.52, 53, 54, 56, 57, 58; cf. 6.32, 49, 50, 51)[66] in order to recognize John's intent. The precise form of this citation has been made to correspond formally to the language of the verses which follow it and explain its significance.

In summary, what we have noted concerning John's care in constructing this citation only serves to confirm the likelihood that he recalls Ps 77.24 OG. In closing, however, it should be added that this discussion of the "general thrust" of Jesus' words[67] does not rule out the possibility that John understood his own church's participation in the Eucharist to be an integral extension and concretization of the import of what is expressed in John 6. That the language the Johannine Jesus utilizes is intended to stimulate and inform secondary associations is (as we have already seen) a feature not uncommon in John's Gospel.

III.

In conclusion, both the form and the function of the crowd's reference to the Old Testament in John 6.31 indicate that John recalls Ps 77.24 OG. The form of this citation is unusual, but can be traced to v. 24 of the psalm and to its immediate context. The selection of the psalm verse for this citation serves two functions in John's narrative: (1) It lends itself best to the crowd's desire to attribute the giving of the bread from heaven to Moses. (2) The psalm verse functions also as the formal basis for the language of the verses in John 6 that follow it and explain its significance.

---

63 Menken, "John 6:31," 55-56, shows how a construction of this type could easily have been capitalized upon in early Jewish exegesis (e.g., Philo). Cf. Richter, "Zitate," 210-15.

64 Menken, "John 6:31," 56.

65 Cf. Prov 3.19; 8.27; 30.4; Wis 9.10; 16.20; 18.15; Sir 24.5 (discussed in Sandelin, Wisdom, 179-80).

66 Cf. Menken, "John 6:31," 44. Note that John characteristically uses τρώγω (6.54, 56, 57, 58; 13.18) as a present tense suppletive to the aorist φαγεῖν (cf. Dodd, Historical Tradition, 37; see also my remarks in chapter nine).

67 Cf. James W. Voelz, "The Discourse on the Bread of Life in John 6: Is it Eucharistic?" ConcJourn 15 (1989): 29-37, esp. 35.

Chapter 4

BREAD FROM HEAVEN (2)

A second citation of the Old Testament in John 6 appears in the second stage of its three-part explication of Ps 77.24 OG.[1] Jesus' protagonists take issue with his suggestion that he, like the manna they hoped to receive (6.30-31) and in fulfillment of that which the manna anticipated, has descended ἐκ τοῦ οὐρανοῦ (6.41-42; cf. 6.31, 32-33, 35, 38). In response, Jesus asserts, "No one can come to me unless the Father who sent me draws him" (6.44; cf. 6.29, 36-39). Elaborating on this statement, Jesus recalls a passage from "the prophets:"

καὶ ἔσονται πάντες διδακτοὶ θεοῦ (6.45a).

The citation is unique to John (cf. 1 John 2.27) and represents the first time in his Gospel that John has Jesus himself cite the Old Testament (cf. 7.37-38; 8.17; 10.34; 13.18; 15.25; 17.12; 19.28). Variant traditions concerning God's eschatological instruction of his people appear elsewhere in the New Testament (1 Thess 4.9; cf. 1 Cor 2.13) and in the literature of both early Christianity (*Barn.* 21.6) and later Judaism.[2] None of these traditions, however, offer more than illustrative independent parallels.

---

[1] On this citation and the character of the ensuing three-part dialogue, see the preceding chapter.

[2] The expression "taught by God" appears in CD 20.4 (cf. 1QH 2.39; 7.10, 14; 8.36). In CD, it is the Messiah of Aaron who will come as the "Interpreter of the Law" and teach the "new Law" (CD 6.7; 7.18-21; cf. 4QFlor 1.11). The literature of the rabbis will be discussed below.

Before turning to a discussion of John's source for his citation, it is necessary first to consider the statement that John 6.45a can be found "written"[3] ἐν τοῖς προφήταις.[4] The plural "the prophets" is for many scholars an indication either (1) that John does not have a particular prophetic source in mind (but instead draws on several texts) or (2) that he may not be certain where his citation comes from.[5] A telling argument against at least the first of these explanations is that John's citation has indeed come from one distinct source.[6] It is also possible, however, to identify elsewhere sufficient parallel references to "the prophets" in formulae which introduce specific and solitary passages from the prophetic literature.[7]

Regrettably, the New Testament evidence is inconclusive. Initially, Matthew's reference in Matt 2.23 to "what was spoken by the prophets" (i.e., "He shall be called a Nazarene") seems just such a parallel.[8] But scholars' inability to conclusively establish a precise source for this citation renders this possibility difficult to establish. Luke's references to "the prophets" (cf. Luke 7.42-43 [Amos 5.25-27]; 13.40-41 [Hab 1.5]; 15.15-18 [Amos 9.11-12]) all come from the Minor Prophets.[9] It is difficult, therefore, to know whether or not Luke has only the Dodecapropheton in mind.[10]

Nevertheless, it is widely acknowledged that the phrase "the prophets" functions in Judaism (as early as the preface to Sir; cf. 2 Macc 15.9; 4 Macc 18.10; CD 7.17; *m. Meg.* 4.15) and in early Christian literature (see esp. John 1.45; cf. Matt 5.17; Luke 24.27, 44; Acts 28.23; Rom 3.21) as a reference to the second division of the Old Testament canon. And those who use this expression in this manner have been known to use it with reference to a solitary and specific

---

3 The entire formula ("It is written in the prophets") occurs nowhere else in the New Testament. On the participial expression γεγραμμένον ἐστίν (2.17; 6.31, 45; 10.34; 12.14; cf. 12.16), see my remarks in chapters two and three.

4 For what follows, see esp. Menken, "John 6,45," 165-67, 71-72.

5 Cf. Bultmann, *John*, 231 n. 3; Goodwin, "Sources," 68; Noack, *Tradition*, 75; C. Smits, *Oud-Testamentische Citaten in het Nieuwe Testament*, Bd. 2, *Handelingen van de Apostelen, Evangelie van Johannes, Apocalyps en Katholieke Brieven*, Collectanea Franciscana Neerlandica, Bd. 8/2 (Bois-le-Duc: L. C. G. Malmberg, 1955), 221 (cited by Menken, "John 6,45," 165 n. 4); Braun, *Jean 2*, 15-16; Freed, *OT Quotations*, 17-18; Brown, *John 1*, 271; Reim, *Studien*, 16. Barrett, *St. John*, 295-96, reverses himself in the second edition of his commentary and abandons his preliminary judgment that John's "vague reference" to the prophets represents a possible indication of "uncertainty regarding the exact source of the quotation."

6 See below.

7 Menken, "John 6,45," 165.

8 Freed, *OT Quotations*, 17-18.

9 Cf. Westcott, *St. John*, 105; Bernard, *St. John*, 204; Bultmann, *John*, 231 n.3; Freed, *OT Quotations*, 18.

10 Menken, "John 6,45," 165-66, refers esp. to "the book of the prophets" in Acts 7.42.

prophetic text. The rabbinic literature has characteristically served to provide illustrations of such use.[11] But additional support for the same appears in the literature of Hellenistic Judaism and of the Christian fathers as well.[12] There is, therefore, more than sufficient warrant for suspecting that John's reference in John 6.45a to "the prophets" may well recall one and only one prophetic passage.[13]

Some may object that John's citation which (as we shall see) comes from Isaiah does not mention the prophet by name (while elsewhere in John [cf. 1.23; 12.38, 39] citations from Isaiah consistently make explicit reference to him). This, however, does not a priori rule out Isaiah as John's intended referent.[14] One must first determine what for John the rule is and what constitutes an exception.[15]

Indeed, in no other instances other than those mentioned above does John identify Old Testament authors by name. And in each of these instances, it is likely that something has prompted John to introduce an exception and to refer specifically to Isaiah. In John's citation of Isa 40.3 in John 1.23, the name of Isaiah is apparently a common and prominent feature of the tradition concerning the Baptist (cf. Matt 3.3; Mark 1.2; Luke 3.4). In John 12.41, John means to contrast Isaiah's prophetic experience as it is described in Isa 6 with the blindness of the Jews. John's two quotations from Isaiah in John 12.38 and 12.39-40 prepare the reader for this contrast and therefore also mention the prophet by name.[16]

The absence of any explicit reference to the name of the prophet in John 6.45, therefore, "is by no means abnormal, and is no argument against one

---

[11] Richter, "Zitate," 253 n. 305, points esp. to Mek. Amalek 2 on Exod 17.14 (cf. p. 269; Schlatter, Der Evangelist, 176) and b. Sanh. 90b. In each of these, a reference to the Law is followed by references to the prophets and the writings (this pattern, significant to Borgen, Bread, is discussed in the preceding chapter).

[12] Menken, "John 6,45," 166-67, finds the evidence from the rabbinic material too dependent upon how one regards Borgen's thesis concerning the presence of a homiletic pattern in John 6.31-58. Sufficient alternative examples appear in Philo (De fuga et inventione 197; De mutatione nominum 169; cf. De plantatione 138; De confusione linguarum 44; Mut. 139; De somniis 2.172), Josephus (Ant. 11.3-4), and Justin Martyr (Dial. 89.3; 119.3).

[13] Cf. Westcott, St. John, 105; Bernard, St. John, 204; Freed, OT Quotations, 18; Richter, "Zitate," 252-53; Lindars, John, 264; Reim, Studien, 16; Bruce, John, 156; Menken, "John 6,45," 167 ("regardless of whether it follows a quotation from the Torah or not").

[14] Cf. Braun, Jean 2, 15-16; Richter, "Zitate," 269.

[15] Menken, "John 6,45," 167. For example, "In den Prophetenzitaten der frühen Rabbinen wird der Name des Propheten meistens nicht genannt" (Richter, "Zitate," 252-53).

[16] See my chapters on these citations below.

precise passage from Isa being the source of the quotation."[17] What text in Isaiah, then, does this citation recall?

I.

The only Old Testament passage which sufficiently corresponds to John 6.45 is Isa 54.13.[18] The two passages, however, differ conspicuously.[19] For this reason, many scholars have sought alternative referents for John's citation. Most scholars have identified Isa 54.13 as John's referent. But Jer 31.33-34 has also attracted some attention (sometimes independent of and sometimes in combination with Isa 54.13). Occasionally, John's citation has been described as a composite of several Old Testament passages having to do with God's eschatological instruction of his people (e.g., Isa 54.13; Jer 24.7; 31.33-34; Joel 2.27, 29; Hab 2.14).[20] Finally, because no one Old Testament passage completely corresponds to the form of John's citation, scholars have argued that he quotes "freely" or from memory.[21]

Recently, however, few scholars have argued for a passage other than Isa 54.13 as John's referent.[22] Scholarly attention has focused on Isa 54.13 alone.

---

[17] Menken, "John 6,45," 167.

[18] Cf. in chapter three my remarks concerning the significance of Isa 55.1-3 for Jesus' presentation of himself as the bread of life.

[19] Note esp. John's substitution of "all" for Isaiah's "all your sons." See further below.

[20] See also Ps 71.17; 119.171; Prov 4.4, 11; Isa 8.16; 11.9; 40.14; 50.4; Ezek 11.19-20; 36.26-27; Mic 4.2; *Pss. Sol.* 17.32a ("and he will be a righteous king over them, taught by God").

[21] Again, Richter's survey of 1972 ("Zitate," 254-62) does a nice job of presenting a detailed sketch of the many proposals that have been made concerning John 6.45. For more recent efforts, see below.

[22] Exceptions to this include Schnackenburg, *St. John* 2, 50-51, who refers first to Isa 54.13, but then also acknowledges the possibility of an allusion to Jer 31.34; Morris, *John*, 372, who cannot decide between Isa 54.13, Jer 31,34, or a combination of the two (in favor of the latter is Longenecker, *Exegesis*, 59, 72; cf. Pancaro, *Law*, 329); and, of course, Richter, "Zitate," 262-71, who again (cf. my remarks in the preceding chapter) argues that John does not work directly with the OT at all, but instead derives his citation from a contemporaneous Jewish haggadah. Richter's hypothesis, however, is called into question by the existence of a Christian variant of this tradition which also predates John's Gospel (cf. 1 Thess 4.9). In favor of such traditions current in early Christianity as the most likely source for John are Noack, *Tradition*, 76; and Reim, *Studien*, 93-94, who posits the influence of sapiential circles (for parallels in the wisdom literature, see Feuillet, *Studies*, 89-91; Pancaro, *Law*, 281); see also Green, *Death*, 118. There is, it seems, "no need to derive Jn 6,45 from this specifically Jewish tradition" (Menken, "John 6,45," 164). Its influence on John is "nur erschlossen, nicht belegt" (Roland Bergmeier, *Glaube als Gabe nach Johannes: Religions- und theologiegeschichtliche Studien zum pradestinatianischen Dualismus im vierten Evangelium*, Beiträge zur Wissenschaft vom Alten

This latest trend is, in fact, the correct one.[23] God's eschatological activity as the Teacher of Israel is the subject of numerous Old Testament passages. But only Isa 54.13 is sufficiently close to John 6.45.

It remains, then, to establish whether the influence of a specific textual tradition is evident in John's citation. The answer to this question, however, is not immediately evident. The evidence seems to point in two separate directions: (1) Seemingly in favor of John's dependence upon a Hebrew *Vorlage* is the construction of his sentence. The nominatives πάντες and διδακτοί represent a possible rendering of the Hebrew of the MT. The OG, on the other hand, appears to differ from both of these in reading (θήσω, Isa 54.12) πάντας . . . διδακτούς.[24] (2) But two features of John's citation seem to suggest his dependence upon the OG. First, διδακτός appears both in John 6.45a and in the OG. Διδακτός is a *hapax* in John's Gospel[25] and appears only two times in the OG (Isa 54.13 and 1 Macc 4.7).[26] And second, John's citation agrees with the OG in its use of θεοῦ rather than κυρίου (which would seem to be the more natural rendering of the Hebrew יהוה).[27] Interestingly, none of these preceding observations provide persuasive evidence for John's dependence upon either of these textual traditions.

First, it is not immediately evident that the structure of the sentences in the MT and in the OG differ. In other words, it is possible that one is to understand Isa 54.13a MT to be governed by the verb in the first part of v. 12.[28]

---

und Neuen Testament, 6. Folge, Bd. 12 [Stuttgart: W. Kohlhammer, 1980], 249-50 nn. 226 and 233).

[23] See, e.g., Lindars, *John*, 264; Aletti, "Jean 6," 190; Reim, *Studien*, 16-18, 90; Pancaro, *Law*, 279, 282 n. 310; Barclay M. Newman and Eugene A. Nida, *A Translator's Handbook on the Gospel of John*, Helps for Translators (London: United Bible Societies, 1980), 204; Hanson, *NT Interpretation*, 160; Haenchen, *John 1*, 292; Becker, *Johannes*, 213; Evans, "Formulas," 80; Bergmeier, *Glaube*, 249 n. 233; Bruce, *John*, 156; Archer/Chirichigno, *OT Quotations*, 124-25; Kysar, *John*, 105; Carson, "John," 246-47; Menken, "John 6,45," 164-72.

[24] Cf. Westcott, *St. John*, xiv; Bernard, *St. John*, 205; Burney, *Aramaic Origin*, 118; Borgen, *Bread*, 84 n. 1; Freed, *OT Quotations*, 18; Reim, *Studien*, 16-17, 90, 223, 279; Aletti, "Jean 6," 190; Archer/Chirichigno, *OT Quotations*, xxvi, 125; Humann, "OT Quotations," 43 n. 41.

[25] Cf. Barrett, *St. John*, 296.

[26] Cf. Schnackenburg, *St. John 2*, 50-51.

[27] See Burney, *Aramaic Origin*, 118, who suggests that a copyist ("possibly the translator from Aramaic into Greek") has introduced θεοῦ from the OG into John's citation which originally came from a Hebrew *Vorlage*. See also Schlatter, *Der Evangelist*, 176; O'Rourke, "OT Citations," 56; Borgen, *Bread*, 84 n. 1; Freed, *OT Quotations*, 18; Anthony T. Hanson, *The Living Utterances of God: The New Testament Exegesis of the Old* (London: Darton, Longman and Todd, 1983), 119-20; Menken, "John 6,45," 168, 170-71; Humann, "OT Quotations," 43 n. 41.

[28] Menken, "John 6,45," 169; cf. Noack, *Tradition*, 76 n. 185; Richter, "Zitate," 254 n. 308.

We have already noted how John feels free to subject the Old Testament passages he cites to certain limited non-essential alterations in order to adapt them to the new and uniquely Johannine contexts in which he places them. Now elsewhere in the New Testament[29] and in, for example, the works of Philo,[30] forms of εἰμί are sometimes used in order to facilitate such alterations. The exegetical procedure responsible for the structure of John's citation of Isa 54.13, then, may well be methodologically similar to what one observes elsewhere in the New Testament and in Philo.[31] In other words, John draws on the OG, deletes the main verb θήσω (Isa 54.12), and inserts the copula.

Consequently, the structure of John's citation cannot be used as an argument in favor of his dependence upon a specific textual tradition. Two scenarios are equally probable: (1) John recalls a Hebrew *Vorlage* and supplements his translation of Isa 54.13a (understood as a nominal phrase) with ἔσονται or (2) he draws on the OG and "does as Philo does."[32]

Similarly, neither διδακτός nor θεοῦ in John 6.45 are especially indicative of the influence of the OG. The term διδακτός is rather scarce in the OG,[33] but is a natural rendering of לִמֻּד.[34] Διδακτός could, therefore, conceivably represent in John 6.45 a rendering of לִמֻּד. Indeed, there is, it seems, no other instance in John's Gospel in which John might have occasion to repeat its use. That it is a *hapax* in John's Gospel, therefore, is not necessarily a significant detail.[35] John's use of θεοῦ is also of questionable significance. It is not unusual for a translator to use θεός to translate the tetragrammeton.[36]

There is, however, one feature of this citation which does seem to suggest John's dependence upon a specific textual tradition. John's citation omits Isaiah's reference to the "sons"[37] of Jerusalem. Now the textual impetus for this modifi-

---

[29] Cf. the citations of Isa 56.7 in Mark 11.17 and Luke 19.46 (discussed in Menken, "John 6,45," 169).

[30] See esp. *Legum allegoria* 1.58; *De plantatione* 44 (these and other references are discussed in Menken, "John 6,45," 169-70).

[31] Menken, "John 6,45," 170.

[32] Menken, "John 6,45," 170.

[33] See Isa 54.13; 1 Macc 4.7; cf. Isa 8.16 Aq.; 29.13 Aq. Symm. Theod.

[34] Menken, "John 6,45," 169 (cf. Isa 8.16 Aq.). Cf. Freed, *OT Quotations*, 18.

[35] Menken, "John 6,45," 169 (who notes John's use of *adiectiva verbalia* in -τος in, e.g., 9.30; 10.12, 13; 18.15, 16; 19.13, 23).

[36] This is especially evident in the OG versions of Prov (keep in mind the sapiential orientation of John) and Isa (cf. Freed, *OT Quotations*, 19 n. 1). Indeed, the expression "taught by God" is a rather common one in Jewish (esp. among the rabbis) and early Christian literature (see above; cf. Borgen, *Bread*, 84 n. 1, 150; Richter, "Zitate," 262-66; Pancaro, *Law*, 285-86).

[37] See above. The reading "your builders" appearing in 54.13b of 1QIsaᵃ reflects in an interesting way the desert community's self-consciousness, but is for John "relatively unimportant" (Menken, "John 6,45," 168 n. 18; cf. Hanson, *NT Interpretation*, 160).

cation could easily have come from the context of the quoted passage in the OG.[38] The OG translator apparently understood the Hebrew גּוּר יָגוּר ("he will stir up strife") in Isa 54.15 in terms of the noun גֵּר ("proselyte; cf. the verb גּוּר "to dwell as a stranger," or, in the middle Hebrew and Jewish Aramaic in the pi'el or pa'el, "to make a proselyte") and translated Isaiah accordingly: "behold proselytes will come to you through me, and will flee to you for protection." The OG's indication that proselytes too will be numbered among the citizens of the new Jerusalem could easily have been regarded by John as sufficient justification for his omission of "your sons" from John 6.45.

The evidence, therefore, is less than conclusive. In what follows, an attempt will be made to determine the extent to which John's apparent intent in quoting this passage confirms or conflicts with what has already been adduced.

II.

It is especially the verses that precede John's citation which illustrate his intent in having Jesus speak as he does. Jesus' protagonists have taken offense at his suggestion that he has descended from heaven (6.41, 42b, cf. 6.31, 32-33, 35, 38).[39] Their "murmuring" (6.41; cf. 6.43, 61; 7.12, 32) recalls similar reactions exhibited by their "fathers" (cf. 6.31, 49, 58) in the wilderness (first at the water of Marah [Exod 15.24], then prior to the giving of the manna [Exod 16.2, 7, 8, 9, 12], and even later [cf. Exod 17.3; Num 11.1; 14.2, 27, 29; and elsewhere]). Their reaction is one of unbelief (Ps 105.24-25 OG)[40] and rebellion against God's word (Exod 16.8; cf. Isa 30.12).[41] The reader of John's Gospel is to infer that "the scene of the rebellious people in the desert is being played out again"[42] in Jesus' own encounter with "the Jews."[43]

---

[38] For what follows, see esp. Hanson, NT Interpretation, 160 (cf. idem, Utterances, 119-20); and Menken, "John 6,45," 171.

[39] On Jesus' heavenly origins, see my remarks in chapter three.

[40] Cf. the immediate context of John's OT referent for his citation in John 6.31 (esp. Ps 78.22, 32).

[41] Cf. Sir 10.25; 46.7; Wis 1.10, 11.

[42] Kysar, John, 104. Cf. Bultmann, John, 229 n. 4; Schnackenburg, St. John 2, 49.

[43] Schnackenburg, St. John 2, 49, rightly remarks, "it is not surprising that the audience is now described (as in 52) as οἱ Ἰουδαῖοι." However, it is not necessary to understand this phrase, as he does, as a "pejorative" (p. 49; cf. idem, St. John 1, 286). This phrase instead functions to heighten the tragic irony of this and other scenes in John's Gospel where Jesus' "own" rebel against the very Savior they should have recognized and embraced (1.11). John's reverting to his usual manner of designating Jesus' opponents (Lindars, John, 262; Kysar, John, 104) has been prompted by his desire to emphasize this crowd's identity both with their "fathers" and with the Jewish people of the present (including their rulers) whose tragic rebellion they now represent (cf. Hoskyns, Fourth Gospel, 296).

It is inconceivable to Jesus' opponents that he could have a father and a mother that they all "know" (6.42a; cf. Matt 13.55; Mark 6.3; Luke 4.22)[44] and, at the same time, be someone who has descended from heaven (6.42b).[45] Jesus, however, refuses to entertain their speculations regarding this presumed impossibility.[46] Instead, Jesus attempts, as he has before,[47] to redirect the focus of their attention. The immediate issue of significance for Jesus involves heavenly, not worldly origins. Specifically, only one whose "origin" is also "heavenly"[48] (i.e., only one who is drawn by the Father in heaven) can come to Jesus (6.44; cf. 6.27, 29, 35-39, esp. v. 37).[49] Only one whose origin is heavenly can embrace

---

[44] In claiming that they "know" (see 1.26; 3.2, 8; 4.10, 22, 32; 7.27-28; cf. 3.11; 6.6, 61, 64; 7.29) Jesus' father and mother (cf. 1.45; 7.27), they identify themselves as fellow natives of Galilee (cf. 2.12; Bernard, St. John, 202-3; Brown, John 1, 270; Schnackenburg, St. John 2, 451 n. 131). On the use of πως, cf. John 3.4, 9; 6.52; 7.15; 8.33; 12.34.

[45] The Jews do not object to the idea that a man could be descended from heaven. Rather, they object to the suggestion that a man of celestial origins could at the same time be "born of earthly semen" (Hugo Odeberg, The Fourth Gospel: Interpreted in Its Relation to Contemporaneous Religious Currents in Palestine and the Hellenistic-Oriental World [Amsterdam: B. R. Grüner, 1968], 264-65 n. 3). Cf. Barrett, St. John, 295: "John nowhere affirms belief in the virgin birth of Jesus, but it is probable that he here ironically alludes to it–if the objectors had known the truth about Jesus' parentage they would have been compelled to recognize that it was entirely congruent with his having come down from heaven." John conspicuously avoids, however, any explicit discussion of Jesus' earthly origins (see further below).

[46] The stressing of Jesus' heavenly origins versus his earthly origins is a characteristic feature of John's Gospel. Indeed, this may well explain the apparent muting of a Davidic Christology (which itself is so heavily saturated with the issue of earthly origins) in John's portrait of Jesus. There is, for example, a similar ironic refusal to pick up and address directly questions pertaining to Jesus' origins in John 7.41b-42 (cf. Jouette M. Bassler, "A Man For All Seasons: David in Rabbinic and New Testament Literature," Int 40 [1986]: 156-69, esp. 166). Note the parallel absence of any typically Davidic birth narrative or genealogy in John's Gospel. Cf. the avoidance in esp. John 20.9 of any reference to the early church's characteristic Davidic proof-texts for Jesus' resurrection (e.g., Acts 2). See below my discussion of John's portrait of Jesus' entry into Jerusalem.

[47] See in chapter three my remarks on the course of the preceding dialogue.

[48] Cf. John 3.3. Jesus' reference in John 3.3 to being born ἄνωθεν is interpreted by Nicodemus as a reference to earthly origins. Jesus' intent, however, involves only a reference to origins which are not of this world. John 3.3, then, refers to an utterly unique heavenly birth which comes "from above" (and for the first time), not to being born "again," or "anew" (cf. the only other uses of ἄνωθεν in John's Gospel at John 3.7, 31; 19.11, 33; contrast my discussion of John 2.19 in chapter two). Translators of ἄνωθεν, therefore, encounter a significant problem. There is no satisfactory English equivalent which bears the latent and deliberate ambiguity of this Greek adverb (cf. the recent dissenting viewpoints of William C. Grese, "'Unless One is Born Again:' The Use of a Heavenly Journey in John 3," JBL 107 [1988]: 677-93, esp. 677 n. 1, 691; Ben Witherington III, "The Waters of Birth: John 3.5 and 1 John 5.6-8," NTS 35 [1989]: 155-60, esp. 159).

Jesus' heavenly origin and receive the food he has to give (6.48-50). All those who come, then, are "taught by God" (6.45a). In other words, they have "heard and learned" (6.45b) from the Father.[50]

But how are they to learn from a Father they cannot see? Jesus has just one answer for them. Because Jesus has come from the Father and alone has seen the Father (6.46; cf. 1.18a; 5.37), to see Jesus (6.36) is to see and hear the Father[51] and be taught by God (6.59; cf. 1.18b; 8.38; 14.7-9. 24).[52] With these verses, Jesus' argument skillfully returns to his claim to be the bread of God which has descended from heaven. Again, he challenges them to believe and receive life (6.47-48; cf. 6.27-40, esp. v. 35).[53]

---

[49] See John 6.37 and 65, where the verb δίδωμι (cf. 1.12-13; 3.16, 27; 4.10; 6.31, 32, 37, 39, 65) is substituted for ἐλκύω (see Cant 1.4; Jer 38.3 OG; Hos 11.4 MT; cf. the irony of Peter's misguided defense of Jesus in 18.10 with his work as a post-resurrection disciple in 21.6, 11). Again, Jesus rules out any suggestion that they can independently "work the work of God" (6.28-29; see my remarks in chapter three).

[50] Jesus' conflict with the Jews over heavenly versus earthly origins reaches a climax in John 8. Here Jesus again asserts their ignorance of him, his origins, and his Father (8.14, 19, 55; cf. 8.21, 23-25) and pronounces their Jewish sonship worthless. They are no more than mere σπέρματα (8.33, 37). Their rejection of him (8.33-59) shows that they are not ἐκ τοῦ θεοῦ (8.47). They have forfeited the opportunity to be τέκνα (8.39; cf. 1.12; 11.52; 13.32) and have, instead, embraced the devil as their father (8.38, 41, 44). Cf. Benny C. Aker, "The Merits of the Fathers: An Interpretation of John 8:31-59" (Ph.D. diss., Saint Louis University, 1984).

[51] To hear Jesus (8.47) is to hear what Jesus has heard (8.26-28, 40; 15.15; cf. Newman/Nida, John, 204: "As in many other contexts, hears involves more than mere 'listening to.' It is really equivalent to learns."). Jesus' argument is masterfully circular (Odeberg, Fourth Gospel, 257-58; Barrett, St. John, 296; Schnackenburg, St. John 2, 51; Pancaro, Law, 283-84; Kysar, John, 105). In order to come to Jesus, one must be drawn by the Father. But it is Jesus himself who is the Father's agent in attracting disciples (see the climax of this operation in 12.32). The solitary role of Jesus in the eschatological drama and God's sole hand in the genesis of faith is unmistakably asserted. One hears/learns/comes (i.e., believes!) only because the Father in Jesus draws/teaches (i.e., generates faith).

[52] In Judaism, it was believed that God himself would come in the eschaton and teach the Torah to the sons of Jerusalem (cf. Schnackenburg, St. John 2, 51; Pancaro, Law, 281-87; Richter, Studien, 262-71; and the Targum of Isa 54.13: "all you sons will be taught in the Law of the Lord"). By applying Isa 54.13 to Jesus, John offers, from the standpoint of Judaism, two surprising assertions: (1) The teaching that God was to provide directly has come in Jesus. In other words, Jesus is God (in, e.g., 5.39, 46-47, Scripture too is able to "instruct," but in the present context the identity of the eschatological Teacher is the immediate concern). (2) The instruction that Jesus offers is not the Torah (it is not a "new" Law). His "teaching" is the exclusive revelation of the Father accomplished in and through himself. Rather than merely returning to the OT, Jesus instead challenges them to believe in him as the consummation of its expectations (cf. Wendy E. Sproston, "'Is Not This Jesus, the Son of Joseph . . .?' [John 6.42]: Johannine Christology as a Challenge to Faith," JSNT 24 [1985]: 77-97).

[53] He adds, "Your fathers ate the manna in the wilderness, and they died. This is the bread which comes down from heaven, that a man may eat of it and not die" (6.49-50; cf.

It is now possible to return to John's citation. To what extent can the form of this citation be explained on the basis of the role John would have it play in his narrative?

Perhaps the best place to begin is with the construction of John's sentence. It would appear that John has shaped his citation so that the substantival use of the adjective πάντες with the copula formally complements the construction of the sentences appearing in the immediate context of John 6.45 (cf. πάντες in 6.45a with οὐδείς in 6.44a; πᾶς in 6.45b; and τις in 6.46a; see also 6.50, 51).[54] This formal parallelism, on the one hand, could not be maintained without the absence in John 6.45 of Isa 54.13's reference to the "sons" of Jerusalem. On the other hand, it facilitates in a distinctive fashion the interconnectedness of the thoughts presented in these verses. What, then, is the significance of πάντες?

Scholars have characteristically explained πάντες in terms of John's so-called "universalism."[55] In other words, salvation is for both the sons of Jerusalem and the Gentiles (see in particular 10.16; 11.51-52; cf. 10.16).[56] Indeed, John 6.45 and its immediate context does seem to complement John's program for the inclusion of the Gentiles. However, scholars have failed to identify an additional, related, and perhaps even more immediate impetus for the omission of "your sons" from John 6.45. This impetus is John's desire to emphasize (especially in this context) the necessity of heavenly rather than earthly origins. John leaves Isaiah's reference to "sonship" out of his citation in order to emphasize that it is only the child of God (1.12-13), born from above (3.3) and taught by God (6.45), who may approach Jesus (cf. 11.51-52)[57] and not die (6.49-50, 58).

6.31-33, 58). The manna was only able to sustain the life of this world which ends with the grave in death. Jesus, on the other hand, gives eschatological life that endures beyond the grave (cf. 11.11).

[54] Cf. John 6.37, 39, 40. Note also the use of the substantival participle in John 6.35b, 37b, 47, 54, 56, 57, 58.

[55] Schlatter, *Der Evangelist*, 176; Lindars, *NT Apologetic*, 266, 270; Freed, *OT Quotations*, 19-20; Schnackenburg, *St. John* 2, 51; Aletti, "Jean 6," 190; Reim, *Studien*, 17; Becker, *Johannes*, 213; Kysar, *John*, 105; Arguing for the relative character of this universality are Richter, "Zitate," 267-68; Bergmeier, *Glaube*, 26, 45 n. 320, 216; Menken, "John 6,45," 170-71.

[56] Cf. the uses of "all" in John 1.7; 5.23; 12.32; 17.21. See also John 1.29; 3.16-17; 4.42; 6.33, 51; 8.12; 9.5; 12.9-20, 47; 1 John 2.2; 4.14.

[57] Those who refuse to hear (6.60; cf. 8.43) and learn (cf. 7.15; Rev 14.3) continue to walk in darkness (cf. 5.24; cf. 8.12). They possess only an identity inherited from an earthly father (cf. the "sonship" of Judas in 6.71; 12.4; 13.2, 26) and rooted in this world (cf. 6.70; 8.44; 13.2, 27). But those drawn by the Father receive a new identity from above through Jesus (contrast 12.32 with 19.26-27; cf. Jesus' indication in 21.15, 16, 17 [note the references to Peter's "sonship"] that Peter in denying Jesus forfeited the identity that Jesus gave him in 1.42). Cf. Matt 23.9.

The appearance in John 6.45 of both θεοῦ and διδακτοί is similarly indicative of John's hand. John's use of διδακτός is quite unusual,[58] but parallels significantly his extensive use of διδάσκω (and related forms) elsewhere in his Gospel.[59] It also seems unlikely that John would use a term other than θεός to refer to God. Why? Θεοῦ appears in John 6.45 not because, as some have suggested, John in his Gospel never refers to God as κύριος,[60] but because the Johannine Jesus never does (see also the formal parallelism of the genitives in 6.28, 29, 33, 45, 46, 69).[61]

In summary, the form of John's citation seems in every respect to be thoroughly Johannine. Unfortunately, the agreement in form between Isa 54.13 OG and John's citation, therefore, proves nothing. John's citation represents a conceivable rendering of a Hebrew Vorlage as well. There is, at best, only limited evidence for the influence of the OG in John's omission of "your sons" from his citation.

III.

In conclusion, Jesus' citation of the Old Testament in John 6.45 comes from Isa 54.13. What little evidence there is for the influence of a specific textual tradition points tentatively in the direction of the OG. John's citation differs conspicuously from the OG. But the form of John 6.45 can be traced to Isa 54.13 OG and to its immediate context. John's citation facilitates two propositions: (1) In order to come to Jesus, one must be taught by God. In other words, one's "origin" must be like Jesus' origin, "heavenly" (John characteristically suppresses matters pertaining to earthly origins). (2) Because Jesus has descended from heaven and alone has seen the Father, his instruction is the instruction of God expected by Isaiah.

---

58 Διδακτός appears in the NT only here and at 1 Cor 2.13.

59 On "teaching" in Judaism and John, consult Pancaro, Law, 77-116. Cf. John 1.38, 49; 3.2, 10, 26; 4.31; 6.25, 59; 7.14-17, 28, 35; 8.20, 28; 9.2, 34; 11.8, 28; 13.13, 14; 14.26; 18.19-20; 20.16; see also 1 John 2.27; Rev 2.14, 20. Jesus is clearly portrayed as the eschatological Teacher. Cf. παιδεία (absent in John's Gospel) in Isa 50.4 OG.

60 So Reim, Studien, 16; cf. the critique of Menken, "John 6.45," 168.

61 Cf. κύριος in John 6.34, 68.

Chapter 5

THE GODS AND THE SON OF GOD

John 10.22-39, the Johannine version of Jesus' final encounter with the religious leaders of the Jews prior to his arrest, finds no direct parallel in the Synoptics. These verses do, however, bear elements which seem to recall the Synoptic accounts of Jesus' trial at the hands of his protagonists (cf. Matt 26.57-75; Mark 14.53-72; Luke 22.54, 63-71). Indeed, these parallels may well be intentional.[1] But there is little evidence for John's dependence upon any of the Synoptics.[2]

A potentially lethal point of contention surfaces in this Jesus' final confrontation. Their claim is that, in saying "I and the Father are one" (10.30), Jesus has become worthy of stoning (10.31) because he has committed blasphemy against God (10.33; cf. 5.18; Lev 24.16).[3] Jesus' response to this suggestion has occasioned a considerable amount of discussion among scholars. What

---

[1] Kysar, *John*, 168 (cf. Jerome H. Neyrey, "'I Said: You are Gods:' Psalm 82:6 and John 10," *JBL* 108 [1989]: 647-63). According to Kysar, such a possibility suggests that "for John the whole of Jesus' encounters with the religious leaders is a kind of trial scene" (cf. A. E. Harvey, *Jesus on Trial: A Study in the Fourth Gospel* [Atlanta: John Knox, 1977]). See further below.

[2] See esp. Dodd, *Historical Tradition*, 88-96. Cf. idem, *Interpretation*, 361-62; Pancaro, *Law*, 64-71; Brown, *John* 1, 405; Schnackenburg, *St. John* 2, 306; Lindars, *John*, 365-71; Barrett, *St. John*, 378-79; Markku Kotila, *Umstrittener Zeuge: Studien zur Stellung des Gesetzes in der johanneischen Theologiegeschichte*, Annales Academiae Scientiarum Fennicae, Dissertationes Humanarum Litterarum, Bd. 48 (Helsinki: Suomalainen Tiedeakatemia, 1988), 87.

[3] On the uncertain character of this offense, see, e.g., Barrett, *John*, 383-84.

precisely is to be made of Jesus' use of the Old Testament to refute his adversaries?

Jesus begins by citing the Old Testament: "Is it not written in your Law,

'ἐγὼ εἶπα θεοί ἐστε;'" (10.34).

The Old Testament passage to which Jesus refers (cf. Jesus' references to the Old Testament in 6.45; 7.37-38; 8.17; 13.18; 15.25; 19.28) appears only here in the New Testament. It does, however, occupy significant attention elsewhere both in the literature of later Judaism and the Christian fathers.[4]

The formula which introduces this citation (cf. 2.17; 6.31, 45; 12.14, 16) is similarly unique to John's Gospel (cf. esp. 1 Cor 14.21).[5] Jesus' indication that his citation comes from the "Law" might initially seem incorrect, for it does not come from the Pentateuch (see below). The difficulty, however, is an illusory one. "Law" is in all likelihood to be taken as a reference to the Old Testament in general.[6] The use of the term is somewhat unusual, but not unknown among the rabbis[7] (cf. 12.34; 15.25; Rom 3.19; 1 Cor 14.21).[8]

Jesus' use of the pronominal adjective ὑμῶν[9] ("your Law") might also initially appear to represent a disavowal of the Old Testament, or at least an attempt to distance himself from it. But Jesus' purpose seems to have been instead to emphasize that the verity of his position is easily substantiated from the Jews' own sacred Scriptures.[10] Thus, John accentuates the irony of their blindness. Their desire to stone him cannot be legitimized from the very Scriptures they claim to know and believe (cf. 6.31; 7.42, 49; 9.28-29; 12.34; 19.7). Instead, the same Scriptures can be called upon in support of their perceived enemy (cf. esp. 5.39, 46-47).

We have already noted that Jesus' citation does not come from the Pentateuch. What, then, is his source? Can it be determined whether or not a specific textual tradition has been influential?

---

[4] See below. Cf. Reim, *Studien*, 24.

[5] On the use in John's formula of the periphrastic participle, see esp. my observations in chapters two and three.

[6] So most scholars.

[7] See Str-B 2:542-43; 3:159, 463. Cf. Schlatter, *Der Evangelist*, 243-44.

[8] Contrast the more usual references to the "Law" in Luke 2.23, 24; 10.26.

[9] The omission of ὑμῶν is supported by P[45] ℵ* D Θ pc it sy[s] and Cyp. It seems that a scribe found John's reference to the Law inappropriate and deleted the problem. John, however, characteristically refers to the Law (either the Pentateuch or the whole OT) as a "given" entrusted to the Jews (see 1.17; 7.19, 22-23, 47-52; 8.17; 12.34; 15.25; 18.31; 19.7; cf. 1.45).

[10] Cf. Barrett, *St. John*, 384; Morris, *Reflections*, 395.

I.

The task of isolating what passage John recalls is a relatively simple one. John 10.34 reproduces word for word the text of Ps 82(81).6. No other Old Testament text has ever been considered by scholars as a possible source.

John's citation agrees word for word with Ps 81.6 OG. The OG, however, does not deviate in any perceptible fashion from the Hebrew of the MT. Only a few scholars, therefore, have ventured to suggest that the influence of a specific textual tradition is evident in this citation.[11] Of the few that have made such an attempt, all have concluded that John's citation reflects the influence of the OG. But only very rarely has an explanation been offered for why the OG may be the more probable source.[12]

As it turns out, the OG is, in fact, John's most probable source. Why? Only in John 10.34 does John use εἶπα. Elsewhere in his Gospel, John always uses εἶπον for the first person aorist indicative. Εἶπα, it would seem, has come from Ps 81,6 OG.[13]

The simple brevity of this citation prevents the possibility of finding in John 10.34 any other features which might suggest the influence of a specific textual tradition. Perhaps an understanding of John's intent in citing this passage will offer additional insights.[14]

---

11 Cf. Burney, *Aramaic Origin*, 118: "the verbal agreement between Jn. and LXX has . . . no special significance, since Heb. could hardly be otherwise rendered." Freed, *OT Quotations*, 61, notes that the Hebrew second person plural pronoun is not translated in the OG "apart from its inclusion in the verb." It is not likely, however, that it would be translated (cf. Isa 41.23).

12 Cf., e.g., the insufficient efforts of Franke, *Alte Testament*, 283; Goodwin, "Sources," 62; Dodd, *Historical Tradition*, 46 n. 1; Reim, *Studien*, 23, 90, 160, 229 (who posits the influence of wisdom circles, pp. 25, 94); Pancaro, *Law*, 175; Humann, "OT Quotations," 42.

13 Menken, "John 1,23," 192. Cf. Noack, *Tradition*, 82: "10.34 . . . zitiert Ps LXX 81,6, und zwar wörtlich bis in Einzelheiten, sogar die Form εἶπα ist die der LXX." Menken (pp. 192-93 n. 8) points out that a limited number of lesser mss. (including A and D) support the reading εἶπον in John 10.34. The reading εἶπα could, then, be regarded as a secondary assimilation to the OG. However, the singularity of εἶπα is to be taken instead as a significant point in favor of its originality. Moreover, the variant εἶπον may reflect the influence of John 10.36: "I said (εἶπον), I am the Son of God."

14 The previously held and formerly popular theory that John quotes here "aus dem Gedächtnis" (cf. Noack, *Tradition*, 84; Goodwin, "Sources," 62) continues to attract contemporary proponents (Kotila, *Zeuge*, 90-91). John, however, is far from haphazard in his reproduction of this passage; neither does he appear unaware of the OT context from which his citation came (see further below).

II.

Jesus' defense of himself in John 10.34-36 has occasioned numerous conflicting interpretations. The most divisive problem for scholars has involved the attempt to delineate who John understands the addressees of the psalm to be. Significantly, in each of the solutions that have been offered evidence from the literature of later Judaism has played a key role.

Scholars have traditionally identified Israel's judges as the understood addressees of the psalm.[15] According to the advocates of this interpretation, Israel's judges are designated "gods" by virtue of their role in executing the divine function of judgment. This role Israel's judges received by divine appointment (cf., e.g., *Midr. Ps.* 82.1; *b. Sanh.* 6b-7a; *b. Sota* 47b). These judges, however, have failed to faithfully execute justice in Israel. The psalm, therefore, indicates that they will die like ordinary men (v. 7).

As an alternative to a more traditional interpretation, some scholars have suggested that the "gods" are understood to be superhuman figures to whom the care for the nations was entrusted. These figures were designated "gods" by the pagan world and "angels" by the Jews.[16] Referred to as "gods" by virtue of this divine commission, they nevertheless failed to execute their trust. As punishment, they became mortal beings, subject to death.[17]

---

[15] Cf. Toy, *Quotations*, 87; Eugen Hühn, *Die messianischen Weissagungen des israelitisch-jüdischen Volkes bis zu den Targumim historisch-kritisch untersucht und erläutert*, 2. Teil, *Die alttestamentlichen Citate und Reminiscenzen im Neuen Testament* (Tübingen: Mohr-Siebeck, 1900), 85; Westcott, *St. John*, 160; Bernard, *St. John*, 367; Brown, *John* 1, 409-11; Morris, *John*, 525-26; Reim, *Studien*, 23; Lindars, *John*, 374; Richard Jungkuntz, "An Approach to the Exegesis of John 10:34-36," *CTM* 35 (1964): 561-65; Bruce, *John*, 235 ("whether of human or angelic rank"); Kysar, *John*, 168-69; Humann, "OT Quotations," 35; Stephen L. Homcy, "'You are Gods'? Spirituality and a Difficult Text," *JETS* 32 (1989): 485-91; W. Gary Phillips, "An Apologetic Study of John 10:34-36," *BSac* 146 (1989): 405-19. See further below.

[16] John A. Emerton, "Some New Testament Notes," *JTS*, n.s. 11 (1960): 329-32, maintains that evidence from the Peshitta, the patristic literature, and the OG supports this understanding of the psalm. Cf. Jan-A. Bühner, *Der Gesandte und sein Weg im vierten Evangelium: Die kultur- und religionsgeschichtlichen Grundlagen der johanneischen Sendungschristologie sowie ihre traditionsgeschichtliche Entwicklung*, Wissenschaftliche Untersuchungen zum Neuen Testament, 2. Reihe, Bd. 2 (Tübingen: Mohr-Siebeck, 1977), 393-94.

[17] Subsequent to Emerton's initial formulation of this interpretation, Marinus de Jonge and Adam S. van der Woude, "11QMelchizedek and the New Testament," *NTS* 12 (1965/1966): 301-26 (trans., p. 303) offered an analysis of a newly discovered Qumran document in which, it was claimed, a similar understanding of Ps 82(81) was evident. V. 1 of the psalm is taken by the desert community as a statement made by Melchizedek. Conversely, those in the psalm designated "gods" and "sons of the Most High," but have been agents of wickedness in the world, are referred to as "Belial and the spirits of his lot" (i.e., evil angels). Naturally, Emerton in turn responded by taking the use of the psalm at Qumran as additional support for a similar understanding of its use in John 10.34-36 (see John A. Emerton,

Still another interpretation that has emerged and has attracted a considerable amount of recent support asserts that John understands the psalm to be an address to the nation of Israel after its reception of the Law at Sinai.[18] If Israel had remained faithful to the Law, this people would not have died. Disobedience, however, was not long in coming. With the making of the golden calf, Israel became subject to death (cf., e.g., *b. Abod. Zar.* 5a; *Midr. Rab. Exod.* 32.7).[19]

Of these proposals, one can be quickly dismissed. It is most unlikely that John refers to angels. The context of John's reference to the psalm makes no reference to angels. Indeed, even the larger context of John's Gospel lacks similar references to such heavenly beings playing roles of comparable significance.[20]

"Melchizedek and the Gods: Fresh Evidence for the Jewish Background of John X.34-36," *JTS*, n.s. 17 (1966): 399-401).

[18] See Str-B 2:543; Anthony T. Hanson, "John's Citation of Psalm LXXXII: John X.33-6," *NTS* 11 (1964/1965): 158-62 (cf. idem, "John's Citation of Psalm LXXXII Reconsidered," *NTS* 13 (1966/1967): 363-67; idem, *Utterances*, 120-21); Nils A. Dahl, "The Johannine Church and History," in *Current Issues in New Testament Interpretation: Essays in Honor of Otto A. Piper*, ed. W. Klassen (New York: Harper & Brothers, 1962), 133; James S. Ackerman, "The Rabbinic Interpretation of Psalm 82 and the Gospel of John: John 10:34," *HTR* 59 (1966): 186-91: Schnackenburg, *St. John* 2, 311; Pancaro, *Law*, 177-85; Barrett, *St. John*, 384-85; Sloyan, *John*, 135; Neyrey, "I Said" (cf. idem, *An Ideology of Revolt: John's Christology in Social-Science Perspective* [Philadelphia: Fortress, 1988], 72-74, 221-24); cf. Homcy, "Spirituality," 489.

[19] Hanson, "Psalm 82," 160-61, has suggested further that the "Word of God" in John 10.35 is to be understood as the pre-existent Logos (cf. Westcott, *St. John*, 160; Lagrange, *Jean*, 290, who describes the "gods" referred to in John 10.35 as "ceux à qui parle le Seigneur dans le passage cité"). The phrase "to whom the word of God came," then, is to be understood to mean "to whom the pre-existent Logos spoke." Jesus' argument, therefore, is to be paraphrased as follows: "If to be addressed by the pre-existent Word justifies men in being called gods, . . . far more are we justified in applying the title Son of God to the human bearer of the pre-existent Word" (cf. Hanson's elaboration of this with reference to the Melchizedek fragment and his response to his critics in "Ps 82 Reconsidered"). Provocative as this suggestion may be, however, it is unlikely that John had this in mind. "The phrase 'to whom the word of God came (ἐγένετο)' is most naturally to be understood as those to whom *the message* was spoken, and is frequently so used in the OT prophets, especially in Jer and Ezek" (Beasley-Murray, *John*, 177 [emphasis his]; cf. Pancaro, *Law*, 185-88; Schnackenburg, *St. John* 2, 312). In Hanson's most recent treatment of this issue (*Utterances*, 121), he offers the additional and even more speculative suggestion that "The last verse (of the psalm) will then be regarded as a prophecy of the resurrection of Christ ('Arise, O God') and the accession of the Gentiles."

[20] Cf. de Jonge/van der Woude, "11QMelchizedek," 313-14: "there is no reason to think of angels; verse 33 even makes a clear contrast between god and men." See also Hanson, "Ps 82 Reconsidered" (and idem, *Utterances*, 121: "[John] would have no sympathy with the identification of Melchisedech with an angel").

Two options, therefore, remain. Most scholars hold that Jesus' argument is typical of the genre *a minori ad majus*, a method common in rabbinic circles.[21] But does John's use of the psalm envision Israel's judges or the nation of Israel? And how does this relate to Jesus' argument?

To answer these questions, one must begin with Jesus' reference in John 10.35 to the "gods" of the psalm as those "to whom the word of God came." Many scholars have found it improbable that words such as these could be used to refer to Israel's judges. These scholars typically point out that the Old Testament never speaks of the "word" coming to Israel's judges. On the other hand, it is argued, this quite naturally qualifies as a description of Israel's reception of the Torah at the foot of Mount Sinai.[22] But the logic of this argument bears little weight when examined in some detail.

The phrase "the word of God came to . . ." is typical of the Old Testament and of Judaism in general.[23] The phrase appears with reference to Abraham (Gen 15.1), Moses and Aaron (*Mek. Exod.* 12.1), Solomon (1 Kgs 6.11), and David (1 Chr 22.8). It is especially prominent, however, in references to later Old Testament prophets[24] (see Jer 1.4, 11; Mic 1.1; Zech 1.1; Ezek 6.1; 17.1; 34.1; *et. al.*; cf. Hos 1.1; Joel 1.1; Zeph 1.1; and the Baptist in Luke 3.2!). Why is this significant? Because this phrase consistently and characteristically seems to single out specific *individuals* who are to function in Israel as spokesmen for God to the nation (cf. Jer 1.7, 9; Zech 1.3; Ezek 6.2-3; 17.2-3; 34.2; Hos 1.2; and the Baptist in Luke 3.3!). This phrase does not, however, at any time appear with reference to the nation itself. Such a reference would not at all correspond to its normal usage. On the other hand, its use with reference to Israel's judges would be completely in keeping with its usual function.[25] For this reason, some version

---

[21] For a useful critique of the various alternatives which have been considered, see Phillips, "John 10:34-36," 410-19. Contrast the differing emphasis of the contribution by Urban C. von Wahlde, "Literary Structure and Theological Argument in Three Discourses with the Jews in the Fourth Gospel," *JBL* 103 (1984): 575-84, who posits a parallelism between the arguments appearing in John 6.31-59; 8.13-59; and 10.22-39.

[22] Cf. Hanson, "Ps 82 Reconsidered," 366-67; Ackerman, "Psalm 82," 187-88; Schnackenburg, *St. John* 2, 311; Pancaro, *Law*, 189-92; Beasley-Murray, *John*, 176-77.

[23] Bultmann, *John*, 389 n. 4. Cf. Str-B 2:543; Schlatter, *Der Evangelist*, 244.

[24] Cf. Ackerman, "Psalm 82," 188 n. 9.

[25] Cf. Marie-Émile Boismard, "Jésus, le Prophète par excellence, d'après Jean 10,24-39," in *Neues Testament und Kirche. Für Rudolf Schnackenburg*, hg. J. Gnilka (Freiburg: Herder, 1974), 161: "il faudrait, pour nous convaincre, qu'ils prouvent que l'expression au singulier 'la parole de Dieu' pouvait désigner la Torah dans le judaïsm contemporain du Christ, ou même de l'évangéliste." He adds (p. 161 n. 4), "La Bible parle souvent de la Torah comme des 'paroles' que Dieu a données à son peuple; elle est 'les paroles de L'Alliance' (Ex 34,28), ou 'les dix paroles' (Ex 34.28; Deut 10,4). Mais on a toujours le mot 'parole' au pluriel." What follows

of a more traditional interpretation of Jesus' reference to the "gods" in John
10.34-36 is to be preferred.

Assuming, then, that this is the case, it is both conspicuous and significant
that Jesus does not refer to Israel's judges as "sanctified and sent" (10.36); neither
does he refer to himself as one "to whom the word of God came" (10.35).[26]
Jesus' desire, it seems, is to set up a contrast between their office and his own. In
describing them as those "to whom the word of God came," and himself as
"sanctified and sent," it is likely that Jesus intends for his audience to associate
him first not with the judges, but with another group of spokesmen prominent
in the Old Testament, the prophets.[27] Indeed, in this particular context it is
probable that the Jews are to understand Jesus' self-predication as a reference to

---

has been significantly influenced by Boismard. Some of the most important points where we
both agree and disagree are indicated below.

[26] In fact, it would be particularly inappropriate from an OT perspective to refer to
Israel's judges as "sanctified and sent" (see further below). Neither would it make sense from
the standpoint of John to refer to Jesus as one "to whom the word of God came." Jesus is the
Logos who is God's Word become flesh and as God's Word has come into the world (1.9, 14-
18). Cf. the use of the same terminology with reference to Jesus and the followers of Jesus in
17.17-19. Jesus' disciples are, like Jesus and through Jesus, sanctified (cf. Acts 20.32; 26.18; 1
Cor 1.2; Heb 2.11; 10.10; 2 Tim 2.21) and sent into the world. As Jesus' emissaries, they work
so that others might also believe through their word (17.20; cf. 14.12) and become one
(17.21-23; cf. 10.16; 11.52; 17.11; 1 John 2.20; 3.24; 4.15).

[27] Boismard, "le Prophète," 162-63 (cf. idem, Moïse, 114-15; Bruce, John, 235; McCaffrey,
House, 233). See esp. Jer 1.4 ("Now the word of the Lord came to me saying . . ."), 5b ("before
you were born I sanctified you; I appointed you a prophet to the nations;" cf. Sir 49.7), and 7
("to all to whom I send you you shall go"). Cf. John 6.69 ("you are the Holy One of God"). On
Jesus as the Holy One par excellence and the use of this title to designate Jesus as
agent/revealer of God and judge, see William R. Domeris, "The Office of the Holy One," JTSA
54 (1986): 35-38, esp. 38 (cf. idem, "The Holy One of God as a Title for Jesus," Neot 19
[1985]: 9-17). There is, it seems, a certain tragic irony in this reference to Jesus'
"sanctification" in the midst of a feast celebrating the "re-sanctifying" of the Jerusalem temple
(10.22; on the synonyms ἁγιάζω and ἐγκαινίζω [cf. vv. 22, 36], see esp. Hoskyns, Fourth
Gospel, 392). The Jews, in the midst of celebrating the restoration of their temple, are destroying it (see chapter two). And in instigating a final confrontation with Jesus prior to his trial,
they reject the coming of God's true temple and fail to see in him the eschatological establishment of true worship and the fulfillment of this festival's hope for God's final deliverance (cf.
Westcott, St. John, 157; Guilding, Worship, 127; Braun, Jean 2, 83; Brown, John 1, 405, 411;
Morris, John, 516-17; Lindars, John, 375; Newman/Nida, Handbook, 346; Kysar, John, 169;
Beasley-Murray, John, 172, 177; McCaffrey, House, 232-35; Egil A. Wyller, "In Solomon's
Porch: A Henological Analysis of the Architectonic of the Fourth Gospel," ST 42 [1988]: 155-
56). Contrast the Jews' coming to Jesus in the middle of "winter" (10.23), the darkest time of
the year, with Nicodemus' coming by night (3.2).

one particular prophet. That prophet is the eschatological prophet, the prophet like Moses.[28]

What is apparently most significant for Jesus' argument, then, is not the equivalence of Jesus' role as the eschatological prophet with that of the "gods" as judges.[29] Instead, what Jesus wishes to emphasize is the significance of the contrasting relationship of each to the person of Moses. When one pauses to compare each with the Old Testament figure of Moses, it becomes immediately apparent that the Jews err grossly in attempting to stone Jesus. Why? Jesus' identity as the eschatological prophet overwhelmingly overshadows that of the judges.

On the one hand, Israel's judges possess an identity which the Old Testament indicates they inherited from Moses.[30] Hence, as was the case with Moses, theirs is a divine charge. Theirs is the judgment of God (cf. Deut 1.7; 19.17; Exod 21.6; 22.9). Now Moses was the premier judge of Israel and the first and only Old Testament individual said to be "like God" (cf. Exod 4.16; 7.1).

---

[28] Cf. Boismard, "le Prophète," 163-66 (cf. idem, Moïse, 2-3, 115). The possibility that John, in recalling the prophet Jeremiah (see above), also evokes images reminiscent of Moses, is confirmed by this. Both Moses and Jeremiah share the following characteristics: (1) Initially, both attempt to refuse God's commission (cf. Jer 1.6 with Exod 3.11; 4.10; 6.30). (2) Both become spokesmen for God (cf. Jer 1.7b with Exod 7.2; see also Exod 4.12). (3) God promises to be with both (cf. Jer 1.8 with Exod 3.12; see also Exod 4.12). (4) Both are sent (cf. Jer 1.7 with Exod 3.10-14). (5) Neither speaks on his own authority (cf. Jer 1.7, 9 with Deut 18.18). That the Johannine Jesus even speaks of the prophet like Moses has already been established (see my remarks in chapter three). That Moses is being recalled in this particular context is suggested not only by vv. 35-36 but also by the following details: (1) The Jews' demand that Jesus identify whether or not he is the Christ (10.24). But Jesus refuses to operate with their categories (Bruce, John, 230). Still, he answers in the affirmative (cf. 4.25-26) by referring to the testimony of his entire life, both words and deeds (v. 25; cf. 5.43). Jesus' deeds (cf. 4.34; 5.17, 20, 36; 7.3; 17.4) would, of course, include his signs (7.21; 9.3, 4; 15. 24; cf. 10.25 with the signs of Moses in Exod 4.1-9 and my remarks on Moses' signs in chapter three). (2) Jesus describes his disciples as sheep that he knows. They hear his voice and follow him (vv. 26-28; cf. 10.3, 4, 10; and Num 27.15-23). Finally, cf. Jesus' sanctification (10.36) with that of Jeremiah in Jer 1.5 and Moses in Sir 45.4.

[29] This is one of the major weaknesses of Boismard, "le Prophète." His attempt to establish that "les fonctions de 'juge' ou de 'prophète' sont quasi identiques" (p. 163; cf. idem, Moïse, 115) tends to obscure both the OT data and the clarity and significance of the contrast Jesus purposes to establish (see further below).

[30] Cf. Boismard, "le Prophète," 168-71 (contrast idem, Moïse, 114). Key to this understanding of the judges in Ps 82(81) is Deut 1.16-17 (cf. 1.12-17; Midr. Ps. 82; b. Sota 47b; b. Sanh. 6b-7a). With the institution of the first judges in Israel (cf. Deut 1.17 and Ps 82[81].3-4), the judgment which belongs to God (Deut 1.17) and was entrusted to Moses (the original solitary judge of Israel) was, in turn, transferred to a select group of Israel's tribal leaders (Deut 1.15; cf. Ps 82[81].7). Cf. the parallel in Exod 18.13-26.

Therefore, because Israel's judges possess a derivative measure of Moses' authority, they are also privy to a similar title, "gods."

Jesus, on the other hand, possesses an identity of incomparable significance.[31] His is *not* an identity derived from Moses. Neither is he simply another Moses.[32] Rather, Jesus is the eschatological prophet like Moses who surpasses infinitely the person of Moses (John 1.17). Moses met with God "face to face" and was given God's word (Deut 34.10; Num 12.6-8; Exod 33.11). But Jesus *is* God's pre-existent Word become flesh (John 1.1,14). Jesus speaks what he has seen and heard from his Father (John 3.31-32; 8.38; 16.27-28) as one who uniquely reposes in the bosom of the Father (John 1.18).[33] Thus, because Jesus' identity exceeds that of Moses, and Moses' identity exceeds that of Israel's judges, the "gods" (John 10.35-36), Jesus is unquestionably worthy of the title "Son of God" (10.36).[34]

---

[31] Cf. Boismard, "le Prophète," 170-71.

[32] Otherwise Boismard, "le Prophète," 166, 171. The Jewish hope for a second Moses has already manifested itself in John's Gospel (see my remarks in chapter three). See further below.

[33] Cf. Barrett, *St. John*, 385: "behind the argument as thus formulated there lies no belief in the 'divinity' of humanity as such, but a conviction of the creative power of the word of God. Addressed to creatures it raises them above themselves; in Jesus it is personally present, and he may therefore with much more right be called divine."

[34] On the significance of the anarthrous predicate nominative υἱός, see James W. Voelz, "The Language of the New Testament," in *Aufstieg und Niedergang der römischen Welt: Geschichte und Kultur Roms im Spiegel der neueren Forschung*, 2. Principat, Bd. 25/2, hg. Wolfgang Haase (New York: de Gruyter, 1984), 957. Jesus had not actually said previously "I am the Son of God." But this statement naturally complements his former claim to be one with the Father (10.30). Why has this title been selected? His statement is an obviously deliberate maneuver to avoid saying "I am God" (see 1.1, 18; 20.28; cf. the rather speculative attempt to find in Ps 45 the OT background for these statements in Günter Reim, "Jesus as God in the Fourth Gospel: The Old Testament Background," *NTS* 30 [1984]: 158-60). As is his custom throughout John's Gospel, Jesus avoids this and continues to affirm that his divinity must be viewed by them in terms of his relationship with the Father (see 1.14, 18; 3.16, 18; 5.25; 11.4; 20.31; cf. 1.34; 11.27; 19.7; the central role of this relationship in Johannine Christology has been recently asserted by W. R. G. Loader, "The Central Structure of Johannine Christology," *NTS* 30 [1984]: 188-216; and Evarist Pinto, *Jesus the Son and Giver of Life in the Fourth Gospel* [Rome: Pontificia Universitaria Urbaniana, 1981]). Also, the use of the Son of God title elsewhere in John's Gospel is associated with royal motifs (1.49; 11.27; 20.31; cf. the attempts to analyze the OT background of this designation in H. Haag, "'Son of God' in the Language and Thinking of the Old Testament," *Concilium* 153 [1982]: 31-36; Pinto, *Son*, 53-62; Boismard, *Moïse*, 108-11). The use of this title fits well, then, in this context where Jesus purposes to establish his superiority over one of Israel's premier rulers, Moses. Finally, it is frequently suggested that Jesus has yet another purpose in referring to himself as the "Son of God" (=God; contrast 1 John 5.20; cf. Pancaro, *Law*, 59-63; Kikuo Matsunaga, "The 'Theos' Christology as the Ultimate Confession of the Fourth Gospel," *AJBI* 7 [1981]: 124-45). Jesus also alludes to and asserts his superiority over the "sons of the Most High" (=the "gods") in v.

One final observation remains. All of the details in John 10.22-39 which seem to suggest that Jesus is to be understood as the prophet like Moses can also be taken as an affirmation of his role as eschatological Judge. This suggests further that Jesus' citing the psalm in response to the Jews' attempt to encircle him and thereby arrive at a final judgment concerning him may be taken as an ironic reversal of the circumstances by Jesus.[35] Israel's leaders[36] desire to offer a final judgment concerning Jesus. Jesus, on the other hand, reveals himself to be the very Judge envisioned in the psalm,[37] standing "in the midst"[38] of Israel's judges, chastising them for their inability to judge justly.[39] If there is no change in their ways, all will end in death.[40]

6b of the psalm. Why, then, is v. 6b not cited? Perhaps because John normally avoids referring to anyone other than Jesus in the Gospel as υἱός (Pancaro, *Law*, 176-77).

[35] Cf. Neyrey, *Revolt*, 66-68 (and idem, "I Said," 650).

[36] The location of this scene (cf. 2.13-22) and the character of the ensuing dialogue suggest that "the Jews" here are to be understood as the religious authorities (Neyrey, *Revolt*, 66; cf. Beasley-Murray, *John*, 20, 173).

[37] See esp. Jungkuntz, "John 10:32-34," 559-65 (cf. Hanson, "Ps 82 Reconsidered," 367). Jungkuntz offers numerous helpful observations concerning the relationship between the concepts "judge," "king," and "shepherd" in OT thought (pp. 563-64). But his attempt to show that the statement "the Scripture cannot be broken" (10.35) is to be rendered "Scripture cannot be kept from fulfillment" does not convince (pp. 559-60, 565; similarly Bernard, *St. John*, 368, to whom Jungkuntz does not refer; and Pancaro, *Law*, 327). Jesus' reference to the "Scripture," like his reference in John 10.34 to the "Law" (on the identity of these terms, see Kotila, *Zeuge*, 92), has in mind the entire OT (see Bultmann, *John*, 389 n. 4; Morris, *John*, 526-27; Lindars, *John*, 374; cf. Pancaro, *Law*, 188 n. 34; Phillips, "John 10:34-36," 409 n. 11). What is true, therefore, of John 10.34 is so because it is derived from the whole (Pancaro, *Law*, 515, 517). The statement that Scripture cannot be broken (cf. 1 Pet 1.25 [Isa 40.8b]; Matt 24.35; Mark 7.13) is meant simply to suggest that Scripture cannot be stripped of its binding force (cf. John 5.18; 7.23; 1 John 3.8; Rev 1.5). Pancaro, *Law*, 188-89, rightly points out that finding in John's Gospel the fulfillment of the psalm does not require great imagination. Unfortunately, Pancaro's solution is not convincing either (for Pancaro, the prophecy is fulfilled when the word of Jesus gives men the right to call themselves gods, sons of the Most High). The psalm simply indicates that God as Judge will come and chide Israel's judges for not making right judgments. This is precisely who Jesus is and what Jesus does in this scene. Whether there are further aspects of the larger context of the psalm John intends to recall in his construction of John 10.22-39 is difficult to know with certainty. In what follows, a few of the more conspicuous details both seem to hold in common are noted.

[38] Note John's reference to Jesus' *walking* (10.23) in the temple and his being *surrounded* (10.24; cf. Ps 7.6-8) by Israel's judges. Cf. the psalm's similar reference to the Judge *standing in the midst* of judges (v. 1). Contrast Jesus in the midst of his enemies in John 1.26; 8.59 (all of these anticipating 19.18) with Jesus in the midst of the true children of God in John 20.19, 20.

[39] Cf. the lack of understanding in v. 5 of the psalm with John 10.6, 14, 15, 25-27 (cf. 6.69), 38 (cf. 1.10).

[40] Note the irony of their desire to kill Jesus in a situation in which it is their own lives that are at stake (8.21, 24).

Far from representing a retreat from his former assertion (10.30), then, every aspect of Jesus' argument serves to reassert his oneness with the Father. At the same time, Jesus also shows his opponents to be without legitimate grounds for stoning him.

It is Jesus, in fact, who has come "for judgment" (9.39; cf. 5.22, 27-30; 8.16, 26; 12.31; 16.11). And they are worthy of such (cf. 3.18-19). Yet Jesus' desire is not to pronounce judgment on them (cf. 3.17; 8.15; 12.47). Instead, Jesus closes by exhorting them one last time to believe in him.

They have rejected his words, but have implicitly acknowledged that the works he has "shown" (cf. 5.20; 14.8-11; 20.20) them are "good" (10.32-33).[41] Jesus, therefore, pleads with them to believe in his works (10.37-38; cf. 10.25, 26). Jesus does this not because one may believe Jesus' works and choose not to believe his words. Rather faith in Jesus' works provokes a κρίσις in which one of two alternatives must be considered. One may, on the one hand, choose not to believe anything at all regarding Jesus.[42] It is Jesus' hope, however, that belief in his works would instead lead to faith in his words as well, especially "that the Father is in me and I am in the Father" (10.38; cf. 14.10-12).[43] The Jews unfortunately choose the former alternative and reject both Jesus' words and his works. They seek to seize Jesus (10.39a),[44] but he eludes them (10.39b)[45] and retreats beyond the Jordan to where his ministry began (10.40).[46] There beyond the Jordan many believe in him (10.41-42).

In summary, this analysis of John's intent has failed to detect any additional evidence for the influence of a specific textual tradition. While John does seem to

---

[41] Pancaro, Law, 75. It is likely that the designation "good" is to be taken as a synonym for "true" (see 2.10; 10.11, 14; cf. my remarks on the eschatological character of John's use of the term "true" in chapter three).

[42] Note in John 10.38 the emphasis on both coming to know and abiding in that knowledge.

[43] Jesus offers not a way around believing in his words, but a way to such faith (cf. Pancaro. Law, 75). Note that v. 38 constitutes the last of three affirmations of Jesus' identity with the Father in this text (Kysar, John, 170; cf. vv. 30 and 36).

[44] Cf. 7.30, 32, 44; 8.20; 11.57. That the Jews do not again attempt to stone Jesus is probably significant. It may be that, even though they reject his claims, on the level of their own understanding (cf. Brown, John 1, 409-10; Boismard, "le Prophète," 170-71; Bruce, John, 235) Jesus' argument has left them with a problem they cannot solve. How can they stone Jesus for blasphemy when the Scripture itself refers to men (like themselves!) as gods? They have no grounds to stone him, but they also have no desire to let him escape.

[45] Cf. Wis 2.12-20.

[46] Convincingly arguing for this (among other details) as an indication that the Fourth Gospel has reached the conclusion of its "erste Hauptteile" is Mathias Rissi, "Der Aufbau des vierten Evangeliums," NTS 29 (1983): 48-54, esp. 50-51 (cf. Brown, John 1, 414; Lindars, John, 377; Wyller, "Solomon's Porch").

be aware of the larger context of the psalm, it is difficult know with precision the extent to which he desires to recall this context in John 10.22-39.

III.

In conclusion, Jesus' citation from the Old Testament in John 10.34 comes from Ps 81.6 OG. The psalm is recalled in order to facilitate an argument in which John apparently wishes to establish the following: (1) The psalm addresses Israel's judges who, because they possess an identity and authority derived from Moses (who is himself "like God"), are referred to as "gods." (2) Because Moses' identity surpasses that of the "gods," and Jesus' identity surpasses that of Moses, Jesus is able to speak as he does of his unity with the Father and is worthy of the title "Son of God."

Chapter 6

THE ARRIVAL OF THE KING

John's account of Jesus' final entry into Jerusalem (John 12.12-19) relates the same event recorded in each of the Synoptics (cf. Matt 21.1-9; Mark 11.1-10; Luke 19.28-40). But John's account appears quite independent of the Synoptics. Indeed, one might go so far as to say that John's version of this event differs from those appearing in the Synoptics "in every point where it is possible to differ in relating the same event."[1]

Still, two references to the Old Testament are especially prominent in John's account (cf. 12.38-40; 19.36-38) and are evident in the Synoptics as well. John writes in his version of Jesus' final journey to Jerusalem that Jesus was greeted by a large crowd with the words of Ps 118(117).25-26 (John 12.13; cf. Matt 21.9; Mark 11.9; Luke 19.38). According to John, Jesus' response to this greeting was to find a young ass and to sit on it (John 12.14; cf. Matt 21.1-3, 6-7; Mark 11.1-

---

[1] Dodd, *Historical Tradition*, 155. Thus, any attempt to explain the Johannine setting on the basis of a comparison with the Synoptics yields, at best, only limited results (p. 154). "It may no doubt be possible to harmonize the two accounts, but it is exceedingly difficult to see how one could be derived from the other" (p. 156). On the independence of John's account from that of the Synoptics, see esp. Dwight Moody Smith, "John 12,12ff. and the Question of John's Use of the Synoptics," *JBL* 82 (1963): 58-64 (who opposes Edwin D. Freed, "The Entry into Jerusalem in the Gospel of John," *JBL* 80 [1961]: 329-38); Bultmann, *John*, 417; Brown, *John 1*, 459-61; Claus-Peter März, "*Siehe Dein König kommt zu Dir* . . . ." *Eine traditionsgeschichtliche Untersuchung zur Einzugsperikope*, Erfurter theologische Studien, Bd. 43 (Leipzig: St. Benno-Verlag, 1980), 151-84; Kiyoshi Tsuchido, "Tradition and Redaction in John 12.1-43," *NTS* 30 (1984): 611-13, 615; Robinson, *Priority*, 229-38; Josef Wagner, *Auferstehung und Leben: Joh 11,1-12,19 als Spiegel johanneischer Redaktions- und Theologiegeschichte*, Biblische Untersuchungen, Bd. 19 (Regensburg: Verlag Friedrich Pustet, 1988), 384-93.

7; Luke 19.29-35). Jesus' act, in turn, is editorially referred to by John as the fulfillment of Old Testament prophecy (cf. 12.38, 39-40; 19.24, 28[?], 36, 37):

μὴ φοβοῦ θυγάτηρ Σίων·
ἰδού ὁ βασιλεύς σου ἔρχεται,
καθήμενος ἐπὶ πῶλον ὄνου (12.15).

John's citation contains numerous puzzling features which are of disputed origin. Indeed, the precise form of John 12.15 is unlike any other extant form of this Old Testament passage either in the versions or elsewhere in Jewish or early Christian literature.[2]

These circumstances have led some scholars to ponder whether or not John's citation is actually his own creation.[3] John 12.12-14 is, we have noted, established traditional material.[4] It may be, therefore, that a reference to the Old Testament passage which John cites was also common to this material (note that both Matt 21.5 and Mark 11.2 ["a colt . . . on which no one has ever sat"] recall this prophecy).[5] John's citation (we shall see) has been conspicuously abbreviated so that only those features which complement its present context remain.[6] Has John adopted the form of his citation from a pre-johannine tradition of some kind? This is indeed possible. The exegetical procedure evident in this citation, however, is also evident in citations elsewhere in John's Gospel. John 12.15, then, may well be John's own creation.[7]

Two additional observations suggest the same conclusion. First, we have already noted that the formula which introduces this citation (καθώς ἐστιν γεγραμμένον, 12.14) is probably John's unique contribution (cf. 2.19; 6.31, 45;

---

2 For references to this OT passage in the rabbinic literature, see Str-B 1:842-44. Cf. *Sib. Or.* 8.325-28; Justin Martyr, 1 *Apol.* 35.11; *Dial.* 53.3 (discussed by Lindars, *NT Apologetic*, 115).

3 See esp. Menken, "Joh 12,15," 194-95.

4 Significantly, vv. 12-14 evince "fast keine johanneischen Stilcharakteristika" (Menken, "Joh 12,15," 194, who refers to the earlier efforts of Eduard Schweizer, *Ego Eimi* . . . . *Die religionsgeschichtliche Herkunft und theologische Bedeutung der johanneischen Bildreden, zugleich ein Beitrag zur Quellenfrage des vierten Evangeleiums*, Forschungen zur Religion und Literatur des Alten und Neuen Testaments, Bd. 56 [Göttingen: Vandenhoeck & Ruprecht, 1939], 100).

5 Cf. Menken, "Joh 12,15," 194.

6 See my development of this below.

7 Cf. Menken, "Joh 12,15," 194-95: "Diese Kurzform mag schon vorjohanneisch sein; sie lässt sich jedoch mit der Form anderer expliziter Anführungen des AT im Joh gut vergleichen: Öfters werden da alttestamentliche Texte verkürzt oder komprimiert, um damit Zitat und Kontext (in weitem Sinn) möglichst gut einander anzugleichen. Man betrachte die Bearbeitung von Jes 40,3 in Joh 1,23; von Ps 78,24 in 6,31; von Jes 54,13 in 6,45; von 6,10 in 12,40; von Ps 34[33],21 in 19,36 [falls dieser Psalmvers dort tatsächlich zitiert wird]. Damit ist also die Auslassung der meisten Attribute des Königs . . . schon erklärt–soweit solche Auslassungen überhaupt zu erklären sind–, und zwar als möglich traditionell, aber zugleich passend im Joh."

10.34; contrast 12.16).[8] And second, on the basis of the grammar and content of vv. 16-19, it is likely that his activity is also to be seen in the unparalleled remarks which follow this citation.[9]

Thus, more than just the unusual character of John's citation suggests that his creative hand has been at work in John 12.15.[10] What, then, has influenced the present form of John 12.15? Is the intent in the offering of this citation evident? And what additional insights do the answers to these questions provide?

I.

John's citation recalls Zech 9.9. But John's citation also differs conspicuously from Zech 9.9. First, John's citation is decidedly shorter: (1) The second half of the exhortation which appears in Zech 9.9a and is addressed to the daughter of Jerusalem is missing. (2) John's version of Zech 9.9b lacks both its indirect object ("to you")[11] and its characterization of the rider as "triumphant," "victorious," and "humble." What remains of the prophet's characterization of the approaching king is only that his mount happens to be an ass. (3) John's description of this ass has been significantly simplified. In place of Zechariah's two parallel references to the king's mount, John 12.15 simply reads πῶλον ὄνου. Second, in place of Zechariah's opening exhortation "Rejoice greatly," John 12.15 begins with "Fear not." And third, unlike Zechariah's king, the Johannine Jesus does not "ride" his ass. Instead, he "sits" on it.

Scholars attempts to establish whether or not a specific textual tradition has contributed to the perplexing form of this citation have been predictably varied. Some scholars have posited the influence of a Hebrew *Vorlage*, maintaining that this is especially evident in Johns reference to Jesus' mount as a πῶλον ὄνου.[12] Others, however, have viewed this same reference as evidence for John's dependence upon Matthew's parallel citation of the same prophecy (Matt 21.5).[13] Still

---

8 See my remarks in chapter two and three. Similarly, Menken, "Joh 12,15," 195, who contrasts John 19.19; Luke 4.17; 20.17; 1 Cor 15.54; and 2 Cor 4.13.

9 Cf. Menken, "Joh 12,15," 195.

10 Cf. Menken, "Joh 12,15," 195: "Die Vermutung, dass das Zitat seine jetzige Form mindestens zum Teil dem Evangelisten verdankt, hat also einiges für sich."

11 The omission of σοι from Zech 9.9 OG in, e.g., ms. 534 probably reflects the influence of John 12.15 (Menken, "Joh 12,15," 193 n. 2).

12 Cf. Burney, *Aramaic Origin*, 120; Bernard, *St. John*, 425; Freed, *OT Quotations*, 78 (a possibility); Brown, *John* 1, 461; Schnackenburg, *St. John* 2, 376; Lindars, *John*, 423-24; Reim, *Studien*, 30, 90, 220; März, *König*, 161-62.

13 Cf. Freed, *OT Quotations*, 80, 121 (pp. 66-81 represent a slightly revised version of his previous essay "Entry" referred to above).

others have pointed to the use of the OG.[14] Even the possibility that both Hebrew and Greek textual traditions have been influential has been considered.[15]

How are these hypotheses to be evaluated? First, we have already noted that there is no compelling evidence for John's dependence upon Matthew.[16] Second, where John 12.15 clearly seems to recall Zech 9.9, it is not possible to determine whether a Hebrew or Greek *Vorlage* is represented:[17] (1) Θυγάτηρ Σιών, ὁ βασιλεύς σου ἔρχεται followed by ἐπί plus the accusative agrees exactly with the OG. (2) But the OG does not here deviate from the Hebrew of the MT. (3) In fact, it is unlikely that a translator would have rendered the Hebrew in any other way. And third, the rest of John's citation either (1) does not seem to correspond precisely to what one observes in any of the extant versions of this passage (καθήμενος; πῶλον ὄνου) or (2) does not seem to come from Zech 9.9 at all (μὴ φοβοῦ).[18]

Faced with what they could not otherwise explain, many scholars have chosen to regard John's citation as a symptom of his imperfect memory.[19] These scholars, however, have not adequately considered whether or not another explanation is possible.[20] First, John's intent in offering this citation must be carefully addressed.

II.

An understanding of especially the uncommon aspects of John's citation is critical in any attempt to characterize his intent in referring to this prophecy. The first (and perhaps the most perplexing) of these aspects is the opening exhorta-

---

14 Cf. Marie-Émile Boismard and A. Lamouille, *Synopse des quatres évangiles en français avec paralleles des apocryphes et des Peres*, tome 3, *L'Évangile de Jean*, 2e édition, (Paris: Éditions du Cerf, 1987), 62.

15 See Menken, "Joh 12,15," esp. 204-9; cf. Longenecker, *Exegesis*, 137, who refers to John 12.15 as a paraphrastic variation of the OG influenced by the Hebrew of the MT.

16 Similarly, Menken, "Joh 12,15," 196.

17 Cf. Menken, "Joh 12,15," 196.

18 Cf. Menken, "Joh 12,15," 196. The textual problems relating to καθήμενος will be discussed below. The Johannine phrase πῶλον ὄνου, if regarded as an abbreviation of that which appears in Zech 9.9, is closer to the Hebrew of the MT (וְעַל־עַיִר בֶּן־אֲתֹנוֹת עַל־חֲמוֹר) than it is to the OG (ἐπὶ ὑποζύγιον καὶ πῶλον ὄνου). But it is hardly an exact translation of the Hebrew of the MT.

19 Cf. Goodwin, "Sources;" Noack, *Tradition*, 74-75, 82, 84; Freed, *OT Quotations*, 78-80 ("tenable"); Barrett, *St. John*, 418-19; Moo, *Passion Narratives*, 179 (a possibility); Kysar, *John*, 191-92 (a possibility); Fortna, *Fourth Gospel*, 146 n. 331; Humann, "OT Quotations," 45 (a possibility).

20 Cf. Menken, "Joh 12,15," 196.

tion μὴ φοβοῦ.[21] The prohibition does not appear to have come from Zechariah. Scholars, therefore, have sought out a possible referent elsewhere in the Old Testament in passages where Israel or Jerusalem is addressed in an equivalent fashion.[22]

Of the possible referents that have been considered by scholars, two in particular have attracted considerable attention: Isa 40.9 and Zeph 3.16. Isa 40.9-10[23] shares with Zech 9.9 both the prediction of an eschatological "coming" (in Zech, the king comes; in Isa, God himself comes) and the following expressions in the OG (which here closely follows the Hebrew of the MT): Σιών, Ἰερουσαλήμ, ἰδού . . . ἔρχεται. Scholars argue, therefore, that John's μὴ φοβοῦ recalls Isa 40.9. John recalls either a Hebrew *Vorlage* (אַל־תִּירָאִי) or the OG (μὴ φοβεῖσθε) and adjusts the plural to the singular.[24]

Zeph 3.14-17,[25] on the other hand, lacks an explicit reference to an eschatological "coming," but shares with Zechariah the vision of an eschatological king in the midst of his people. Also, the opening exhortation in Zech 9.9 OG is

---

[21] The difference between the nominative θυγάτηρ in John 12.15 (a hapax in the Johannine literature) and the vocative θύγατερ in Zech 9.9 OG (appearing elsewhere in the NT only at Matt 9.22) is, for our purposes, of no significance. Cf. Menken, "Joh 12,15," 193 n. 1: "An beiden Stellen (und an vielen anderen derartigen Stellen) schwankt die Textüberlieferung zwischen Nominativ und Vokativ; ein Wechsel findet leicht statt, beim Abschreiben oder Zitieren. Der Unterschied besagt also nichts in bezug auf eine mögliche johanneische Abhängigkeit von der LXX."

[22] See, e.g., Isa 10.24 [cf. v. 32]; 35.4; 40.9; 41.10, 13; 43.1, 5; 44.2, 8; 51.7; 54.4; Jer 46.27-28; Zeph 3.16.

[23] Those who have made some reference to this text include Franke, *Alte Testament*, 286; Hühn, *Citate*, 87; Noack, *Tradition*, 75, who adds, "es wäre aber an sich auch denkbar, dass die Wendung μὴ φοβοῦ so bekannt und beliebt war, dass sie sozusagen von selbst auftauchte" (similarly, Morris, *John*, 586 n. 46; Moo, *Passion Narratives*, 179-80); Stendahl, *St. Matthew*, 119-20; Freed, *OT Quotations*, 67, 78; Reim, *Studien*, 29-31, 162; Longenecker, *Exegesis*, 155; Barrett, *St. John*, 418-19; Ernst Haenchen, *John 2: A Commentary on the Gospel of John Chapters 7-21*, trans. R. W. Funk, ed. R. W. Funk with U. Busse, Hermeneia–A Critical and Historical Commentary on the Bible (Philadelphia: Fortress, 1984), 93; Bruce, *John*, 277 n. 11; Becker, *Johannes*, 378; Kysar, *John*, 192; Carson, "John," 246; Humann, "OT Quotations," 45 n. 52; see esp. Menken, "Joh 12,15," 198.

[24] This would, of course, complement John's other reference to this same context in John 1.23 (cf. also Isa 40.11 with John 10.1-18, 26-29; 11.52; 21.15-17).

[25] Cf. Franke, *Alte Testament*, 286; Hoskyns, *Fourth Gospel*, 422; Lindars, *NT Apologetic*, 26 n. 2, 113 (cf. idem, *John*, 424); Bultmann, *John*, 418 n. 4; Braun, *Jean 2*, 19; Freed, *OT Quotations*, 78-80, 121; Brown, *John 1*, 458, 462; Schnackenburg, *St. John 2*, 376, 525 n. 46; Pancaro, *Law*, 329; Barrett, *St. John*, 419; Rudolf Pesch and Reinhard Kratz, *So liest man synoptisch: Anleitung und Kommentar zum Studium der synoptischen Evangelien*, Bd. 6, *Passionsgeschichte: Erster Teil* (Frankfurt am Main: Verlag Josef Knecht, 1979), 71; Becker, *Johannes*, 378; Kysar, *John*, 192; März, *König*, 161; Fortna, *Fourth Gospel*, 146 n. 331; Robinson, *Priority*, 232 n. 60; Humann, "OT Quotations," 45-46; see esp. Menken, "Joh 12,15," 198.

virtually identical to the same in Zeph 3.14.[26] Shared terminology includes both the noun βασιλεύς (מֶלֶךְ)[27] and the verb σώζω (יָשַׁע). Scholars have argued that John must, therefore, recall a Hebrew *Vorlage*. The OG renders אַל־תִּירָאִי with θάρσει.[28] Others, however, have objected that this is not entirely certain. The verb φοβέομαι is a well-established synonym for θαρσέω and could have been substituted for the latter because it better complements its eventual Johannine context[29] (θαρσέω appears in the Fourth Gospel only at 16.33).

Neither of these alternatives, however, is particularly compelling. Instead, a third alternative represents a much better explanation, Isa 44.2. Isa 44.2 has generally received little attention from scholars[30] because initially it appears to have less in common with Zech 9.9 than other passages. But the merits of this alternative are especially evident when first the relationship of John 12.15 to its preceding context is properly defined.

According to John 12.9-11 (cf. vv. 17-18), the crowd that came out to meet Jesus that day did so because it had heard of Lazarus' resurrection from the dead. Jesus, therefore, was to be heralded as the eschatological King of Israel promised by God (12.12-13).[31] Tragically, however, their understanding of Jesus' signifi-

---

[26] The degree of correspondence between the two in the MT is much more limited. Note, however, that σφόδρα in Zeph 3.14 OG is not textually certain. "Die Identität beider Anfangszeilen in der LXX ist möglicherweise auch das Ergebnis der Verbindung analoger Schriftstellen" (Menken, "Joh 12,15," 198 n. 21).

[27] Identifying Zeph 3.15 (OG: βασιλεὺς Ἰσραήλ; MT: מֶלֶךְ יִשְׂרָאֵל) as a possible source for or referent of the title "the King of Israel" in John 12.13 (ὁ βασιλεὺς τοῦ Ἰσραήλ) are Hühn, *Citate*, 87; Freed, *OT Quotations*, 78; Lindars, *John*, 424; Pesch/Kratz, *So liest man*, 71; Barrett, *St. John*, 418-19; Menken, "Joh 12,15," 198; Humann, "OT Quotations," 46.

[28] Cf. Lindars, *NT Apologetic*, 26 n. 2; Brown, *John* 1, 458; Schnackenburg, *St. John* 2, 525 n. 46; Kysar, *John*, 192; Menken, "Joh 12,15," 198; Humann, "OT Quotations," 45 n. 51, 46.

[29] See the detailed remarks of Freed, *OT Quotations*, 78-80, 121 (contrast Humann, "OT Quotations," 45). Cf. also Zeph 3.13 OG: καὶ οὐκ ἔσται ὁ ἐκφοβῶν αὐτούς. Fear is provoked on numerous occasions in John's Gospel (see 6.19; 7.13; 9.22; 19.8, 38; 20.19). The prohibition μὴ φοβοῦ in John 12.15 complements these references, as well as John's indication elsewhere that Jesus comes to dispel, not to provoke fear (6.20; cf. Rev 1.17; 2.10). However, any attempt to suggest that μὴ φοβοῦ was introduced into John 12.15 in order to address the fear of this crowd provoked by the resurrection of Lazarus (Menken, "Joh 12,15," 199-200) exceeds what can be established on the basis of the text. Note also that the substitution of "Fear not" for "Rejoice greatly" complements John's assertion that, with the exception of the Baptist (3.29), the disciples of Jesus do not understand (12.16) and therefore do not "rejoice" until after Jesus' glorification (see 20.20; cf. 14.28; 16.22).

[30] Cf. Hoskyns, *Fourth Gospel*, 422; Goodwin, "Sources," 68; Bultmann, *John*, 418 n. 4; Barrett, *St. John*, 418-19; Humann, "OT Quotations," 45 n. 52.

[31] Their greeting ("Hosanna! Blessed is he who comes in the name of the Lord") represents not a citation *per se* (similarly, Matt 21.9; Mark 11.9; Luke 19.38), but a rendering of a popular Jewish festal greeting which itself was derived from Ps 118(117). With the exception of the term ὡσαννά (cf. Matt 21.9, 15; Mark 11.9, 10), their greeting corresponds

cance as king is heavily conditioned by their nationalistic fervor. Several aspects of John's description of this scene make this clear.

Their nationalism is especially evident, however, in their use of palm branches to greet Jesus. The palm was for the Jews a symbol which, at least from the time of the Maccabees, stood for the nation and functioned as an expression of their hope for an imminent national liberation (see 1 Macc 13.51; 2 Macc 10.7; cf. Test. Naph. 5.4; Rev 7.9).[32] Jesus' response to their greeting is to find an ass and to sit on it (12.14). Why? Jesus' purpose is to show that his royal status must be understood not in terms of their nationalism, but in terms of Zechariah's prophecy (12.15).[33]

Why is an understanding of this sequence important? The precise form of the royal title attributed to Jesus by this crowd (ὁ βασιλεὺς τοῦ 'Ισραήλ)

---

word for word with what one observes in Ps 117.25-26 OG (which here represents the most natural rendering of the Hebrew of the MT). The presence of ὡσαννά (a transliteration of the Heb./Aram., not the OG's paraphrase σῶσον δή) probably reflects the actual form of the untranslatable opening to this popular greeting. It cannot, therefore, be taken as an indication of John's dependence upon a Hebrew Vorlage.

[32] See esp. William R. Farmer, "The Palm Branches in John 12:13," JTS, n.s. 3 (1952): 62-66; cf. Brown, John 1, 461-63; Schnackenburg, St. John 2, 374-75; Barrett, St. John, 417; Moo, Passion Narratives, 182; Bruce, John, 258-59; Kysar, John, 191; Robinson, Priority, 231; Menken, "Joh 12,15," 200. Contrast the rather speculative attempt to show some connection here with the phoenix myth by John Spencer Hill, "Τὰ βαΐα τῶν φοινίκων (John 12:13): Pleonasm or Prolepsis?" JBL 101 (1982): 133-35. Later, palms served as national symbols on the coinage minted by Jewish insurgents during the first and second revolts against Rome. The palm was evidently so well established as a symbol for the Jewish nation that Rome in turn stamped it on their own coins which they produced to celebrate the crushing of the Jewish insurgency. This interpretation of the crowd's intent in using palm branches to greet Jesus is supported further by the character of the very words they choose in order to welcome him. In Ps 118(117), these words (vv. 25-26) are addressed to a triumphant figure (v. 7) who has just cut off the hostile nations (vv. 10-17) and now purposes to enter the gates of the city (vv. 19-20) with a festal procession and branches (v.27; on the messianic interpretation of this psalm elsewhere in the NT, cf. v.6 with Heb 13.6; v. 22 with Matt 21.42; Mark 12.10-11; Luke 20.17; Acts 4.11; 1 Pet 2.4, 7; v. 26 with Matt 23.39; Luke 13.35; contrast the rabbinic references in Str-B 1:845-50, 876; 2:256). Finally, even John's description of the crowd's going out εἰς ὑπάντησιν, a characteristic Greek expression for the reception of just such a royal personality, seems to participate in this scheme (see Josephus, Wars 7.100; Ant. 11.327, 329; cf. Erik Peterson, "Die Einholung des Kyrios," ZST 7 [1930]: 682-702; Bultmann, John, 417-18 n. 8; Brown, John 1, 461-62; Feuillet, Studies, 142-43; Schnackenburg, St. John 2, 374, 524 n. 38; Wagner, Auferstehung, 388 n. 116; Robinson, Priority, 232; Menken, "Joh 12,15," 200).

[33] Similarly, Hoskyns, Fourth Gospel, 420-22; Brown, John 1, 461-63; Schnackenburg, St. John 2, 375; Morris, John, 586; Lindars, John, 420, 423; Barrett, St. John, 416, 418; Moo, Passion Narratives, 182; Bruce, John, 259-60; W. A. Visser't Hooft, "Triumphalism in the Gospels," SJT 38 (1985): 491-504; Becker, Johannes, 378-79; Kysar, John, 191-93; Robinson, Priority, 230-32; Beasley-Murray, John, 210; Menken, "Joh 12,15," 200-1.

appears only once in the OG, in Isa 44.6 (MT: **מֶלֶךְ יִשְׂרָאֵל**).[34] This observation, together with an understanding of the significance of John 12.13-15, suggests persuasively that John here recalls Isa 44.6 OG.[35] But this is not all. It also suggests that the presence of μὴ φοβοῦ in John 12.15 is to be attributed to the influence of Isa 44.2 OG (μὴ φοβοῦ; MT: **אַל־תִּירָא**).

If this is the case, then μὴ φοβοῦ in John 12.15 plays a significant twofold role in an already apparent Johannine scheme in which Jesus' actions are presented as his attempt to affirm yet inform the crowd's reference to him as "the King of Israel." On the one hand, μὴ φοβοῦ calls attention to, affirms, and informs in terms of Isa 44 the crowd's reference to Jesus as king (i.e., Jesus is the God-King).[36] On the other hand, its position in John's citation indicates that μὴ φοβοῦ also functions as a kind of bridge which establishes the connection that is to be seen between the title "the King of Israel" (12.13) and Zech 9.9 (12.15).[37]

Thus, "The purpose of this piece of prophetic symbolism is clear. It is to say: 'King of Israel–yes (cf. 1.49); but not that sort of king (cf. 18.36f.).'"[38] Jesus' deed of power on behalf of Lazarus had, as in a previous instance (cf. 6.14-15),[39] led the crowd to conclude that Jesus was the prophet like Moses. Jesus, therefore, was the royal Messiah they had long hoped for,[40] a warrior-king who would liberate them from the Romans.[41] On this other occasion, Jesus had simply

---

[34] I have been unable to find a single researcher who makes this observation. Of those who have considered the possibility that Isa 44.2 has influenced John 12.15, none that I know of have gone on to discuss the possible influence of Isa 44.6 on John 12.13.

[35] Jesus receives now at the end of his final journey to Jerusalem the same title he received at the beginning of his first journey (1.49). Note John's characteristic use of articles with similar titles in John 1.49; 18.33, 39; 19.3, 19, 21.

[36] It is unlikely that those who referred to Jesus as king would have had a specific OT text in mind, especially Isa 44.6. Such a reference viewed in its OT context would, however, significantly complement John's efforts elsewhere to show that Jesus is the Creator (Isa 44.2), God himself (44.6b, 8b; cf. Rev 1.17; 2.8; 22.13), source of life-giving water (44.3a), who sends the Spirit (44.3b) and calls witnesses (44.8a).

[37] Any attempt to reproduce the second of the parallel exhortations in Zech 9.9 (κήρυσσε, θύγατερ Ἰερουσαλήμ) would only obscure what John purposes to accomplish with this citation (the verb κηρύσσω is conspicuously absent in John's Gospel). It is, therefore, appropriately deleted.

[38] Robinson, *Priority*, 232.

[39] It seems likely that John's unique description of the crowd that here greets Jesus (12.12) deliberately recalls for the sake of contrast the crowd in this previous incident (cf. 6.2, 5).

[40] See my remarks in chapter three.

[41] As for the Pharisees, they too seem to expect that Jesus will lead a nationalist rebellion (12.19; cf. 11.48; Job 21.32-33 OG). What they fear, however, is that he will fail in this attempt. Their hyperbolic statement ("the world has gone after him") is full of irony and unconscious prophetic significance. Jesus' popularity will be decidedly short-lived. And their

refused them (6.15). In this instance, however, he accepts the title they offer him. But he does so only on his own terms.[42] And he is quick to point out those terms.

In one sense, they are correct. Jesus has, in fact, come for the sake of conflict. But Jesus' purpose is to drive out "the ruler of this world" (12.31), not the Romans. Jesus comes, then, to dispel darkness (cf. 8.12), to liberate from sin (cf. 8.31-36) and death (cf. 5.24). He comes to save, not to destroy (cf. 3.16-17). Jesus selects an ass as his mount, then, not to demonstrate his humility.[43] Instead, he does this to show that the victory he brings will come not by means of horses and chariots (cf. Zech 9.10a; contrast Zech 1.8; Rev 19.11-21), the instruments of war, but in the form of the unexpected and paradoxical figure before them. This king brings peace rather than war for both Israel and the nations (cf. Zech 9.10b with John 11.51-52; 12.20-21, 32).

John adds in John 12.16 that these events were not understood by Jesus' disciples until after his death. What this seems to mean is that the enigmatic form of Jesus' arrival in Jerusalem both anticipated and illustrated the paradoxical irony of Jesus' ultimate crucifixion as the King of the Jews.[44] But it was only in the light of the cross that Jesus' disciples were finally able to see this.[45]

---

attempt to save their own nation will, in fact, further Jesus' campaign to save both it and the rest of the world.

[42] Jesus is ready on this occasion to accept the title "king" (cf. 1.49) because the agenda of his "confessors" will not impede his own agenda (12.23; contrast 6.15).

[43] In keeping with this, John's citation of Zechariah's prophecy lacks Zechariah's reference to the king as "humble" (retained in Matt 21.5). Similarly, Zechariah's characterization of the king as "triumphant" and "victorious" adds nothing to John's portrait of Jesus. It, therefore, is also deleted (and is deleted in Matthew's Gospel as well). Cf. Humann, "OT Quotations," 46.

[44] See Kysar, *John*, 191, 193; cf. Marie de Merode, "L'accueil triomphal de Jésus selon Jean 11-12," *RTL* 13 (1982): 61-62. It is unlikely that there is in John's Gospel any difference implied in the designations "King of Israel" (see 1.31, 47, 49; 3.10; cf. Rev 2.14; 7.4; 21.12) and "King of the Jews." Rather, this use probably reflects a well-established social convention among the Jews in which the term "Israel" was used by Jews only when speaking with fellow Jews. See P. J. Tomson, "The Names Israel and Jew in Ancient Judaism and in the New Testament," *Bijdragen* 47 (1986): 12-40, 266-89.

[45] Even at the conclusion of Jesus' time with them, his disciples continue to exhibit no more of an understanding of what they have witnessed than they had at the beginning (cf. 2.22; Schnackenburg, *St. John* 2, 376-77). From the beginning, his royal status was apparent to them (1.49), but its character and its purpose were not. It is only later that they will remember (cf. 2.22; 14.25-26; 15.20, 26; 16.4) and understand (see 14.20; 16.13; cf. 7.39). Only then will they comprehend the things that the crowd did that day on Jesus' behalf (ταῦτα ἐποίησαν αὐτῷ; cf. 12.12-13) and the things that were written in the OT about him (cf. the formula in 12.14). The intent, then, of John 12.16 is "to say that everything Jesus did must be understood, can properly be seen, only in the light of what is still to come" (Fortna, *Fourth Gospel*, 147). Thus, "the only anointing that Jesus receives is an anointing for death (xii 7); the only crown he will wear is the crown of thorns (xix 2); the only robe he will wear is the

Because Jesus refused to be the kind of king the Jews wanted him to be, they abandoned him. Ironically, it was especially in their rejection of him that Jesus revealed himself to be the King of the Jews and brought to completion that which he as such came to accomplish (see esp. 19.17-22, 28-30).[46]

Two final elements of John's citation of Zech 9.9 require detailed analysis: (1) the substitution of "sitting" for Zechariah's "riding;" and (2) the description of Jesus' mount as a πῶλον ὄνου.[47]

We have already noted that καθήμενος appears in none of the extant Greek versions of Zech 9.9. Is it possible, then, that it represents in John's citation a rendering of the Hebrew רכב? The Hebrew verb רכב qal is usually rendered in the OG with either ἐπιβαίνω or (in the case of the participle) ἀναβάτης or ἐπιβάτης. The hiph'il forms of this verb are normally rendered with either ἀναβιβάζω or ἐπιβιβάζω. In both Zech 9.9 OG and in the later Greek versions of this passage, ἐπιβεβηκώς is the only rendering which appears for the participle רכב. Indeed, on only one occasion does the OG ever render the verb רכב

---

cloak of mockery; and when thus anointed and robed, he stands before his people and is presented as their king, the crowd will *shout*, 'Crucify him!' (xix 14-15). Thus, they will lift him up to draw all men" (Brown, *John* 1, 463).

[46] Cf. the reference in Zech 9.11 to the "blood of the covenant" which frees those who are trapped in the waterless pit. Contrast Rev 7.9-10.

[47] Menken, "Joh 12,15," 201-4, 208, has attempted to show that John's omission of σοι from his citation is "durch analoge Schriftstellen berechtigt (i.e., Isa 40.9-11; Gen 49.1-11) und vornehmlich theologisch durch den johanneischen Gedanken der universalen Bedeutung des Kommens Jesu motiviert" (p. 208; cf. 1.9; 3.19; 6.14; 9.39; 11.27; 12.46; 16.28; 18.37). Even without σοι, however, John's citation of Zech 9.9 emphasizes precisely what Menken suggests it is avoiding. I.e., it is especially in Jesus' final coming to Zion that he comes to his own (1.11a) and is ultimately rejected by his own (1.11b). In this coming the benefits of what he accomplishes are made available to all (1.12-13; cf. the new Zion in Rev 14.1). John's omission of σοι does not alter the sense of this passage and is not, therefore, theologically motivated. It is tempting to suggest that John's omission of σοι is, instead, to be explained on the basis of a consistent feature of Johannine style. In John's Gospel, whenever Jesus "comes" (ἔρχομαι) to a place, his destination is always specified with the prepositional phrase εἰς plus the accusative (cf. the above references to Jesus' coming into the world with 1.11; 3.22; 4.5, 45, 46, 54; 6.17; 11.30, 38; 12.1). On the other hand, when Jesus "comes" to a person (or persons) the person he comes to is always specified with the prepositional phrase πρός plus the accusative (cf. 1.29; 13.6; 14.18, 23, 28; 16.7). Zechariah's σοι does not fit into this pattern (on the expansion of the sphere of the preposition in the Koine so that prepositional phrases were then used where classical Greek had formerly employed a simple case form, see Voelz, "Language," 953). It may be, however, that the omission of σοι reflects nothing more than an attempt to carefully balance the meter of the resulting citation (Freed, *OT Quotations*, 79-80).

with κάθημαι (Isa 19.1). This evidence seems to indicate that John's καθήμενος does not represent a rendering of רכב.[48]

Still, the possibility that καθήμενος represents a rendering of a Hebrew *Vorlage* should not be too quickly dismissed. There are, in fact, several occasions in which either (ἐπι)κάθημαι or (ἐπι)καθίζω (followed by ἐπί plus the genitive or the accusative) appears in the OG or in Theod. as a rendering of רכב.[49] Also, there is little difference in meaning between these terms and a more usual rendering of רכב. Thus, it must be acknowledged that it is indeed a possibility that καθήμενος in John 12.15 represents a rendering of רכב (although the evidence for this cannot be said to be great).[50]

In order to adequately address this problem, however, one must reckon with the question of intent. Why has this unusual verb form been selected? I am persuaded that this element of John's citation is best explained as something which, like the citation itself, appears in order to illustrate Jesus' royal status. Κάθημαι (and similar forms) is characteristically used in the OG (as a rendering of the Hebrew ישׁב), with Josephus, and in the New Testament to describe a king (or God) sitting on his throne.[51]

Is it possible, then, that some other Old Testament passage has supplied the rationale for the use of this verb in John's citation? There is, in fact, an Old Testament episode which exhibits features strikingly similar to what one observes both in Zech 9.9 and in John's Gospel. 1 Kgs 1 is the first part of the story of Solomon's inheritance of the throne from his father David. David summons Zadok, Nathan, and Benaiah and charges them to place Solomon on David's own mule and to bring him to Gihon. There they are to anoint him king and then herald him as such as he returns to Jerusalem to assume his throne (vv. 28-35). These events, in turn, provoke fear on the part of Adonijah (who himself wished to be king) and his compatriots (vv. 38-53).

---

[48] Freed, *OT Quotations*, 80. For Freed, the presence of καθήμενος in John 12.15 is to be attributed to the influence of ἐκάθισεν in John 12.14 (see further below).

[49] Menken, "Joh 12,15," 205. In the OG, רכב qal is rendered with κάθημαι in Isa 19.1; with καθίζω in Lev 15.9 A and 2 Sam 22.11; with ἐπικάθημαι in 2 Sam 16.2; and with ἐπικαθίζω in 2 Sam 13.29 and 22.11 A. The OG renders רכב hiph'il with ἐπικαθίζω in 1 Kgs 1.38, 44 and 2 Kgs 10.16 (cf. Theod. Isa 58.14).

[50] Cf. Reim, *Studien*, 30; Archer/Chirichigno, *OT Quotations*, 131.

[51] See the numerous examples identified by Menken, "Joh 12,15," 205 nn. 46-48 (cf. Humann, "OT Quotations," 46). Menken adds (pp. 205-6), "Es fällt auf, dass wenigstens an einigen der Stellen, wo die LXX *rkb* mit κάθημαι oder ähnlichem übersetzt, das Verb sich auf das Reiten bzw. Sitzen des Königs oder wie ein König bezieht (2 Reg 13,29: die Söhne des Königs auf Eseln; 16,2: das Haus des Königs auf Eseln; 22,11: Gott auf den Cherubim; 3 Reg 1,38. 44: Salomo auf den königlichen Maultier; Jes 19,1: Gott auf einer Wolke). Καθήμενος als Übersetzung von *rokeb* in Joh 12,15 könnte also auch sehr wohl dazu dienen, Jesu königliche Würde hervorzuheben."

1 Kgs 1 is especially significant because it portrays Solomon's act of sitting on the king's mule as something which singled him out as the one designated to sit on the throne.[52] The language of the OG especially seems to reflect this idea. In the midst of numerous instances of the use of either κάθημαι or καθίζω to describe the act of sitting on the throne, the OG, describing Solomon's act of sitting on his father's mule, renders רכב hiph'il with ἐπιβιβάζω in v. 33, but with ἐπικαθίζω in vv. 38 and 44.[53]

The parallels between this text and John's Gospel certainly seem to suggest that 1 Kgs 1 has been influential.[54] Thus, it has been argued that καθήμενος in John 12.15 represents a rendering of רכב and reflects the influence of the rendering of רכב hiph'il with ἐπικαθίζω in 1 Kgs 1.38, 44 OG.[55] But this is hardly the only possibility. An awareness of the conspicuous juxtaposition of the verbs ἐπιβιβάζω, καθίζω, and κάθημαι in 1 Kgs 1 OG and the intent apparent in their use may have led instead to a citation of Zech 9.9 OG in which καθήμενος (cf. esp. 1 Kgs 1.35, 48 OG) was substituted for ἐπιβεβηκὼς (cf. 1 Kgs 1.33 OG; contrast ἐκάθισεν in John 12.14 with 1 Kgs 1.38, 44, 46 OG). Which is the more likely scenario? At the moment, it is difficult to say (see further below). In either case, however, as Jesus approaches Jerusalem (viewed as an act anticipating his crucifixion) he shows that he is going to the cross as the anointed one, the rightful bearer of his Father's throne.[56]

The description of Jesus' mount at the conclusion of John's citation remains. We have already noted that πῶλον ὄνου does not seem to correspond precisely with any other extant version of Zech 9.9 (whether it offers a condensation of

---

[52] Cf. Menken, "Joh 12,15," 206 (who refers to similar examples in Josephus, Ant., 8.386-87; 12.171-72). Contrast Judg 5.10; Jer 17.25; 22.4.

[53] Cf. Menken, "Joh 12,15," 206.

[54] Cf. Merode, "Jean 11-12," 56; Harald Sahlin, Zur Typologie des Johannesevangeliums, Uppsala universitetsarskrift, Bd. 1950/4 (Uppsala: Lundequistska Bokhandeln, 1950), 47-48; März, König, 110-11.

[55] Menken, "Joh 12,15," 206-7, 208, 209.

[56] Contrast the sacrificial character of Jesus' "anointing" on the sixth day before the Passover (the day the Passover lamb was traditionally selected) in John 12.1-8 (see esp. v. 7; cf. ὀσμή in v.3 with Eph 5.2; Phil 4.18; 2 Cor 2.14, 16). Cf. the plot to kill Jesus in John 11.50-53; 12.10. Contrast John 19.13 and the irony of Pilate's "sitting" and presuming to possess the authority to judge the eschatological King/Judge (cf. Rev 3.21; 19.4; 20.11; 21.5; contrast John 6.3). It should be noted, however, that John stops short of suggesting that Jesus is to be recognized as the Son of David (see esp. Matt 21.9; Mark 11.10; Luke 19.35 [cf. 1 Kgs 1.44-45]). Indeed, as has been the case elsewhere (cf. my remarks in chapter four), John avoids describing Jesus in terms of Davidic motifs "because they do not fit his unique view of Jesus as king" (Freed, OT Quotations, 74).

Zechariah's parallel references to this mount or not). There is, however, an "analoge Schriftstelle" which qualifies as a probable referent, Gen 49.10-11.[57]

Gen 49.10-11, a passage which as early as Qumran was interpreted messianically,[58] shares with Zech 9.9 more than just aspects of its general contents. The two passages also utilize language conspicuously reminiscent of each other.[59] Consequently, in both Jewish and early Christian literature the two passages were brought together and seen to be anticipating the same event.[60]

Now Gen 49.11b OG is the only place in the OG where the expression $\pi\hat{\omega}\lambda o\nu$ $\check{o}\nu o\nu$ appears (the precise form of this expression is $\tau\grave{o}\nu$ $\pi\hat{\omega}\lambda o\nu$ $\tau\hat{\eta}\varsigma$ $\check{o}\nu o\nu$ $a\mathring{v}\tau o\hat{v}$, a rather inexact rendering of the Hebrew בני אתנו[61]). These observations suggest persuasively that $\pi\hat{\omega}\lambda o\nu$ $\check{o}\nu o\nu$ in John 12.15 has come from Gen 49.11 OG.[62] Presumably, one is to see in this too another attempt to illustrate Jesus' royal identity.[63]

In summary, it is doubtful that the present form of John 12.15 was somehow derived from a pre-johannine tradition.[64] John's citation is thoroughly integrated into its present literary and theological context.[65] Also, in this citation $\mu\grave{\eta}$ $\phi o\beta o\hat{v}$ in particular is especially Johannine in appearance. Thus, John 12.15 can with some confidence be seen as John's own creation.[66]

---

57 See esp. Menken, "Joh 12,15," 201-2, 207-8, 209; cf. Freed, OT Quotations, 78; J. Duncan M. Derrett, "Law in the New Testament: The Palm Sunday Colt," NovT 13 (1971): 255; Schnackenburg, St. John 2, 376; Pancaro, Law, 329; Moo, Passion Narratives, 182 n. 1.

58 See the many texts referred to by Menken, "Joh 12,15," 201-2, esp. n. 33.

59 The conclusion of Zech 9.9 refers to the colt of an ass (MT: עיר בן־אתנות; OG: $\pi\hat{\omega}\lambda o\nu$ $\nu\acute{e}o\nu$). The beginning of Gen 49.11 refers to a similar animal (MT: עירה ... אתנו בני; OG: $\tau\grave{o}\nu$ $\pi\hat{\omega}\lambda o\nu$ $a\mathring{v}\tau o\hat{v}$ ... $\tau\grave{o}\nu$ $\pi\hat{\omega}\lambda o\nu$ $\tau\hat{\eta}\varsigma$ $\check{o}\nu o\nu$ $a\mathring{v}\tau o\hat{v}$). In Gen 49.10, the שילה "comes" (MT: יבא; OG: $\check{e}\lambda\theta\eta$). In Zechariah, as we have noted, the king also "comes" (MT: יבוא; OG: $\check{e}\rho\chi\epsilon\tau a\iota$).

60 See Menken, "Joh 12,15," 202.

61 In fact, $\pi\hat{\omega}\lambda o\varsigma$ renders בן in the OG only at Gen 49.11.

62 In the process of substituting this expression from Gen 49.11 OG, the articles and the personal pronoun contained in it were deleted, apparently because the expression this one replaces in Zech 9.9 lacked such features. What results is a significantly abbreviated and carefully metered citation which highlights only those features of interest to the account in which it now appears.

63 It is difficult, however, to establish with any certainty how much of this OT context John recalls. Particularly congenial to the Johannine perspective is, of course, v. 10's reference to the king as the "expectation of nations" (cf. John 11.48, 50-52; 18.35). Less certain are (1) v. 9's reference to the "lion of Judah" (cf. Rev 5.5) and (2) v. 11's reference to the "vine" (cf. John 15.1, 4-5) and its prophecy that the king "will wash his robe in wine, and his garment in the blood of the grape."

64 According to Fortna, Fourth Gospel, 146-48, v. 15 was derived by John without change from his source.

65 Cf. Menken, "Joh 12,15," 209.

66 Contrast Menken, "Joh 12,15," 208-9.

Whether or not a specific textual tradition is represented in John's citation is less certain. Where John recalls Zechariah, John's citation, the OG, and the Hebrew of the MT all agree with each other. Other elements of this citation, however, at least twice suggested the influence of the OG: μὴ φοβοῦ (Isa 44.2 OG) and πῶλον ὄνου (Gen 49.11 OG). No evidence for the influence of a Hebrew *Vorlage* was detected. The limited evidence that we have, therefore, suggests that the rest of John's citation also recalls the OG.[67]

III.

In conclusion, John's editorial reference to the Old Testament in John 12.15 comes from Zech 9.9. What little evidence there is for the influence of a specific textual tradition points tentatively in the direction of the OG. The uncommon aspects of this citation have not come from the larger context of Zechariah, but have instead come from analogous Old Testament contexts. John's exegetical procedure augments significantly an already apparent scheme in John 12.12-15 in which Jesus' actions in v. 14 are presented as an attempt to affirm yet inform the crowd's reference to Jesus as the King of Israel. Jesus has come not to lead a popular revolt against Rome, but to go to the cross and thereby bring freedom from sin.

---

[67] Cf. Menken, "Joh 12,15," 209.

Chapter 7

HIS OWN PEOPLE RECEIVED HIM NOT

Neither the Fourth Gospel's combination of editorial references to the prophet Isaiah in John 12.37-41 nor its account of Jesus' final attempt to persuade his own people to believe in him (see esp. 12.35-36) finds a direct parallel in the Synoptics. The two passages from Isaiah cited by John (cf. 12.13-15; 19.36-37) appear independently elsewhere in the New Testament.[1] But no other New Testament writer refers to the scene appearing here in John's Gospel. And no other New Testament work refers to both of the Old Testament passages that are here juxtaposed.

The focus of attention in the present chapter will be the first of John's two references to the prophet Isaiah appearing in John 12.38 and 12.40. In John's account of Jesus' final attempt to move the Jews to believe in him, John reflects on the degree to which Jesus was ultimately successful: "Though he (Jesus) had done so many signs before them, yet they did not believe in him" (12.37; cf. 1.11). Jesus' lack of success is interpreted by John (cf. 12.15; 19.24, 28 [?], 36,

---

[1] The first line of the citation in John 12.38 appears in precisely the same form in Rom 10.16 (cf. Justin, *Dial.* 42). This has prompted some scholars to conclude that this OT passage belonged to an early anthology of passages utilized in primitive Christian preaching and teaching. Cf. Dodd, *Scriptures*, 39 (and idem, *Interpretation*, 380); Lindars, *NT Apologetic*, 161 (and idem, *John*, 436-37); Bultmann, *John*, 452 n. 2; Brown, *John* 1, 485; Tsuchido, "John 12.1-43," 614; Roman Küschelm, "Verstockung als Gericht: Eine Untersuchung zu Joh 12,35-43; Lk 13,34-35; 19,41-44," *BibLit* 57 (1984): 242; Sloyan, *John*, 161-62; Fortna, *Fourth Gospel*, 138; contrast Schnackenburg, *St. John* 2, 413-14. For parallels to John 12.40, see the following chapter.

37) as the "fulfillment" of "the word" of the prophet Isaiah.[2] Experiencing similar frustrations, Isaiah anticipated the frustrated efforts of Jesus as well in offering the following lament:

κύριε τίς ἐπίστευσεν τῇ ἀκοῇ ἡμῶν ;
καὶ ὁ βραχίων κυρίου τίνι ἀπεκαλύφθη ;   (12.38).

The quotation formula which precedes John's citation is unique to his Gospel.[3] Perhaps the most conspicuous feature of this formula is the appearance in it of John's first use of the verb πληρόω to indicate the fulfillment of Old Testament prophecy.[4] Interestingly, beginning with John 12.38 each citation of the Old Testament in the Fourth Gospel includes a similar explicit reference to the "fulfillment" of Scripture.[5] These references are included in order to signal and emphasize the fact that beginning with John's summary remarks in John 12.37-41 Jesus' "hour" has indeed come (cf. 12.23, 31-33). In Jesus' hour one views the final outcome of Jesus' coming. One views the climactic fulfillment not only of Old Testament prophecy but also of Jesus' own prophetic words (cf. 18.9, 32) and deeds.[6] Tragically, however, this emerging outcome will include the anticipated rejection of Jesus by his own people.[7]

---

[2] We have already noted John's pattern of explicitly referring to the prophet Isaiah (see my remarks in chapter four).

[3] The rather unusual reference to the fulfillment of Isaiah's "word" (see also 15.25; cf. Rev 1.3; 22.7, 9, 10, 18-19; contrast Luke 3.4; Acts 15.15) contributes significantly to this singularity. On the question of whether the character of this formula betrays the hand of a different writer, see the following chapter.

[4] See esp. Evans, "Formulas," 80-81; cf. Brown, *John* 2, 554; Pancaro, *Law*, 354-63; Carson, "John," 248; Humann, "OT Quotations," 38-39, 50. Fulfillment formulas are lacking both in the Qumran literature (cf. Fitzmyer, "OT Quotations," 303-4) and in the Mishna (cf. Metzger, "Formulas, 306-7). Cf. Str-B 1:74. In Matthew, such formulas occur frequently. Outside of Matthew and John, however, they occur only sparingly (Freed, *OT Quotations*, 84 n. 1; John J. O'Rourke, "John's Fulfillment Texts," *SciencesEccl* 19 [1967]: 433 n. 3).

[5] Note the use of πληρόω with ὁ λόγος in John 12.38 and 15.25; and with ἡ γραφή in 13.18; 17.12; 19.24, 36 (contrast 7.8). The citations appearing in John 12.40 and 19.37 seem initially to represent exceptions to this pattern. Πληρόω does not appear in the formulas that introduce them. But, "in view of the close relationship and proximity of these texts with the ones cited immediately before them (in John 12:38 and 19:36, respectively) the introductory formula ἵνα πληρωθῇ of the lead texts is surely meant to be applied to the second quotations. This understanding is supported by noting the presence of the word πάλιν which links the second quotations to the first ones" (Evans, "Formulas," 80 n. 2; cf. Carson, "John," 248; Humann, "OT Quotations," 50).

[6] Among Jesus' deeds, it is especially the signs of Jesus that have been shown to be anticipatory in character (see my remarks in chapter two). Thus, the use of πληρόω in formulas beginning with John 12.38 signals a division between that part of Jesus' ministry which preceded and was primarily anticipatory in character and that which now follows and brings to completion both what the OT and Jesus himself anticipated. Indeed, these final moments

What passage from Isaiah, then, is being recalled? Is the influence of a particular version of this passage evident in John's citation? And what can be determined concerning the intent of John in citing this passage in its present form?

I.

The task of establishing which passage from Isaiah John cites and which version of this Old Testament passage he recalls is a relatively simple one. John 12.38 corresponds in every detail with the text of Isa 53.1 OG. Isa 53.1 OG, in turn, is unusual in one key respect. The OG contains one element not reflected in any potential Hebrew *Vorlage*, the prefixed vocative κύριε.

Some scholars have argued for John's dependence upon the OG without making this observation.[8] Many others have correctly noted that the influence of the OG is especially evident when John 12.38 and Isa 53.1 OG agree in prefixing κύριε.[9] In any case, scholars are virtually unanimous in their judgment that the OG is represented in this citation.[10]

---

themselves are also said to reach their own striking climax. In John 19.28-30, the selection of yet another conspicuous verb (τελειόω, 19.28) signals that Jesus' fulfillment of Scripture (ἡ γραφή, 19.28) has reached its all-encompassing conclusion (similarly τελέω in 19.28, 30; cf. the anticipatory uses of τελειόω in 4.34; 5.36; 17.4, 23; and τελέω in 13.1).

[7] This result is tragic precisely because, in spite of the fact that it is foreseen, it is not desired and not necessary. Thus, "Perhaps we should not press the conjunction *hina* so as to make it yield its full classical sense of purpose ('*in order that* the saying of Isaiah might be fulfilled'); here the meaning may be no more than that their unbelief fulfilled the prophet's saying" (Bruce, *John*, 270; cf. Lindars, *John*, 437). See further below.

[8] Cf. Hühn, *Citate*, 88; Stendahl, *St. Matthew*, 163; Bultmann, *John*, 452 n. 2; Josef Blank, *Krisis: Untersuchungen zur johanneischen Christologie und Eschatologie* (Freiburg im Breisgau: Lambertus-Verlag, 1964), 299; Brown, *John* 1, 485; Lindars, *John*, 437; Longenecker, *Exegesis*, 137; Evans, "Formulas," 80 (and idem, "The Function of Isaiah 6:9-10 in Mark and John," *NovT* 24 [1982]: 136); Küschelm, "Verstockung," 236 n. 7; Becker, *Johannes*, 409; Kysar, *John*, 201; Sloyan, *John*, 162; Ronald L. Tyler, "The Source and Function of Isaiah 6:9-10 in John 12:40," in *Johannine Studies: Essays in Honor of Frank Pack*, ed. James E. Priest (Malibu, Ca.: Pepperdine University Press, 1989), 211-12, 217.

[9] Cf. Franke, *Alte Testament*, 283, 286; Toy, *Quotations*, 88; Burney, *Aramaic Origin*, 120; Bernard, *St. John*, 450; Hoskyns, *Fourth Gospel*, 428; Dodd, *Scriptures*, 39; Goodwin, "Sources," 62; Freed *OT Quotations*, 84, 122, 126; O'Rourke, "Fulfillment," 434, 442; Reim, *Studien*, 34, 90, 217; Archer/Chirichigno, *OT Quotations*, 121; Bruce, *John*, 270; Menken, "John 1,23," 193; Humann, "OT Quotations," 42.

[10] A curious exception is Barrett, *St. John*, 28, 431. Barrett notes that both John and the OG agree in prefixing κύριε, yet finds that no conclusion can be drawn from this concerning the OG as a source.

This is as far as most have ventured. There is, however, an additional feature of John 12.38 which suggests the same conclusion, but has only very rarely caught the attention of scholars. For the idea of "revealing," John's Gospel agrees with the OG in its use of the verb ἀποκαλύπτω. This, however, is the only time in John's Gospel that this verb appears. Elsewhere, φανερόω is the verb of choice.[11] Here too, then, the influence of the OG is apparent.[12]

John 12.38 has not yet represented a difficult challenge. The task of characterizing John's intent in including this citation in his Gospel, however, is a different matter. And this will have far-reaching implications for how the citation in John 12.40 as well is to be understood.

II.

John's intent in citing Isa 53.1 OG has proved to be a difficult thing for scholars to characterize. The reason for this is that John 12.38 seems to fit poorly where it appears in John's Gospel.[13] John's citation seems especially ill-adapted to the verse that immediately precedes it.

We have already noted that line one of Isa 53.1 speaks of faith in what has been preached (cf. OG Isa 6.9; 52.7); line two refers to the revelation of "the arm of the Lord." Most scholars rightly point out that, for John, line one represents a reference to the words of Jesus;[14] line two refers to Jesus' signs.[15] The problem is this: John 12.37 makes no reference to Jesus' words and, instead, speaks only of

---

11 Cf. John 1.31; 2.11; 3.21; 7.4; 9.3; 17.6; 21.1, 14; 1 John 1.2; 2.19, 28; 3.2, 5, 8; 4.9; Rev 3.18; 15.4. The verb ἀποκαλύπτω is, in fact, lacking in both the Johannine epistles and Revelation as well. The noun ἀποκάλυψις appears only at Rev 1.1.

12 Cf. Franke, Alte Testament, 290; Menken, "John 1,23," 193. Robinson, Priority, 327, recognizes that ἀπεκαλύφθη is a hapax, but fails to attribute this to the influence of the OG.

13 It is difficult to detect any clear indication that John wishes here to recall the larger context of Isa 53 as well. Cf., however, Brown, John 1, 485, who among others maintains that in the case of John 12.20-36, "much of the terminology John uses to describe the hour of Jesus' being lifted up in glory has its basis in the Suffering Servant hymns of Deutero-Isaiah."

14 For Paul, line one represents a reference to the "gospel" (Rom 10.16). Cf. "our report" in John 12.38 with Jesus' use of the first person plural "we" in John 3.11.

15 Cf. Westcott, St. John, 184-85; Bernard, St. John, 450; Schlatter, Der Evangelist, 274; Hoskyns, Fourth Gospel, 428; Freed, OT Quotations, 85, 122; Brown, John 1, 485; Barrett, St. John, 431; Bruce, John, 270-71; Schnackenburg, Johannes 4, 149 (pp. 143-52 appeared originally as "Joh 12,39-41: Zur christologischen Schriftauslegung des vierten Evangelisten, in Neues Testament und Geschichte: Historisches Geschehen und Deutung im Neuen Testament. Oscar Cullmann zum 70. Geburtstag, hg. H. Baltensweiler und B. Reicke [Zürich: Theologischer Verlag, 1972], 167-77); Küschelm, "Verstockung," 236; Beasley-Murray, John, 216; Menken, "Joh 12,40," 197; Humann, "OT Quotations," 36, 42.

a lack of faith in Jesus in spite of his many signs. How, then, is John 12.38 to be reconciled with John 12.37?[16]

First, it should be noted that two essential ideas appearing in John 12.37 do, in fact, reappear in John 12.38. Both John 12.37 and line one of John's citation speak of believing. Both John 12.37 and line two of John's citation refer to the arm of the Lord (i.e., to Jesus' signs). Thus, for John the key word in line one that linked John 12.38 to John 12.37 was ἐπίστευσεν. And taken together, lines one and two do complement that which is asserted in John 12.37.[17]

There is, however, in John 12.38 the matter of the additional and seemingly extraneous reference to Jesus' "report." Some scholars suggest that this element of John's citation is to be taken as largely incidental.[18] But John does not wish for his addressees to treat ἀκοῇ as a basically superfluous element of his citation. It is especially John's second reference to the prophet Isaiah in John 12.39-40 that makes this clear. It is in the following chapter, therefore, that this issue will be resolved.

In summary, a provisional understanding of John's intent has not offered additional insights into his source for this citation. But this will figure significantly in the following chapter. Any attempt to understand John's second reference to the prophet Isaiah must take into account his as yet unexplained reference to the content of Jesus' proclamation.

III.

The preliminary conclusions are these. John's editorial reference to the prophet Isaiah in John 12.38 has come from Isa 53.1 OG. The Jewish rejection of

---

16 John 12.38 also does not seem to fit well with the citation that follows it. In the next chapter it will be discovered that the original OT passage cited in John 12.40 contained references to Israel's ability to "hear" which are absent in John's citation.

17 Cf. Menken, "Joh 12,40," 198. John 12.37 also appears to have been constructed in order to suggest that Jesus, the prophet like Moses, was no more successful in persuading Israel than was his predecessor. See esp. Deut 29.2-4 (cf. Brown, *John* 1, 485; Barrett, *St. John*, 430; Kysar, *John*, 201; contrast Exod 4.1-9, esp. v. 5; Num 14.11; Ps 78.32). The transition from John 12.37 to John 12.38-40, then, is an even more natural one (cf. Craig A. Evans, "Isaiah 6:9-10 in Early Jewish and Christian Interpretation" [Ph.D. diss., Claremont Graduate School, 1983], 221 n. 93 [hereafter, "Isa 6:9-10"]). Contrast Deut 5.15, where the "arm" of the Lord is an expression appearing with reference to God's agency in the signs that were performed during the Exodus (cf. Brown, *John* 1, 485; Humann, "OT Quotations," 36 n. 16; see also Exod 8.19; Wis 16.16; Acts 13.17).

18 See, e.g., Menken, "Joh 12,40," 198: "Die erste Zeile handelt also nicht speziell von Jesu Verkündigung." Cf. Fortna, *Fourth Gospel*, 138: "'our report' must be the pre-Johannine account of Jesus' signs, simply paralleling after the manner of Hebrew poetry the revealing of 'the arm of the Lord.'"

Jesus and his signs signals not only the fulfillment of this prophecy of Isaiah but also the emerging climax of John's entire Gospel. In the final stages of John's Gospel, Jesus will bring to final completion both Old Testament prophecy and what he himself has anticipated in his former words and deeds. John's subsequent reference to a second prophecy from Isaiah in John 12.39-40, however, must be carefully considered in relation to his first citation of Isaiah in order to arrive at a full understanding of his intent in referring to either passage.

Chapter 8

SO THAT THOSE WHO SEE MAY BECOME BLIND

In John's second reference to the prophet Isaiah in John 12.37-41, John states that Isaiah did more than simply foresee that the Jews would reject Jesus. Isaiah even anticipated the cause of their folly. The Jews were unable to believe because, according to Isaiah (12.39),

> τετύφλωκεν αὐτῶν τοὺς ὀφθαλμοὺς
> καὶ ἐπώρωσεν αὐτῶν τὴν καρδίαν,
> ἵνα μὴ ἴδωσιν τοῖς ὀφθαλμοῖς
> καὶ νοήσωσιν τῇ καρδίᾳ
> καὶ στραφῶσιν, καὶ ἰάσομαι αὐτούς (12.40).[1]

Virtually every aspect of John 12.39-40 is unique to John's Gospel. For example, the formula which parenthetically identifies the source of John's

---

[1] Scholars have frequently misinterpreted the thrust of the construction διὰ τοῦτο . . . , ὅτι . . . in John 12.39 (cf. 5.16; 1 John 3.1). John's intent is to state not that the Jews were unable to believe because Isaiah predicted that they would lack this facility, but because (in accordance with Isaiah's prophecy) τετύφλωκεν . . . (12.40; cf. 3.3, 5, 27; 5.44; 6.44, 65; 14.17; 15.4, 5). When God commissioned Isaiah, he warned him "that indeed all his words would be counter-productive and make them close their ears the more decisively. This would be the effect of his ministry, but it was not its purpose (its purpose was that they might 'turn and be healed'); it is expressed, however, as though God were actually sending him *in order that* his hearers would not listen to him. This Hebraic fashion of expressing result as though it were purpose has influenced John's wording" (Bruce, *John*, 271; similarly, John 12.38).

citation (πάλιν εἶπεν 'Ησαίας) appears only here in the New Testament.[2] We have already noted of this formula that especially πάλιν indicates that the introductory formula ἵνα . . . πληρωθῇ in John 12.38 is to be inferred here as well (cf. John 19.36-37).[3]

It is especially the form of John's citation itself, however, that is conspicuously unique. The prophecy of Isaiah to which John refers was well-known in both Jewish and early Christian circles. References to this prophecy appear with great frequency both in the New Testament (see especially the citations appearing in Matt 13.14-15 and Acts 28.26-27)[4] and elsewhere.[5] The form of John 12.40, however, is remarkably uncommon. Initially, John's citation appears in all respects to be a thoroughly independent creation.[6]

How, then, is the conspicuous form of this citation to be explained? What has contributed to it? And how does this citation reflect John's intent?

I.

The task of isolating what has contributed to the form of John's citation in John 12.40 is a decidedly complex one. The passage referred to is Isa 6.10. But John's citation differs markedly from every other extant version of this passage.

The unparalleled features of John's citation of Isa 6.10 are unusually numerous. Perhaps the most conspicuous of these features has to do with the overall structure of John's citation.[7] To be sure, scholars' analyses of the citation frequently begin with two observation concerning its structure: (1) John's version

---

[2] Cf. Rom 15.12 (see also vv. 10 and 11); contrast Matt 15.4, 7; 19.5, 18-19; 22.24; Mark 7.10; Acts 2.25; Rom 10.16.

[3] See my remarks in chapter seven.

[4] Cf. Mark 4.12; 8.17-18 (see also 3.5; 6.52); Luke 8.10; contrast Rom 9.18; 11.25, 78 (Isa 29.10); 2 Cor 3.14; 4.4; Eph 4.18-19; 1 John 2.11.

[5] For a detailed discussion of the transmission of Isa 6.9-10 in the early Jewish and Christian textual traditions, in rabbinic, patristic, and gnostic literatures, and in the New Testament, see Evans, "Isa 6:9-10" (cf. his short essays "The Text of Isaiah 6:9-10," *ZAW* 94 [1982]: 415-18; "Isaiah 6:9-10 in Rabbinic and Patristic Writings," *VC* 36 [1982]: 275-81; "Jerome's Translation of Isaiah 6:9-10," *VC* 38 [1984]: 202-4). Cf. Joachim Gnilka, *Die Verstockung Israels: Isaias 6,9-10 in der Theologie der Synoptiker*, Studien zum Alten und Neuen Testament, Bd. 3 (München: Kösel-Verlag, 1961).

[6] Cf. Dodd, *Scriptures*, 38 (and idem, *Historical Tradition*, 58 n. 1); O'Rourke, "OT Citations," 43 n. 31; Braun, *Jean 2*, 26; Evans, "Function," 125-26; Küschelm, "Verstockung," 242; Schnackenburg, *Johannes 4*, 152: "Seine (i.e., John's) originale Deutung des Verstockungszitats findet weder in jüdischer Exegese noch auch in vorgängiger urchristlicher Auslegung ein Vorbild" (similarly, Menken, "Joh 12,40," 202-3).

[7] The following development of this point has been significantly influenced by Menken, "Joh 12,40," 195.

of Isa 6.10 deletes the lines in this Old Testament passage referring to the "ears" of the Jews and to their capacity to "hear." (2) At the beginning of John's citation, the sequence of the lines is also unusual.[8] John's citation, therefore, dispenses completely with an original concentric structure evident in both the Greek and Hebrew textual traditions.[9] The MT, for example, (translated in a rather literalistic fashion, and with its final line deleted) exhibits the following structure which is, with some minor variations, preserved in the OG as well:

a   Make fat the *heart* of this people,
b   and its *ears* make heavy,
c   and its *eyes* shut,
c'   lest it sees with its *eyes*,
b'   and with its *ears* it hears,
a' and its *heart* understands.

But in John 12.40, lines b and b' are absent and lines a and c (again, with some minor variations) are reversed. The following sequence results: c a c' a'. The parallelism thus established is enhanced even further in this citation by the consistent placing of the key nouns "eyes" and "heart" at the end of each line (in both the MT and the OG, these nouns follow the verb only in lines a and c').[10]

These preliminary observations alone are sufficient to establish the singularity of John's version of Isa 6.10. Such observations, however, prove to be but a prelude to the many idiosyncrasies that are to be observed in John 12.40. A close examination of the more individual details of John 12.40 reveals numerous additional curiosities. When the individual aspects of John's version of Isa 6.10 are compared with the various extant versions of this Old Testament passage, it is discovered that, at times, John appears to reflect the influence of the OG; on other occasions, John seems to reflect the influence of a Hebrew *Vorlage*; in still other instances, John offers what appears to be a thoroughly independent reading.

The most important data can be summarized as follows: (1) In lines one and two of John 12.40, the two indicatives τετύφλωκεν and ἐπώρωσεν[11] differ from

---

8 In both cases, John's Gospel differs from all other extant versions of Isa 6.10.

9 Cf. Lindars, *John*, 438; Humann, "OT Quotations," 43; contrast O'Rourke, "OT Citations," 43 n. 31.

10 There is an additional consequence of the Fourth Gospel's conspicuous placement of the substantives at the conclusion of each line. While in John 12.40 αὐτῶν precedes the noun it modifies in lines one and two, in lines two and three of the OG αὐτῶν follows the substantive it modifies.

11 The reading ἐπώρωσεν appears in A B* L Θ Ψ f[13] 33 *al* (πεπώρωκεν in B2 f[1] and the Majority text represents a secondary assimilation to the perfect τετύφλωκεν in line one). There is, however, another reading which requires some attention. The aorist ἐπήρωσεν

the MT, where we encounter the hiph'il imperatives הַשְׁמֵן and הָעֵשׁ (with the prophet as addressee), and from the OG as well. The OG offers a version of Isa 6.9 in the indicative and treats the blinding and hardening of the Jews as a *fait accompli* (ἐπαχύνθη . . . ἡ καρδία) for which the people are themselves responsible (τοὺς ὀφθαλμοὺς αὐτῶν ἐκάμμυσαν).[12] (2) In line three, ἵνα μή appears to represent a translation of the Hebrew פֶּן (=MT) against the reading of the OG μήποτε.[13] (3) In line four, τῇ καρδίᾳ seems to reflect the OG rather than the

---

appears in P66.75 ℵ K W pc (again, πεπήρωκεν in 63 122 185 and 259 represents a secondary assimilation to the perfect in line one). The orthographic and lexigraphic differences between πωρόω and πηρόω are slight. Still, Menken, "Joh 12,40," 192-194, has recently shown that early Christian literature in general exhibits a distinct preference for the former (together with the corresponding substantive πώρωσις) rather than the latter. Not only this, "aber in allen Fällen ausser Joh 12,40 sind Varianten mit πηρ- in griechischen Handschriften . . . entweder nicht vorhanden oder sehr selten" (p. 193; such variant readings appear in the case of Mark 3.5; 8.17; Rom 11.7; *Herm.* 30.1 [=Man. 4.2], but are lacking in Mark 6.52; Rom 11.25; 2 Cor 3.14; Eph 4.18; *Herm.* 47.4 [=Man. 12.4]; Theophilus, *Ad Autolycum* 2.35). Menken's analysis reveals that "trotz der starken Ähnlichkeit der Stämme πωρ- und πηρ- die Überlieferung des griechischen Textes überraschend wenig Variation zeigt" (pp. 193-94). A striking exception, however, is John 12.40, the only instance in the NT for which significant textual support for a reading with πηρ- exists. Some scholars have suggested that ἐπήρωσεν represents a secondary attempt to supply a somewhat more suitable verb with τὴν καρδίαν (Barrett, *St. John*, 432; cf. Freed, *OT Quotations*, 87 n. 4; Lindars, *John*, 439; Evans, "Isa 6:9-10," 67 n. 42). Menken (p. 194 n. 24) responds, "Rücksicht nehmend auf Mk 3,5; 6,52; 8,17; Eph 4,18, muss man sagen, dass πωρόω eine bessere Chance hat, 'the somewhat more suitable verb' zu sein" (attention is also directed to Justin, *Dial.* 33). Similarly, de Waard's suggestion (*Comparative Study*, 8; cf. Longenecker, *Exegesis*, 33) that " ἐπήρωσεν goes back to the reading *hsm* in 1QIsᵃ" is held by Menken to be "schwer beweisbar" (p. 194 n. 24). Menken's conclusion, therefore, is this: "Sehr wahrscheinlich wurde in unserem Vers ἐπήρωσεν, ungewöhnlich innerhalb des NT, abgeändert zum gewöhnlichen ἐπώρωσεν. Man kann sich die umgekehrte Bewegung kaum vorstellen, wenn man berücksichtigt, dass es in den anderen Fällen von πωρ- im NT fast keine Variation mit πηρ- gibt, auch nicht da, wo, wie in Joh 12,40, im Kontext von Blindheit die Rede ist (Mk 8,17; Rom 11,7; 2 Kor 3,14, vgl. 4,4; Eph 4,18)" (p. 194). That ἐπήρωσεν was original is indeed possible. However, Menken's argument against an "umgekehrte Bewegung" carries weight only if one assumes that such a substitution would have been necessarily intentional (cf. Acts 5.3 v.l.; contrast *Test. Levi* 13.7 and Theophilus, *Ad Autolycum* 1.7, where πώρωσις appears as a v.l. for πήρωσις). The issue is difficult to resolve with any certainty. What follows will operate with the more commonly held assumption that ἐπώρωσεν was the original reading. An opposite conclusion would not, however, significantly alter the character of the present investigation.

[12] The translation of Symmachus is, in part, similar, but its terminology is conspicuously different. Evans, "Isa 6:9-10," 10-51, shows that the overall tendency in the early translations and versions was to soften the seemingly harsh telic force of this passage and/or emphasize the aspect of the righteous remnant (cf. idem, "Text").

[13] The rest of line three corresponds precisely to the text of the OG. This, however, cannot be afforded any great significance since the OG does not here deviate, e.g., from the

Hebrew לְבָבוֹ (=MT; the subject). But νοήσωσιν differs from the OG συνῶσιν and seems a possible rendering of the Hebrew יָבִין (=MT).[14] (4) In line five, στραφῶσιν appears to reflect the Hebrew שָׁב (=MT) rather than the OG ἐπιστρέψωσιν.[15] But καὶ ἰάσομαι αὐτούς agrees with the OG against the Hebrew וְרָפָא לוֹ (=MT).

The evidence is indeed varied and perplexing. And the conclusions scholars have derived from this data have been similarly confused. Some have preferred to refer to John 12.40 as a more or less free reference reflecting either a Hebrew *Vorlage* alone[16] or the OG alone.[17] Others have suggested that, in fact, both versions of the Old Testament are represented in the Fourth Gospel's citation.[18] Still others, however, have postulated the use of some other version of this text, perhaps an early Christian testimony.[19] And finally, even the possibility that

---

MT (cf. Menken, "Joh 12,40," 203, who rightly points out that the same is true for τοὺς ὀφθαλμούς and τὴν καρδίαν in lines one and two). See further below.

[14] Both συνίημι and νοέω appear in the OG as translations of the Hebrew בִּין in the qal, hiph'il, and hitpolel. The former is much more frequent than the latter. But for Menken, "Joh 12,40," 205, a Hebrew *Vorlage* remains plausible: "Man könnte versuchen, die Wortwahl hier durch einen Verweis auf den Umstand zu erklären, dass der Ausdruck νοέω (ἐν) τῇ καρδίᾳ in der LXX einige Male vorkommt: Hiob 33,23; Jes 44,18; 47,7, vgl. Koh 2,3 Aq + Symm (καρδία ist als Subjekt mit νοέω verbunden in 1 Reg 4,20; Spr 16,23; Jes 32,6), während συνίημι (ἐν) τῇ καρδίᾳ dort nicht mehr gefunden wird (vgl. jedoch Dan 10,12 Theod und die Verbindungen von Derivaten von συνίημι mit καρδία, wie z.B. in Ex 31,6; Hiob 34,10. 34)."

[15] See Menken, "Joh 12,40," 206. In the OG, ἐπιστρέφω appears as the preferred translation of the Hebrew שׁוּב (appearing as such more than four hundred times). The verb στρέφω does, however, appear as a translation of שׁוּב three times (each time as a variant reading in place of composites of στρέφω; cf. Isa 38.8; Jer 41[34].15; Ezek 47.6; see also Isa 38.8 Theod.; Ezek 47.6 Theod.).

[16] See, e.g., Burney, *Aramaic Origin*, 121; Barrett, *St. John*, 29, 431; Archer/Chirichigno, *OT Quotations*, 95.

[17] See, e.g., Franke, *Alte Testament*, 283-84; Hoskyns, *Fourth Gospel*, 428-29; Goodwin, "Sources," 71.

[18] See, e.g., O'Rourke, "Fulfillment," 436, 442; Longenecker, *Exegesis*, 137; Schnackenburg, *Johannes 4*, 146-47; Kysar, *John*, 202; Menken, "Joh 12,40," 198-209. Both Braun, *Jean* 2, 12-13, 20-21, and Reim, *Studien*, 38, 90-91, 217, suggest that it is an editor who has added those features based on the OG. Freed, *OT Quotations*, 85, 122, however, finds it impossible to be certain whether a Greek or Hebrew *Vorlage* has been influential (similarly, Tyler, "John 12:40," 215, 220).

[19] See, e.g., Dodd, *Scriptures*, 39 (cf. idem, *Historical Tradition*, 58 n. 1); Lindars, *John*, 437-38 (cf. idem, *NT Apologetic*, 98 n. 1, 159-67); Dwight Moody Smith, "The Setting and Shape of a Johannine Narrative Source," *JBL* 95 (1976): 239; Sloyan, *John*, 162; J. M. Lieu, "Blindness in the Johannine Tradition," *NTS* 34 (1988): 87-88.

other Old Testament passages were somehow influential has been considered.[20] How, then, are these various proposals to be evaluated?

First, it should be noted that there is a particular aspect of the present problem that has not been encountered in the citations that have preceded. This is the first time in this investigation that a citation has appeared for which a reasonable case can be made, at least in part, for the influence of a Hebrew *Vorlage*.

Indeed, on the one hand, it would seem that the case for the influence of a Hebrew version of Isa 6.10 on John 12.40 can be taken rather far. For example, in addition to what we have already noted it is possible to explain τετύφλωκεν and ἐπώρωσεν in John 12.40 on the basis of an unvocalized Hebrew passage. In this case, the verb forms השע and השמן would have been read as perfects (the latter spelled defectively).[21] The translation of השע with a Greek perfect and השמן with a Greek aorist is somewhat unexpected given the original *parallelismus membrorum* of the Hebrew. But this is certainly not inconceivable for John. The same juxtaposition of tenses occurs with considerable frequency elsewhere in his Gospel.[22]

Also, τῇ καρδίᾳ in line four cannot be held to automatically suggest the influence of the OG. The reading בלבבו is attested especially in 1QIsaᵃ. This reading also finds indirect support in the Peshitta and the Vulgate. A comparable expression appears in Targum Jonathan as well (בליבהון). It is, therefore, possible that a Hebrew *Vorlage* is reflected in τῇ καρδίᾳ.[23]

A Hebrew *Vorlage* explains much of the construction of John's citation. It does not, however, explain all of John's citation.

An obvious example of what seems to be evidence for the influence of the OG in John's citation of Isa 6.10 is the last three words of John 12.40 (καὶ

---

[20] See, e.g., Freed, *OT Quotations*, 87-88; Stendahl, *St. Matthew*, 131 n. 2; Brown, *John* 1, 486; Evans, "Function," 134-35; Menken, "Joh 12,40," 205-6, 208-9; Lieu, "Blindness," 88.

[21] Cf. Burney, *Aramaic Origin*, 121 (who suggests as an alternative that the two Hebrew verb forms were read as infinitive absolutes used in place of perfects); Freed, *OT Quotations*, 87 (a possibility); O'Rourke, "Fulfillment," 436; Reim, *Studien*, 38; Barrett, *St. John*, 431; Archer/Chirichigno, *OT Quotations*, 95; Schnackenburg, *Johannes* 4, 146 (see also idem, *St. John* 2, 416); Menken, "Joh 12,40," 199, 209; see also Humann, "OT Quotations," 44.

[22] See esp. Menken, "Joh 12,40," 199, who calls attention to such texts as John 3.32; 6.31-32; 8.38, 42; 12.46-47; 14.25-26; 17.2; 18.20-21. See further below.

[23] See Menken, "Joh 12,40," 204-5. Contrast O'Rourke, "Fulfillment," 436, who concludes from the high degree of correspondence between the final twelve words of John 12.40 and the OG that John had the wording of the OG in mind when he wrote (cf. Freed, *OT Quotations*, 88). Menken (p. 203 n. 48), however, offers the following appropriate critique: "Ihr Argument hat aber nur Wert für die drei letzten Wörter des Zitates, die keine korrekte Übersetzung des hebräischen Textes abgeben." See further below.

ἰάσομαι αὐτούς).[24] John 12.40 agrees with the OG against every other extant version of this passage. A less obvious example has to do with the possessives in John 12.40. As is the case in the OG, possessives modify τοὺς ὀφθαλμούς and τὴν καρδίαν in John 12.40 (lines one and two), but are lacking in the case of τοῖς ὀφθαλμοῖς and τῇ καρδίᾳ (lines three and four). This pattern is not something one would expect to see in a translation of a Hebrew Vorlage in which pronominal suffixes appear with each substantive in each line. John's use of possessives suggests, therefore, that the OG is being recalled.[25]

The case for the influence of a Hebrew Vorlage on John 12.40 is, upon closer examination, strained from the very beginning. Virtually every scholar who argues that τετύφλωκεν and ἐπώρωσεν represent translations of the Hebrew השמן hiph'il and העש hiph'il fails to note that elsewhere in the extant Greek versions of the Old Testament similar translations are not to be found.[26]

These details suggest that there is a better solution to this problem. The key to a final resolution of this problem lies in a careful analysis of John's intent in citing Isa 6.10.[27]

---

[24] Cf. Franke, Alte Testament, 284, 286-87; Hoskyns, Fourth Gospel, 428-29; Schlatter, Der Evangelist, 275; Goodwin, "Sources," 71; Lindars, NT Apologetic, 160 (and idem, John, 438); Braun, Jean 2, 12; Stendahl, St. Matthew, 131; Brown, John 1, 486; O'Rourke, "Fulfillment," 436; Schnackenburg, St. John 2, 415 (and idem, Johannes 4, 146-47, 150); Reim, Studien, 38, 90-91, 217; Newman/Nida, Handbook, 418; Bergmeier, Glaube, 230; Küschelm, "Verstockung," 236 n. 8; Lieu, "Blindness," 85; Menken, "Joh 12,40," 206, 208-9; Humann, "OT Quotations," 44. There is no reason to doubt that all of line five is governed by the subordinating conjunction in line three (Morris, John, 604 n. 106; Schnackenburg, St. John 2, 415 [cf. idem, Johannes 4, 150]; Menken, "Joh 12,40," 208).

[25] Menken, "Joh 12,40," 203, differs and maintains that the lack of possessives in lines three and four in John 12.40 is "kein Indiz für den Gebrauch der LXX; das Possessivum ist schon in den Zeilen 1 und 2 gebraucht worden, und es kann ausbleiben, wenn die vom Pronomen angedeutete Person mit dem Subjekt des Satzes identisch ist. Solche Auslassung kommt öfters im Joh vor" (cf. 6.5; 7.30, 44; 11.41, 11; 13.10; 19.30; 20.20). Menken fails, however, to note that, while such omissions are indeed possible, the creation of the precise pattern noted above is not to be expected.

[26] Menken, "Joh 12,40," 199-200, is alone in noting this problem, but still insists on a Hebrew Vorlage. According to Menken, John "paraphrases" the original.

[27] For Schnackenburg, Johannes 4, 146, "Der Evangelist benutzt die Schrift offenbar in freier Weise. Ob er ungenau aus dem Gedächtnis zitiert, ist höchst ungewiss (consult Goodwin, "Sources," 71; Noack, Tradition, 83-84; Barrett, St. John, 431; Newman/Nida, Handbook, 418); vielmehr ist zu fragen, ob er nicht trotz guter Kenntnis absichtlich abändert, kombiniert, oder resumiert" (cited by Menken, "Joh 12,40," 190; cf. Burney, Aramaic Origin, 121). Indeed, most other scholars also seem to presuppose that either John or the tradition that preceded him altered Isa 6.10 in order to facilitate some kind of theological agenda (those who have used the term "pesher" with reference to John 12.40 include Lindars, NT Apologetic, 265-72; O'Rourke, "Fulfillment," 436-37; Longenecker, Exegesis, 156; Menken, "Joh 12,40," 209; on the limitations of such a designation, see Stendahl, St. Matthew, 201-2; cf. Marshall,

II.

Perhaps the most important aspect of any attempt to characterize John's intent in citing Isa 6.10 is the task of identifying the understood subject of the verbs τετύφλωκεν and ἐπώρωσεν in lines one and two of John 12.40. Several solutions have been thus far offered. Each, however, has its problems.

The majority of scholars conclude, usually without argument, that God is the understood subject in lines one and two of John 12.40. There are, however, at least two problems with this solution. First, while God is known to blind or harden both in the Old Testament and in the New Testament,[28] such an activity for God is foreign to the eschatological orientation of John's Gospel. In John's Gospel, "the Father judges no one, but has given all judgment to the Son" (5.22; cf. v. 27).[29] And second, it is difficult to see how God can be the subject in lines one and two of John 12.40 when the understood subject of ἰάσομαι in line four is likely to be Jesus.[30] The reason this solution seems unlikely is that the original

---

"Assessment," 10-15). Menken, "Joh 12,40," 191, rightly remarks, "Es scheint mir, dass Schnackenburg unser Verstehen von Joh 12,40 wirklich gefördert hat, indem er die Aufmerksamkeit auf die johanneische Redaktion des Zitates gelenkt hat. Es bleibt jedoch in diesem Zitat einiges zu untersuchen übrig, sowohl was die konsequente Durchführung der Redaktionskritik angeht, als auch in der Verbindung dieser mit der Quellenkritik."

[28] Menken, "Joh 12,40," 198 n. 34, offers numerous diverse examples of this from both Jewish and early Christian literature. The overall problem is discussed in some detail by Schnackenburg, St. John 2, 270-74; Heikki Räisänen, The Idea of Divine Hardening: A Comparative Study of the Notion of Divine Hardening, Leading Astray and Inciting to Evil in the Bible and Qur'ān, Publications of the Finnish Exegetical Society, vol. 25 (Helsinki: Finnische Exegetische Gesellschaft, 1976), 45-98; Bergmeier, Glaube; Don A. Carson, Divine Sovereignty and Human Responsibility: Biblical Perspectives in Tension, New Foundations Theological Library (Atlanta: John Knox Press, 1981).

[29] Similarly, Blank, Krisis, 302-3: "Die Schwierigkeit, die entsteht, wenn man bei Johannes Gott als Subjekt der Verblendung und Verstockung annimmt, besteht weniger darin, dass in der Schrift eine solche Möglichkeit überhaupt undenkbar wäre, als vielmehr darin, dass diese Aussage im Johannesevangelium sich nur ausserordentlich widerstrebend in den Gesamtzusammenhang einfügen würde." He adds, "Man frage sich einmal, ob ein solcher Sinn johanneisch denkbar ist?" Blank grants that, according to John 6.44, one cannot come to Jesus unless the Father draws him. "Aber dafür, dass Gott selbst das Nicht-Glauben-Können bewirkte, gibt es sonst im vierten Evangelium keinen Beweis" (in the same vein, we have already noted that John makes frequent reference to passages from Ps 69[68] [see my remarks in chapter two], but the psalm's call on God to blind the eyes of the unfaithful in v. 23 [cf. Rom 11.7-10] is not to be found in John's Gospel).

[30] That Jesus is the subject of ἰάσομαι is especially evident in John's reference to the glory of Jesus in John 12.41 (cf. Schnackenburg, Johannes 4, 147, 150-51; Bergmeier, Glaube, 263 n. 471; Becker, Johannes, 409-10; Beasley-Murray, John, 217; Humann, "OT Quotations," 44). Some scholars conclude from John 12.41 that the Targum of Isa 6.1, 5 ("I saw the glory of the Lord . . . the glory of the Shekinah of the eternal king, the Lord of hosts") is being recalled (cf. Bernard, St. John, 452; Barrett, St. John, 432; Brown, John 1, 486-87; Evans, "Function," 134 n.

subject of ἰάσομαι in the OG was God. The solution proposed by these scholars, therefore, suggests the existence of an original Old Testament passage containing a grammatical impossibility: "He (God) blinded . . . and I (God) heal them."[31]

Understandably, some scholars have argued instead that Jesus is the subject in lines one and two of John 12.40.[32] But this solution is fraught with the same difficulties. Such a solution is again in conflict with the eschatological orientation of John's Gospel. In John's Gospel, Jesus comes as duly empowered eschatological Judge. Jesus says, "For judgment I came into this world" (9.39; cf. 5.22, 27, 30; 8.16, 26; 12.31; 16.11). But Jesus also makes it clear that he does not, in fact, pronounce judgment on the Jews (cf. 3.17-19; 8.15; 12.47). More importantly, however, this solution suggests the same grammatical impossibility: "He (Jesus) blinded . . . and I (Jesus) heal them."

Other scholars, then, have sought a less immediate subject and have found a likely candidate in John's previously mentioned "ruler of this world" (12.31).[33]

48; Bruce, *John*, 272; Schnackenburg, *Johannes* 4, 147; Becker, *Johannes*, 411; Carson, "John," 261 n. 9). There is, however, no reason to rule out the influence of the references to the "glory" of the Lord in Isa 6.1, 3 OG (see Freed, *OT Quotations*, 84 n. 5; cf. Hans H. Malmede, *Die Lichtsymbolik im Neuen Testament*, Studies in Oriental Religions, vol. 15 [Wiesbaden: Otto Harrassowitz, 1986], 15). In either case, John asserts that the prophet saw in his temple vision the preexistent Jesus (cf. 1.18; 6.46; 1 John 4.12; see also similar references to the preexistent Jesus in 1 Cor 10.4; Philo, *De somniis* 1.229-30; Justin, *Dial.* 126-28; 1 *Apol.* 62-63; contrast John 5.46; 8.56). Jesus, then, is understood as the one who addresses the prophet in Isa 6.9-10. Note also that John 12.41 together with the presentation in John 12.40 of Jesus as the one who "heals" complements nicely the portrait of Jesus elsewhere in John's Gospel as the one who especially in his healing signs (cf. 4.46-54; 5.1-9; 9.1-7; see esp. the use of ἰάομαι in 4.47 and 5.13) offers a foretaste of the healing he will secure for all at the cross (cf. Menken, "Joh 12,40," 207). In other words, the "glory" (on this as a reflection of the sapiential orientation of the Gospel, see Willett, "Wisdom," 207-27) Jesus reveals in his signs (cf. 2.11; 11.4, 40; contrast Burge, *Community*, 80) anticipates the glory he will reveal in a climactic fashion at the cross (cf. 1.14; 7.39; 12.16, 23, 28; 13.31-32; 14.13; 17.1, 4-5, 24; contrast 21.19).

31 Similarly, Blank, *Krisis*, 304-5. The end result is an original "unerträgliche grammatische Spannung, die, wenn man Gott durchgehend als Subjeckt setzen würde, eine offenkundige Absurdität beinhalten würde: 'er hat verblendet . . . und *ich* sie heile'" (cf. Bruce Hollenbach, "Lest They Should Turn and Be Forgiven: Irony," *BT* 34 [1983]: 317). In opposition to Blank, Menken, "Joh 12,40," 207, argues that John's reproduction of Isa 6.10 in John 12.40 achieves an effect similar to what one observes in Isa 6.12 OG. In this passage, God speaks of himself in the third person singular. Menken fails, however, to resolve the difficulty of suggesting that in one sentence it is comprehensible for God to refer to himself in *both* the third person singular and the first person singular.

32 Cf. Freed, *OT Quotations*, 87; Hollenbach, "Irony," 313, 317; Bruce, *John*, 272; Lieu, "Blindness," 86.

33 Cf. Blank, *Krisis*, 301-5; R. A. Holst, "The Relation of John, Chapter Twelve, to the So-Called Johannine Book of Glory" (Ph.D. diss., Princeton Theological Seminary, 1974), 204-9; John Painter, "Eschatological Faith in the Gospel of John," in *Reconciliation and Hope: New Testament Essays on Atonement and Eschatology Presented to L. L. Morris on His 60th Birthday*, ed.

Once more, however, this solution fits poorly with the rest of John's Gospel. Elsewhere in John's Gospel (cf. 6.70; 8.43-44; 13.2), individuals are said to be the progeny of the devil and act in consort with him. But nothing in John's Gospel suggests that the devil might possess or exercise the power to blind or harden.[34] We have already noted that the deliberate substitution of subjects in references to Scripture is an observable phenomenon in Jewish and early Christian exegesis.[35] But to see the devil as the subject in lines one and two of John 12.40 would be an exegetical maneuver seriously in conflict with the original sense of the passage John cites.[36]

There is, in fact, a more likely subject for lines one and two of John 12.40 which appears in the immediate context of John's citation. This subject is John's yet unexplained reference in John 12.38 to Jesus' "report" ($\dot{\alpha}\kappa o\acute{\eta}$).[37] This solution is to be preferred for two reasons.

First, this solution complements both the immediate context of John 12.40 and the context of John's Gospel as a whole. The Jews, in spite of Jesus' many signs, did not believe in Jesus (12.37) because they were unable to accept his "report" (12.38). For what reason were they unable to believe? (12.39). Because the content of Jesus' proclamation blinded their eyes and hardened their hearts (12.40; cf. 8.43!).[38] How is this to be understood? Jesus has indeed come for judgment, "that those who see may become blind" (9.39). But the judgment that Jesus brings is not something he either desires (3.17) or personally executes. Instead, it is a judgment he provokes: "this is the judgment, that the light has come into the world and men loved darkness rather than light" (3.20). Provoked by Jesus' self-revelation, Jesus' protagonists show themselves to be "condemned already" (3.18). In other words, those who "see" (i.e., those who presume that

---

Robert J. Banks (Exeter: Paternoster Press, 1974), 46; this solution is one which can be traced back to the literature of the early church (see Schnackenburg, *Johannes* 4, 148 n. 18); contrast 2 Cor 4.4.

[34] Similarly, Becker, *Johannes*, 410 (quoted by Menken, "Joh 12,40," 198 n. 34). One is tempted to infer from the statement in John 12.35 ἵνα μὴ σκοτία ὑμᾶς καταλάβῃ (cf. 1.5!) that the "darkness" possesses such power (cf. 1 John 2.11!). Lieu, "Blindness," 90-92, however, is probably correct in only seeing in 1 John 2.11 evidence of a rich and complex tradition within Johannine Christianity which is able to embrace various distinct propositions concerning the source of blindness. The proposition in 1 John 2.11, however, is one which does not appear in the Fourth Gospel.

[35] See my remarks in chapter three.

[36] Similarly, Menken, Joh 12,40," 198 n. 34, who adds, "dabei hätte man in diesem Fall irgendeine Anweisung in diese Richtung im Text des Joh erwarten dürfen, zumal da im vorhergehenden Zitat in 12,38 der Prophet bzw. Jesus zu Gott spricht."

[37] Tyler, "John 12:40," 207, ponders briefly this possibility ("Is it the word he preached [which hardens]?"), but fails to offer it any serious attention.

[38] See also John 4.42; 5.24-25; 6.45, 60; 8.47; 10.3-4, 16, 27; 12.47.

they are able to see) show themselves to be actually blind and thereby "become blind" (9.39).[39] Properly construed, then, line one of John 12.40 might be paraphrased as follows: "Jesus' report provoked a response from the Jews which led to the loss of their presumed sight."[40]

Second, this solution is also the one which best corresponds to what one observes in the Old Testament context from which John's citation has come. We have already noted that in Isa 6 as well it is the content of the prophet's proclamation that causes offense and thus "blinds" the people of God. Isaiah does not mean to suggest that an impersonal agent is ultimately responsible for the fate of the Jews. Quite the opposite, as is the case elsewhere in the Old Testament and in the New Testament there is a personal will which is held to be responsible for this blindness. In the case of Isa 6, it is the will of the Jews. John's citation of Isa 6.10 makes this understanding of Isa 6 explicit.[41]

Isa 53.1, therefore, is cited in John 12.38 in order to specify the understood catalyst of this blinding. A final observation, then, is worthy of consideration. The substantive ἀκοή appears only three times in Isa OG, at Isa 6.9; 52.7; and 53.1. This suggests finally that it was John's knowledge of the OG that prompted his juxtaposition of Isa 53.1 and 6.10 in John 12.38 and 40 and informed the role he has these passages play in relation to one another.[42]

With these preliminary observations in mind, it is now possible to describe the editorial intent reflected in the numerous other enigmatic features of John 12.40. As for the overall structure of John's citation, many scholars have already noted that John's omission of the lines in Isa 6.10 which refer to the "ears" of the Jews and to their capacity to "hear" complements his construction of John 12.37.

---

[39] These observations complement in a significant fashion what we have already noted (see esp. my remarks in chapter five). It is not so much the works of Jesus as it is his words which consistently cause offense in John's Gospel. Jesus' works are "good," but his words are intolerable to his opponents (see esp. 10.32-33). Jesus' words are so intolerable to them that even his final plea with them to find in his works sufficient reason to also believe his words is refused (10.37-39a). John therefore writes, "Though he had done so many signs before them, yet they did not believe in him" (12.37).

[40] That a construct of the sort appearing in line one of John 12.40 is, in fact, able to be paraphrased in this fashion is confirmed by what we have already noted concerning another of John's citations. John 2.17, a similar construct, was paraphrased in a remarkably similar fashion: "Jesus zeal will provoke a response from the Jews which will lead to the loss of his life."

[41] There are, as we have noted, those scholars who would object to interpreting the text of Isa 6 MT in this fashion. To see Isa 6 MT as harshly telic, however, would only underline the likelihood that John recalls Isa 6.10 OG: "they have closed their eyes" (see further below).

[42] These two contexts in Isaiah share numerous other features as well (on this, see esp. Evans, "Isa 6:9-10," 209-15, 220-21). It is difficult, however, to establish with any certainty the extent to which this too may have been influential.

Since John 12.37 refers to the signs of Jesus which are seen with the eyes, John deletes the lines in Isa 6.10 referring to ears and hearing.[43] Several scholars have also seen in John's reversal of the original sequence of the remaining lines an indication that, for John, the acts of God begin with the external and then proceed to the internal.[44] But this reversal involves nothing more than an assimilation of the sequence of ideas appearing in John 12.40 to that appearing in John 12.37.[45]

As for the individual aspects of John 12.40 lines one and two, here too one encounters editorial innovations apparently introduced by John in order to further his theological agenda. In the case of τετύφλωκεν, for example, it seems probable that John refers to a passage also in Isaiah and analogous to Isa 6.9-10. One such passage is Isa 42.18-20 OG.[46] Scholars have considered the possibility that John refers to this and other passages from the larger context of Isaiah.[47] The verb τυφλόω, however, appears only once in Isaiah, at Isa 42.19 OG.[48] Passages elsewhere in Isaiah bear only very little in common with Isa 6.9-10.[49] Isa 42.18-

---

[43] Cf. Hoskyns, *Fourth Gospel*, 429; Lindars, *NT Apologetic*, 160-61 (see also idem, *John*, 438); Freed, *OT Quotations*, 88; Schnackenburg, *St. John* 2, 415 (see also idem, *Johannes* 4, 148-49); Reim, *Studien*, 38; Smith "Setting," 240; Barrett, *St. John*, 431; Becker, *Johannes*, 409; Fortna, *Fourth Gospel*, 139; Lieu, "Blindness," 85; Menken, "Joh 12,40," 195-96; Humann, "OT Quotations," 43.

[44] Cf. Schlatter, *Der Evangelist*, 275; Lindars, *NT Apologetic*, 160-61 (see also idem, *John*, 438); Schnackenburg, *St. John* 2, 415 (see also idem, *Johannes* 4, 148-49); Lieu, "Blindness," 85; Menken, "Joh 12,40," 195-96.

[45] In v. 40, line one's reference to the blinding of their eyes (contrast line three) parallels nicely v. 37's reference to their exposure to the signs of Jesus. It is especially Menken, "Joh 12,40," 197, who has pointed out that line two's reference to the hardening of their hearts (contrast line four) is probably to be taken as a reference to what was traditionally understood as the seat of faith (see esp. John 14.1; see also 13.2; 14.27-29; 16.6, 22; 1 John 3.19-24; cf. Mark 11.23; Luke 8.12; 24,25; Acts 8.37 v.l.; 15.9; Rom 10.8-10; Eph 3.17; 1 Tim 1.5; Heb 10.22). Line two, therefore, parallels nicely v. 37's reference to their inability to believe.

[46] Similarly, Freed, *OT Quotations*, 87.

[47] Contrast Evans, "Function," 134-35, who refers to Isa 29.10; 42.18, 19; and 56.10; and Menken, "Joh 12,40," 200, who considers the possibility that Isa 42.18-19; 43.8; or 56.10 may have been influential; suggesting simply that the more common term for blindness in Isaiah has been read back into Isa 6.10 is Lieu, "Blindness," 88.

[48] Τυφλόω in Isa 42.19 OG appears to loosely render a Hebrew construction in which an adjective rather than a verb describes the condition of blindness. It is therefore less likely that a Hebrew *Vorlage* was influential.

[49] In Isa 29.10, it is the Lord who blinds. In Isa 43.8, God as redeemer gathers the blind (cf. 29.18; 35.5; 61.1; see also Ps 146[145].8). It is tempting to find significance in the fact that Isa 56.10 refers to a condition similar to what one observes in Isa 6.9-10 (and in the perfect tense as does line one of John 12.40). The actual degree of similarity between Isa 56.10 and 6.9-10, however, is not great. Also, while τυφλόω is the verb of choice for John,

20 OG, on the other hand, bears much in common with Isa 6.9-10. Isa 42.18-20 OG, like Isa 6.9-10, laments over those who have turned back (ἀπεστράφησαν εἰς τὰ ὀπίσω, 42.17) and does this in a strikingly similar manner:

> Hear, you deaf, and look up, you blind, to see. And who is blind, but my servants? and deaf, but they that rule over them? Yea, the servants of God have been made blind. You have often seen and have not taken heed; your ears have been opened and you have not heard.[50]

Why, then, does John choose the verb τυφλόω? John's choice allows for the use of a verb in his citation which corresponds to the language he uses elsewhere in his Gospel to refer to the "blindness" of the Jews (esp. John 9).[51]

In the case of πωρόω, the prominence of this term elsewhere in Christian circles[52] has suggested to some scholars that its currency among Christians (especially in references to Isa 6.9-10) was what prompted its inclusion in John's citation.[53] This, however, would not coincide with what one observes in explicit citations of the Old Testament elsewhere in John's Gospel. Instead, it is likely that John again betrays his sapiential orientation. The verb πωρόω appears only once in the OG, at Job 17.7[54] (cf. Prov 10.20 A). Recalling this passage, John

---

ἐκτυφλόω appears in Isa 56.10 (it is likely that the sequence of tenses appearing in lines one and two of John 12.40 has again been fashioned in order to recall the same in John 12.37).

[50] Note also the larger context of Isa 42 which bears much in common with John's Gospel. In Isa 42, God's chosen servant bears the Spirit and brings judgment (42.1, 3). He is a light for the Gentiles, who opens their eyes and in whom the Gentiles trust (42.4, 6-7). Then follows a series of promises. God will give his glory (42.8), fulfillment (42.9), and peace (42.13). He will bring the blind and will turn darkness into light for them (42.16).

[51] See esp. Menken, "Joh 12,40," 200-1 (cf. my previous remarks on the relationship of John's citation to John 9; contrast John 5.3; 10.21; 11.37). The OG's καμμύω appears in the NT only at Matt 13.15 and Acts 28.27. It may be, however, that one should consider also the possible influence of the wisdom literature. Freed, OT Quotations, 87, refers to the use of τυφλόω in Wis 2.21 (cf. 2.10-20; see also Job 29.1-3, 15a; the only other occurrence of τυφλόω in the OG is at Tob 7.7). This possibility is strengthened significantly by the fact that both what has preceded and what is yet to follow bears much in common with the thematic concerns of the wisdom literature.

[52] See esp. Mark 3.5; 6.52; 8.17; Rom 11.7, 25; 2 Cor 3.14; Eph 4.18.

[53] Cf. Schnackenburg, Johannes 4, 149-50; Evans, "Isa 6:9-10," 68; Lieu, "Blindness," 86-88; contrast Menken, "Joh 12,40," 201.

[54] Contrast the significant v.l. πηρόω (supported by A ℵs al; appearing elsewhere in the OG only at 4 Macc 18.21; cf. Deut 28.28 Aq.). Thus, even if one concludes that ἐπήρωσεν is the preferred reading for John 12.40 (see above), the possibility that Job 17.7 was influential remains.

inserts πωρόω into his citation in place of a term foreign to the Johannine literature.[55]

In the case of John's placing of αὐτῶν before rather than after the substantives in both lines one and two, we have already noted that John has done this for the sake of the distinctive structure of his citation.[56] It remains to point out that a similar tendency regarding the placement of genitives of personal pronouns is evident elsewhere in John's Gospel.[57] Not only this, John's substitution (against both the MT and the OG) of "their heart" for "the heart of this people" also complements his use of the term λαός only in positive references to those for whom Jesus is about to die (cf. 11.50; 18.14).[58] Altogether, then, what we have noted in lines one and two of John 12.40 confirms that John is responsible for their form.[59]

As for line three, it has been suggested that ἵνα μή appears because it is less susceptible to misunderstanding than is the OG's μήποτε.[60] It may be, however, that John feels free to substitute this common synonym simply because it corre-

---

[55] Similarly, Freed, OT Quotations, 87-88; contrast Dodd, Scriptures, 37 n. 2. The OG's παχύνω appears in the NT only at Matt 13.15 and Acts 28.27.

[56] Similarly, Menken, "Joh 12,40," 195, 201.

[57] That John exhibits an unusual tendency to place genitives of personal pronouns before substantives (esp. with parts of the body) and their articles was noted long ago. See, e.g., Edwin A. Abbott, Johannine Grammar (London: A. & C. Black, 1906), nrs. 2558-69, 2776-84. Recently, however, Menken, "Joh 12,40," 201-2, has attempted to demonstrate this with a greater degree of precision. His study suggests persuasively that, among the Gospels and Acts, this unusual tendency is, in fact, evident in John's Gospel. Indeed, this is especially evident in the case of the two substantives appearing in John 12.40, ὀφθαλμός and καρδία (see esp. John 9.6, 10, 11, 14, 15, 17, 21, 26, 30; what we have already noted concerning the relationship between John 12.40 and John 9 is thus significantly facilitated).

[58] Cf. Schnackenburg, Johannes 4, 148 (cited by Menken, "Joh 12,40," 202, who rightly adds, "Dass er die 3. Person Pl. gebraucht, um auf die Ungläubigen hinzuweisen, ist nur logisch und besagt nichts über Abhängigkeit von einer Version"). Note also the resulting balanced meter of lines one and two.

[59] Similarly, Menken, "Joh 12,40," 202-3; cf. Blank, Krisis, 303-4.

[60] Menken, "Joh 12,40," 204, rightly points out that μήποτε, unlike ἵνα μή, is able to function as an interrogative particle. In this case, "könnte man die Jes-Stelle so verstehen, dass Gott (sic) ihre Augen geblendet und ihr Herz verstummelt hat, ob sie nicht vielleicht doch sehen mit den Augen und verstehen mit dem Herzen" (cf. Rabbi Johanan's similar understanding of this text discussed by Evans, "Rabbinic and Patristic Writings," 275-76).

sponds to what is characteristic of his style elsewhere.[61] In any case, the hand of John is again evident.[62]

As for line four, it is likely that John's νοήσωσιν recalls yet another analogous passage from Isaiah, Isa 44.18 OG.[63] Isa 44.18 OG is strikingly reminiscent of Isa 6.9-10: "They have no understanding to perceive; for they have been blinded so that they should not see with their eyes, nor perceive with their heart (τοῦ νοῆσαι τῇ καρδίᾳ αὐτῶν; contrast Isa 32.6; 47.7 OG).[64] And both John's citation and Isa 44.18 OG conspicuously share a construction in which the verb νοέω is paired with καρδία in the dative. John recalls Isa 44.18 OG[65] in order to liken the Jews to their idolatrous forbearers (cf. Isa 44.9-17; contrast John 19.15).[66]

And as for line five, it is likely that the simplified and synonymous expression στραφῶσιν[67] appears because it accords with John's preference elsewhere in his Gospel for *verba simplicia* (cf. 1.38; 20.14, 16).[68] Again, the hand of John is evident.

---

61 There is only one instance of μήποτε in John's Gospel, as an interrogative particle (7.26). Cf. Menken, "Joh 12,40," 204: "Zu ἵνα μή im besonderen kann man bemerken, dass es im JohEv 18X vorkommt, gegen 8X in MT, 6X in Mk, 9X in Lk und 3X in Apg."

62 Cf. Bernard, *St. John*, 450 (cited by Humann, "OT Quotations," 44 n. 47); Schlatter, *Der Evangelist*, 275 (cited by Bergmeier, *Glaube*, 267 n. 520); Freed, *OT Quotations*, 88; Menken, Joh "12,40," 204.

63 Both Hoskyns, *Fourth Gospel*, 429; and Bergmeier, *Glaube*, 231, refer to Isa 44.18 as a parallel passage in their attempts to explicate John 12,40. It is especially Menken, "Joh 12,40," 205-6, 208-9, however, who has asserted that νοέω in John 12,40 has actually come from this analogous context.

64 See also Isa 44.22: "Turn (ἐπιστρέφω) to me, and I will redeem you." We have already noted that the larger context of Isa 44 OG (see esp. vv. 2 and 6) is recalled elsewhere in John's Gospel (see my remarks in chapter six). Note also the verses that follow Isa 44.18 and also bear much in common with John's Gospel. In spite of the blindness of the Jews, the Lord who has created all things will come as redeemer (44.24) to blot out sin as darkness (44.22), to give glory (44.23), to build up, and to lay the foundation of a holy house (44.28).

65 The OG translates not בִּין but שׂכל hiph'il with νοέω (cf. Prov 1.3; 16.23). The probability that, independent of Isa 44.18 OG, John would both select the verb νοέω and order a translation of the construction מהשׂכיל לבתם ... שׂם (=Isa 44.18 MT) in a manner similar to the OG is not great (cf. Menken, "Joh 12,40," 205-6). The verb νοέω occurs only here in the Johannine literature. In this same body of literature, συνίημι (Isa 6.10 OG) is not to be found.

66 Similarly, Menken, "Joh 12,40," 206. It may also be that, again, John betrays his sapiential orientation (cf., e.g., OG Job 33.23; Prov 16.23).

67 The variant readings for John 12.40 in which forms of ἐπιστρέφω appear probably represent scribal assimilations to Isa 6.10 OG (Menken, "Joh 12,40," 206 n. 59).

68 Similarly, Schnackenburg, *St. John* 2, 415 (cf. idem, *Johannes* 4, 150); Menken, "Joh 12,40," 206, 208 (ἐπιστρέφω appears only in John 21.20). Again, there may also be a connection with wisdom. The verbs στρέφω and ἰάομαι appear together in OG Prov 12.7-8,

In summary, there is no concrete evidence for the influence of a Hebrew *Vorlage* on John's citation. Instead, John's two editorial references to analogous passages from Isa OG suggest that his citation of Isa 6.10 has also come from the OG.[69] The extent of John's editorial activity is striking. This activity, however, is consistent with his theological agenda[70] and with his exegetical procedure elsewhere in his Gospel.[71] This confirms that the form of this citation, therefore, is indeed John's own creation.[72] For John, the final rejection of Jesus by his own people was a fate anticipated by that of the many prophetic personalities that preceded him.[73]

III.

In conclusion, John's editorial reference to the prophet Isaiah in John 12.40 comes from Isa 6.10. What immediate evidence there is for the influence of a particular textual tradition is indicative of the OG (twice aspects of John's citation recall analogous contexts in Isa OG). For the first time in his Gospel, John feels free to substitute synonymous expressions for aspects of the passage he cites in order to adapt his citation to its eventual literary and theological context. John's citation of Isa 6.10 OG takes up and develops his as yet unexplained reference to Jesus' "report" in his citation of Isa 53.1 OG in John 12.38. The arm of the Lord (Isa 53.1) was rejected because Jesus' prophetic report (Isa 6.9; 53.1; cf. 52.7) provoked offense rather than faith and thus "blinded" the Jews (Isa 6.10).

18; 26.14, 18. Cf. the use of the latter in OG Job 5.18; 12.21; Eccl 3.3; Sir 38.9; Wis 16.11-12 (contrast ἐπιστρέφω in v. 7; βραχίων in v. 16).

[69] Keep in mind that the citation in John 12.38 which John 12.40 complements has also come from Isa OG.

[70] Esp. his portrayal of Jesus as the "light" (cf. Schnackenburg, *St. John* 2, 271; Beasley-Murray, *John*, 216).

[71] See my remarks in chapters one and six.

[72] Cf. Schnackenburg, *St. John* 2, 415; Menken, "Joh 12,40," 208-9. There is, therefore, no need to see more than one hand at work in John 12.37-41. See the dissenting viewpoints of Faure, "Zitate," 103-4; Bultmann, *John*, 452 n. 2; Becker, *Johannes*, 409; contrast Lindars, *John*, 437-38.

[73] Cf. Bruce, *John*, 271-72: "the unreceptive hearing which Isaiah was promised was not exhausted in the circumstances of his personal ministry; it was experienced by one prophet after another and found its definitive fulfillment in the unreceptive hearing given to him of whom the prophets spoke." See also Brown, *John* 1, 484; Schnackenburg, *St. John* 2, 274; Longenecker, *Exegesis*, 156; Becker, *Johannes*, 409; Beasley-Murray, *John*, 215.

Chapter 9

THE BETRAYAL

At the conclusion of the Fourth Gospel's unparalleled account of Jesus' washing of his disciples" feet (John 13.1-20), Jesus speaks of his impending betrayal by Judas (contrast 13.2, 10b-11, 21-30). Jesus promises his disciples that they will be "blessed" (13.17). But Jesus adds immediately that he is not now addressing all of his disciples. Utilizing a formula now well-established in the emerging climax of John's Gospel (but absent elsewhere in the New Testament),[1] Jesus says, "I am not speaking of you all; I know whom I have chosen; but (Judas was chosen)[2] in order that the Scripture may be fulfilled:

ὁ τρώγων μου τὸν ἄρτον ἐπῆρεν ἐπ᾽ ἐμὲ τὴν πρέρναν αὐτοῦ" (13.18).

In the Synoptics, Jesus makes similar predictions on the night before his crucifixion (cf. Matt 26.20-25; Mark 14.17-21; Luke 22.21-23). Mark 14.18 even seems to allude to the same Old Testament passage cited here by Jesus (cf. John 6.45; 7.37-38; 8.17; 10.34; 15.25; 19.28).[3] But John's unique portrayal of

---

[1] See my remarks in chapter seven.

[2] The ellipsis ἀλλ᾽ ἵνα is characteristic both of rabbinic usage and of John (see, e.g., Bultmann, *John*, 48-49 n. 3; 477-78 n. 9; Noack, *Tradition*, 23-24; cf. BDF 448.7). Contrast John 1.8, 31; 9.3; 14.31; 15.25; 1 John 2.19. Jesus speaks of those he has "chosen" to be "the twelve" (6.70).

[3] On the rabbinic understanding of this passage, see Str-B 2:558-59 (cf. Schlatter, *Der Evangelist*, 285). The possibility that John was influenced by the rabbis or by a reading of this passage similar to what one observes at Qumran (see 1QH 5.23-24; cf. 5.35) is discussed below.

this evening (13.30) and of Judas suggests that his composition is independent of what one observes in the Synoptics.[4]

Why, then, does this citation appear here in John's Gospel? And how does the form of the Old Testament citation appearing in John 13.18 participate in John's portrait of Judas?

I.

The Old Testament passage cited in John 13.18 is Ps 41(40).10. But the textual tradition represented in this citation is not immediately evident. Scholars' attempts to identify this tradition have been hampered by evidence which does not seem to point in any one direction. On the one hand, several features of John's citation go against the OG and appear to indicate that John translates a Hebrew *Vorlage*: (1) τρώγων rather than the OG's ἐσθίων; (2) the singular "bread" rather than the OG's "breads;" (3) the placing of μου before rather than after ἄρτον as in the OG;[5] and (4) πτέρναν rather than the OG's πτερνισμόν.[6]

---

[4] For Freed, *OT Quotations*, 92, 123, John cites the OT to supplement the Synoptics. On the independence of John 13.1-30 from the Synoptics, see the recent contribution of Green, *Death*, 111-25. See also Dodd, *Historical Tradition*, 36-37; Brown, *John* 2, 571; Max Wilcox, "The Composition of John 13.21-30," in *Neotestamentica et Semitica: Studies in Honour of Matthew Black*, eds. E. Earle Ellis and Max Wilcox (Edinburg: T. & T. Clark, 1969), 144-45, 155-56 (who argues that John's supper sequence bears more in common with the eucharistic tradition cited by Paul in 1 Cor 11): Reim, *Studien*, 41; Schnackenburg, *St. John* 3, 26; Moo, *Passion Narratives*, 237, 240; de Waard, *Comparative Study*, 66; Menken, "John 13.18," 64-65.

[5] John's citation would be even more distant from the OG if one read μετ᾽ ἐμοῦ (Ƥ66 ℵ A D W Θ Ψ f[1.13] Maj lat sy bo; Eus Epiph) rather than μου (B C L 892 pc (q) sa; Or). For de Waard, *Comparative Study*, 66-67, the presence of the former reading in John's citation and in the fourth century OG papyri 2013 and 2050 suggests the influence of a common Hebrew *Vorlage* similar to 1QH 5.23-24, where עלי follows לחמי (acknowledged as a possibility by Moo, *Passion Narratives*, 237; cf. Longenecker, *Exegesis*, 137 n. 6). But de Waard too easily dismisses the possibility that Mark 14.18 (ὁ ἐσθίων μετ᾽ ἐμοῦ) has influenced both these OG papyri (Menken, "John 13.18," 74 n. 7) and the variant reading in John 13.18 (so Bruce M. Metzger, *A Textual Commentary on the Greek New Testament* [London: United Bible Societies, 1971], 240, together with many commentators). Also, "Apart from the translational problem, de Waard overlooks that 1QH 5.23-24 is not a quotation, but a free paraphrase (as also the change of the subject from singular to plural indicates)" (Menken, "John 13.18," 74 n. 7). The reading μετ᾽ ἐμοῦ, then, probably represents an editorial adjustment of the citation to the situation of the supper scene (Menken, "John 13.18," 61). It has been suggested that μου represents instead a learned correction from the OG (Goodwin, "Sources," 66; Freed, *OT Quotations*, 91 [possible]; Barrett, *St. John*, 444). In this case, however, one would expect μου to appear behind τὸν ἄρτον, as it does in the OG (Menken, "John 13.18," 61; contrast Humann, "OT Quotations," 39 n. 25). See further below.

[6] The substantive πτέρνα never appears in the OG as a translation of a Hebrew term other than עקב.

But on the other hand, John's citation seems entirely independent (1) when ἐπῆρεν appears rather than the Hebrew הִגְדִּיל (=MT)[7] or the OG's ἐμεγάλυνεν[8] and (2) when John supplies the otherwise absent possessive αὐτοῦ.

Overall, scholars have held that a Hebrew *Vorlage* represents at least a more probable source for John's citation than the OG.[9] For some, John deviates from the Hebrew only where the OG renders it literally. This is done in order to offer an improved rendering for the Greek reader.[10] Others have preferred to see John's citations as a "free adaptation, perhaps from memory."[11] Still others, however, have questioned the citation's Johannine authorship, preferring instead to attribute its form either to a non-OG translator of the psalm[12] or to an early Christian tradition inherited by John.[13] Few, however, have seriously considered the possibility that the OG was somehow influential.[14]

Initially, much of the evidence certainly seems to suggest that this citation represents a rendering of a Hebrew version of the psalm passage.[15] Still, the difference between the Hebrew "bread" and OG "breads" should not be afforded

---

[7] Neither in the OG nor in any of the other extant Greek translations of the OT does ἐπαίρω (or the simplex or a compound form) appear as a translation of a form of גדל. "Ἐπῆρεν is apparently not simply an alternative rendering of *higdîl*" (Menken, "John 13.18," 67).

[8] The verb μεγαλύνω appears frequently in the OG as the preferred translation of גדל hiph'il.

[9] Cf. Westcott, *St. John*, xiv, 193; Burney, *Aramaic Origin*, 121; Bernard, *St. John*, 467; Schlatter, *Der Evangelist*, 285; O'Rourke, "OT Citations," 57; Braun, *Jean* 2, 13, 20; de Waard, *Comparative Study*, 65-67; Freed, *OT Quotations*, 89, 91, 123, 126; Wilcox, "John 13:21-30," 145, 155; Brown, *John* 2, 571; Morris, *John*, 622 n. 42; Reim, *Studien*, 40, 90, 220; Schnackenburg, *St. John* 3, 26; Barrett, *St. John*, 444; Hanson, *Utterances*, 130; Moo, *Passion Narratives*, 237, 354, 368 n. 2; Becker, *Johannes*, 430; Kysar, *John*, 212; Green, *Death*, 121; Humann, "OT Quotations," 39-40; Menken, "John 13.18." For Franke, *Alte Testament*, 285; Bultmann, *John*, 478 nn. 1-2; and Stendahl, *St. Matthew*, 163, it is sufficient to indicate that the OG was not John's source.

[10] Schnackenburg, *St. John* 3, 28; cf. Barrett, *St. John*, 444; de Waard, *Comparative Study*, 66. See further below.

[11] Freed, *OT Quotations*, 92.

[12] Dodd, *Historical Tradition*, 37 (a possibility); cf. Wilcox, "John 13.21-30," 145-46.

[13] Cf. Noack, *Tradition*, 78; Lindars, *NT Apologetic*, 98. 267 (cf. idem, *John*, 454); Dodd, *Historical Tradition*, 37.

[14] A notable exception is Goodwin, "Sources," 66, who finds that "Though John's wording differs from the LXX, it is not closer to the Hebrew, and it is closer to his own style" (contrast Archer/Chirichigno, *OT Quotations*, xxvi-xxvii). In favor of the OG as John's source are Toy, *Quotations*, 89; Longenecker, *Exegesis*, 73; Francis J. Moloney, "The Structure and Message of John 13:1-38," *AusBR* 34 (1986): 7.

[15] The various recensions of the OG bear little in common with John 13.18 (Menken, "John 13.18," 62). Cf. Aquila and Theodotion: κατεμεγαλύνθη μου πτέρνᾳ; Symmachus: συνεσθίων μοι ἄρτον ἐμὸν κατεμεγαλύνθη μου ἀκολουθῶν.

great significance. The plural of לחם does not occur in the Hebrew. The OG frequently translates the singular with ἄρτοι. [16] And yet to be explained are those aspects of this citation which appear entirely independent of both the Greek and Hebrew textual traditions.

A satisfactory resolution to the overall problem of this citation, then, must first establish that John indeed plays a role in citing the psalm. And then this role must be characterized.

II.

Over the years, scholars have contested not only John's authorship of the citation appearing in John 13.18 but also his authorship of the entire footwashing scene.[17] One of the chief arguments against John's authorship of this entire scene has been that a two-fold interpretation of Jesus' washing of his disciples' feet is evident in it (cf. vv. 6-10 with vv. 12-17). Each interpretation, it is argued, is independent of the other. Each seems to contradict the other (cf. vv. 7 and 12). And each concludes with a reference to Judas (cf. vv. 10b-11 and 18-20). Hence, vv. 6-11 and vv. 12-20 are frequently attributed to different literary strata. The former is generally regarded as the work of John, the latter the work of a redactor.

Two principal observation, however, militate against viewing these verses in this way. First, virtually every verse of John 13 manifests features characteristic of Johannine style.[18] And second, there is no need to regard vv. 12-20 as incompatible with the preceding interpretation of Jesus' washing of his disciples' feet. The scene in John 13 begins with Jesus' act of love which anticipates his death on the cross. Jesus asserts thereby that those who participate in him will be made clean through his death.[19] To participate in him means also, he adds, that they will follow his example (vv. 12-17).[20] Unfortunately, Jesus' disciples understand

---

[16] See de Waard, *Comparative Study*, 66; and Menken, "John 13.18," 74 n. 8, who points to Gen 14.18 and 21.14 as examples of this.

[17] Scholars' latest efforts to address this issue are aptly described and evaluated by Menken, "John 13.18," 63-64. What follows closely parallels his judgments.

[18] Menken, "John 13.18," 64, correctly identifies several features characteristic of John in John 13.18 (without referring to the citation itself): λεγεῖν περί, οἶδα, elliptical ἀλλ' ἵνα, γραφή in the singular, and ἵνα ἡ γραφὴ πληρωθῇ.

[19] Similarly, many recent commentators. John's construction of v. 4 in particular suggests that the footwashing is to be understood as an act anticipating Jesus' death. The verbs τίθημι and λαμβάνω in v. 4 are the same verbs used in John 10.17-18 to describe Jesus' act of "laying down" his life so that he might "take it" again (cf. 10.11, 15; 13.37, 38; 15.13; 1 John 3.16).

[20] On the nature of this example, see esp. John A. T. Robinson, "The Significance of the Footwashing," in *Neotestamentica et Patristica: Eine Freundesgabe, Herrn Professor Dr. Oscar*

none of this till later (vv. 7 and 12). And regrettably, not all of them are clean or will be made clean by what Jesus is about to do (vv. 10b-11); not all of them will follow Jesus' example (vv. 18-20). Vv. 12-17, therefore, meaningfully complement the preceding interpretation of the footwashing.[21] Vv. 18-20 reaffirm the tragic irony of Judas' impending betrayal. In vv. 21-30, then, the identity of Jesus' betrayer is revealed to Jesus' disciples and Judas departs in order to betray Jesus. The sequence is coherent and distinctly Johannine. There is, therefore, no reason to doubt John's authorship of John 13.18.

Thus, in the midst of John's portrayal of Jesus' final moments with his disciples prior to his crucifixion, John offers a carefully nuanced portrait of Judas as well. The thing to observe is that John's Judas is subtly distinct from the Judas one meets elsewhere in the New Testament.[22] For John, Judas' identity is known "from the beginning" (6.64). Judas is the representative defector, the symbol of apostasy, *the disciple* who then turns and betrays Jesus (6.64, 70-71; 12.4). Appropriately, Judas appears later in a context of mass defection. Like the other disciples, Judas was given to Jesus by the Father (6.37-39). But unlike the others, Judas does not repent of his defection (17.12). Jesus and the Father abide with the faithful (14.20,23), but Satan abides with Judas. Judas is the instrument of

---

Cullmann zu seinem 60. Geburtstag überreicht, ed. W. C. van Unnik, Supplements to Novum Testamentum, vol. 6 (Leiden: E. J. Brill, 1962), 144-47; Herold Weiss, "Footwashing in the Johannine Community," *NovT* 21 (1979): 298-325. Jesus' act is no mere lesson on the meaning of the Christian sacraments. Robinson (pp. 144-45) writes, "if there is any sacramental reference, the 'bathing' is to be seen as the act of universal baptism that Jesus is about to accomplish in his death, which in turn is to be the ground of the Church's sacramental action (the 'washing') and will make it sufficient for salvation." Jesus' act is also no mere lesson in humility. To see it as purely exemplary is to overlook its deepest significance. The key lies instead in recognizing these verses as the Johannine equivalent of Mark 10.32-45. If Jesus' disciples are to have any part in him, it can only be as they drink the cup he drinks and are baptized with his baptism (cf. 13.35-37; contrast the εἰς τέλος of 13.1 with the τετέλεσται of 19.30). The washing of the disciples' feet, then, is analogous to Mary's anointing of Jesus' feet in John 12.1-8 (the only two supper scenes in John's Gospel). Jesus' disciples will, like Jesus, love Jesus' sheep and feed them in dying for them (cf. 15.13; 15.18-16.4a; contrast 21.15-19; see the informative treatment of these texts by William C. Weinrich, *Spirit and Martyrdom: A Study of the Work of the Holy Spirit in Contexts of Persecution and Martyrdom in the New Testament and Early Christian Literature* [Washington, D.C.: University Press, 1981], 25-31, 86-89, esp. 88-89 n. 50; see also 1 John 3.16).

[21] Menken, "John 13.18," 64, points out that the same combination of christological/ soteriological and paraenetic interpretations of the cross appears elsewhere in the New Testament (see, e.g., 1 John 4.9-11; Mark 8.31-38 parr.; 9.31-37//Luke 9.44-48; Mark 10.41-45//Matt 20.25-28; Eph 5.1-2, 25-27; 1 Pet 3.17-18).

[22] For the following description of the figure of Judas in John's Gospel, see Culpepper, *Anatomy,* 124-25; cf. Wendy E. Sproston, "'The Scripture' in John 17:12," in *Scripture: Meaning and Method. Essays Presented to Anthony Tyrrell Hanson for His Seventieth Birthday,* ed. Barry P. Thompson (Hull: Hull University Press, 1987). 24-36, esp. 26.

the devil (13.27). Judas is one of the devil's children (cf. 8.44). Indeed, Judas is himself a devil (6.70).

It is appropriate now to turn to the citation appearing in John 13.18. How does this citation participate in John's portrait of Judas? How is the hand of John evident in its form?

Initially, the opening phrase in John's citation of Ps 41(40).10 (ὁ τρώγων μου τὸν ἄρτον) seems a likely translation of the Hebrew phrase אוכל לחמי (=MT). The OG ὁ ἐσθίων ἄρτους μου differs in almost every respect. But a careful examination of the role John has played in the forming of this citation calls into question whether the influence of a Hebrew *Vorlage* is so evident.

First, we have already noted that the use of τρώγω in the Fourth Gospel is typical of John's style.[23] John consistently uses τρώγω (6.54, 56, 57, 58; 13.18) as the present tense suppletive to the aorist φάγομαι.[24] The two verbs τρώγω and φάγομαι, then, are for John equivalent in meaning (this is especially evident in the antithetic parallelism of John 6.53-54).[25] How is this significant? John's preference for τρώγω rather than ἐσθίω suggests an alternative to regarding τρώγων in John 13.18 as John's translation of the Hebrew אכל. Equally plausible is the possibility that John substituted the (for him preferable) synonym τρώγων for the OG's ἐσθίων.[26]

Second, the position of the pronoun μου before rather than after τὸν ἄρτον can similarly be explained in terms of John's stylistic preferences. We have already noted also that John exhibits a perceptible tendency elsewhere in his Gospel to place the genitives of personal pronouns before substantives and their articles.[27] As was the case in John 12.38, then, the position of the personal pronoun does not militate against a possible reference to the OG.

---

[23] See my remarks in chapter three (John's authorship of John 6.52-59 is also discussed in chapter three). See also Humann, "OT Quotations," 40; Menken, "John 13.18," 65.

[24] Cf. 4.31, 32, 33; 6.5, 23, 26, 31, 49, 50, 51, 52, 53, 58; 18.28. Contrast βέβρωκα in 6.13.

[25] Menken, "John 13.18," 65. Ceslaus Spicq, "Τρώγειν: Est-il synonyme de φαγεῖν et d'ἐσθίειν dans le Nouveau Testament?" *NTS* 26 (1979/1980): 414-19, and others have attempted without success to show that these verbs are not synonymous (cf. Matt 24.38 and Luke 17.27). Τρώγω appears frequently in the everyday speech of John's time as an acceptable equivalent for ἐσθίω. See LSJ 1832; cf. Freed, *OT Quotations*, 91; Schnackenburg, *St. John 3*, 26; Burge, *Community*, 182-83; Humann, "OT Quotations," 40.

[26] See esp. Moloney, "John 13:1-38," 7; cf. Longenecker, *Exegesis*, 73. John is not thereby recalling some additional analogous passage from the OG (where τρώγω never appears). Instead, he feels free to simply substitute this synonym. He does, however, have more in mind than merely maintaining a consistent style (see further below).

[27] See my remarks in chapter eight. Cf. Goodwin, "Sources," 66; Menken, "John 13.18," 65-66.

Finally, even the form of the substantive τὸν ἄρτον does not rule out the possibility that John cites the OG.[28] Indeed, it is not unlikely that John substitutes τὸν ἄρτον for the OG's ἄρτους in order to recall an analogous Old Testament passage which has already served as a source for an earlier citation in his Gospel, Ps 77.24 OG (John 6.31: ἄρτον . . . ἔδωκεν αὐτοῖς φαγεῖν). Why recall this passage? Because John wishes to recall the issues he raised in John 6 (see esp. John 6.58: ὁ τρώγων τοῦτον τὸν ἄρτον).[29] In an effort to elaborate on his portrait of Judas, John recalls an earlier context in his Gospel in which Judas was spoken of for the first time (6.64, 70-71).[30] In John 6, to eat the true bread which is Jesus himself means to believe in Jesus.[31] John, then, asserts in John 13.18 not that Judas participated in the supper on the night before Jesus' death,[32] but that Judas at one time believed.[33] Thus, John highlights the tragedy of Judas' apostasy. Against the background of John 6, John 13.18 refers to Judas as one who formerly believed. But now Judas only outwardly belongs to Jesus' disciples.[34]

Ps 40.10 OG thus far represents an entirely possible referent of John 13.18. A careful examination of John's role in shaping the rest of this citation lends even greater credibility to this possibility.

We have already noted that John's ἐπῆρεν seems to represent a departure from the Old Testament passage he cites. In order to grasp why John feels free to

---

[28] Symmachus, like John, reads ἄρτον (similarly, Tertullian and the Psalterium of Hieronymus), but differs otherwise.

[29] Many scholars see in John's use of the present tense substantival participle ὁ τρώγων in John 13.18 a connection with the same use in John 6.54, 56, 57, and 58 (the only two places where John uses this verb; see, e.g., Bernard, St. John, 468; Reim, Studien, 40-41; Wilcox, "John 13:21-30," 145-46; otherwise Schnackenburg, St. John 3, 26). But few scholars note that the entire opening phrase in John 13.18 recalls these passages in John 6 (see, however, Borgen, Bread, 93; Menken, "John 13.18," 72). Indeed, the form of the opening phrase in John 13.18 is exceedingly reminiscent not only of John 6.58 but also of the equivalent expressions ὁ τρώγων μου τὴν σάρκα and ὁ πίνων μου τὸ αἷμα appearing in John 6.54 and 56!

[30] Cf. Menken, "John 13.18," 72.

[31] See my remarks in chapters three and four.

[32] Judas, it seems, does participate in this supper, but John makes no specific reference to Judas' having actually eaten (see esp. 13.26-27).

[33] Noteworthy is the irony of John's reference to Judas' eating in the context of a supper scene in which Judas later leaves in order to betray Jesus. Note also that whenever John refers to Jesus as the eschatological bread, he refers to him as the bread (τὸν ἄρτον; see 6.32, 33, 34, 35, 41, 48, 50, 51, 58; cf. 13.18; contrast the anarthrous ἄρτον in 6.31 [the OT manna was not the true bread]). In connection with this, it is perhaps significant also that the absence in John 13 of any reference to the institution of the Eucharist avoids leaving the reader with the impression that John's references to Jesus as the eschatological bread are to be taken as references to the Eucharist (cf. my remarks at the conclusion of chapter three).

[34] Menken, "John 13.18," 72.

alter the form of the passage he cites one must first note that Ps 41(40).10 and 56(55).13-15 were interpreted in rabbinic literature as references to the figure of Ahithophel.[35] Ahithophel was the counselor of David (2 Sam 15.12) who betrayed his king and conspired with Absalom to destroy David (15.31). But when Ahithophel's plan for destroying David was not followed, he hanged himself (16.20-17.23).

It is easy to see why exegetes in the first century might interpret Ps 41(40).10 in terms of the figure of Ahithophel.[36] Indeed, there is ample evidence to suggest that both in John's Gospel and elsewhere in the New Testament the portrait of the betrayal of Jesus by Judas has been influenced by the Old Testament portrait of Ahithophel's betrayal of David.[37] First, there is of course in both portraits the same general description of a royal figure who is betrayed by his confidant. But there are also numerous additional shared details: (1) Knowing that Ahithophel means to betray him, David retreats across the brook Kidron (2 Sam 15.23); John's passion account also begins with Jesus crossing the Kidron (John 18.1). (2) On the Mount of Olives, David agonizes over his fate and calls on God for help (2 Sam 15.30-31); on the same mount, Jesus also agonizes over what is about to come and prays to his Father (Mark 14.32-42; Luke 22.39-46; cf. John 18.1b; contrast 17.1-26). (3) Ahithophel plans to come by night and take David by surprise so that David's men will flee and David will be killed (2 Sam 17.1-4); Judas comes by night to seize Jesus, causes the disciples to flee, and thus sets into motion the events that will lead to Jesus' death (Matt 26.47-56; Mark 14.43-52; Luke 22.47-53; John 18.2-12). (4) In the midst of Ahithophel's betrayal, it is asserted that the death of David will bring peace to the nation (2 Sam 17.3); in the midst of Judas' betrayal, it is asserted that the death of Jesus will prevent the nation from perishing (John 18.14; cf. 11.50). (5) Both Ahithophel and Judas hang themselves in despair (cf. 2 Sam 17.23 and Matt 27.3-10).[38] Thus, Judas was compared with Ahithophel very early on. And

---

35 Menken, "John 13.18," 69. See the references to Ps 41.10 in *b. Sanh.* 106b; Ps 55.13-15 in *b. Sanh.* 106b; *Tg.* Ps 55, *Num. Rab.* 18.17; *Midr. Teh.*, and *m. 'Abot* 6.3 (see also *Tg.* Ps 140.10). My development of this point closely parallels that of Menken. We differ, however, on how this finally plays a role in John's citation of the psalm (see further below).

36 Menken, "John 13.18," 69, concludes that "In view of the pre-Christian tendency to connect psalms with David's biography and the later explicit 'Ahithophelian' interpretations of parts of Psalms 41 and 55, it is only reasonable to suppose that such an interpretation of Ps. 41.10 was usual at the time the fourth evangelist wrote his gospel. In this interpretation, Psalm 41 and the stories about Ahithophel in 2 Samuel become cognate passages from Scripture."

37 See Menken, "John 13.18," 70-71 (for additional references to the secondary literature, see n. 47).

38 Cf. esp. 2 Sam 17.23 OG (ἀπῆλθεν . . . καὶ ἀπήγξατο) with Matt 27.5 (καὶ ἀπελθὼν ἀπήγξατο). Apart from certain OT battle scenes, Ahithophel's suicide is without parallel in the OT; Judas is the only NT figure who takes his own life.

John's Gospel also reflects this tradition.[39] The possibility, then, that John also had in mind the figure of Ahithophel in 2 Sam when he cited Ps 41(40).10 is worthy of some consideration.

Now the thing to note is that there is in the story about Ahithophel in 2 Samuel a passage analogous to Ps 41(40).10. This passage is 2 Sam 18.28. Following the death of Absalom, Ahimaaz runs to tell David the news of Absalom's defeat (2 Sam 18.19-27). In 2 Sam 18.28, Ahimaaz greets David with the cry "Peace!" He then bows before his king with his face to the ground and declares, "Blessed be the Lord your God, who has delivered up the men (i.e., Absalom and those who followed him, including Ahithophel) who lifted their hand against my lord the king."[40]

2 Sam 18.28 is analogous to Ps 41(40).10 not only because the two passages and their immediate contexts share aspects of their general contents but also because they share specific terminology. For example, in both passages one encounters similar references to "peace" (MT: שָׁלוֹם; OG: εἰρήνη).[41] In both passages, the rebels are referred to as "men" (MT: אִישׁ; 2 Sam 18.28 OG: ἀνήρ; Ps 40.10: ἄνθρωπος). The blessings appearing in 2 Sam 18.28 and Ps 41(40).14 are also very similar. And in 2 Sam 18.32 and Ps 41(40).6, there are parallel references to "enemies" (אֹיֵב; ἐχθρός) who seek "evil" against the king (רָעָה; κακός).

It is, therefore, conceivable that because John regarded these two passages as analogous, he replaced "has made great" in his citation of the psalm with "lifted" from 2 Sam 18.28. But if this is the case, then it is not the OG that has influenced John. The OG reads τοὺς ἄνδρας τοὺς μισοῦντας τὴν χεῖρα αὐτῶν ἐν τῷ κυρίῳ μου τῷ βασιλεῖ. The OG translator apparently translates שׂנאו rather than נשׂאו. The variant readings ἐπαραμένους and ἀντάραντας represent attempts to correct the OG on the basis of the Hebrew נשׂאו. The appearance of ἐπῆρεν in John's citation of the psalm, then, represents a possible indication that John is recalling either a Hebrew version of 2 Sam 18.28 or a corrected Greek translation of this passage.[42]

There is, however, another possible solution to this problem. The story of Ahithophel's collaboration with Absalom is followed in 2 Sam by an additional account relating a second instance of rebellion against David. In 2 Sam 20.1-26,

---

39 It is once again conspicuous, however, that while John recalls an OT context from the biography of David, the figure of David remains in the background of John's Christology (cf. my remarks in chapters four and six).

40 The translation is based on the MT. See further below.

41 See also 2 Sam 19.24(25), 30(31).

42 This is the conclusion of Menken, "John 13.18," 70, 73. Cf. also John 4.35; 6.5; 17.1 with 2 Sam 18.24.

the Benjaminite Sheba also instigates a revolt against his king. The two juxta-posed accounts, therefore, share obvious immediate aspects of their general contents. That the revolt of Sheba is, in fact, to be understood in terms parallel to that of Ahithophel and Absalom is confirmed by two additional observations. First, 2 Sam 20.6 explicitly compares the significance of the two revolts. And second, 2 Sam 20.21 describes Sheba's betrayal of his king in terms analogous to 2 Sam 18.28 (Sheba is "a man" who "has lifted his hand against king David").[43]

These observations suggest that John may have felt justified in turning from 2 Sam 18.28 and in drawing on 2 Sam 20.21 in his citation of Ps 41(40).10. A comparison of 2 Sam 20.21 with John 13.18 lends further support to this pos-sibility. The influence of 2 Sam 20.21 explains not only the substitution of "lifted" (נשא; ἐπῆρε) for "made great" in John's citation of the psalm[44] but also the addition of the seemingly superfluous possessive "his" to the direct object "heel" (cf. ידו; τὴν χεῖρα αὐτοῦ).[45]

Nothing yet rules out the possibility that John refers to the OG. Indeed, the preceding discussion of μου and of John's predilection for placing the genitives of personal pronouns before substantives and their articles suggests that the influence of 2 Sam 20.21 OG is in fact evident in John's τὴν πτέρναν αὐτοῦ.[46]

This inference, in turn, leads one to suspect finally that πτέρναν need not represent John's translation of the Hebrew עקב. One suspects that John may be recalling yet another analogous passage in his citation of the psalm by substitut-ing πτέρναν for the OG's πτερνισμὸν. The expression "his heel" occurs only once in the OG, at Gen 3.15.[47] However, it may be only that John substitutes an acceptable equivalent because he wishes to avoid the use of the OG's πτερνισμόν.[48] The OG can be interpreted to mean that the betrayed was

---

[43] This is particularly evident in the MT. The idiom which appears in 2 Sam 20.21 MT (נשא ידו במלך) appears elsewhere in the MT only at 2 Sam 18.28.

[44] For Schnackenburg, St. John 3, 26, ἐπῆρεν may have been selected in order to convey the idea that Judas' action "was blasphemous or scornful with respect to God" (cf. Sir 48.18; Ps 37[36].35; 75[74].5). This too is possible (similarly, Menken, "John 13:18," 78 n. 46). Indeed, it may be that John again utilizes language indicative of his sapiential orientation (see esp. Prov 24.17 OG [contrast υἱὸς ἀπωλείας in 24.22 with John 17.12]; cf. 3.5; 19.18; 30.13; Sir 6.2; 11.4; 32.1; contrast 48.18 with 2 Sam 20.21!). A reference of this sort, however, would not account for why John alters the passage he cites.

[45] Menken's attempt ("John 13:18," 67, 70, 73) to show that the addition of "his" to "heel" has come from "their hand" in 2 Sam 18.28 does not convince.

[46] Menken, "John 13:18," 70, 73, suggests the possible influence of the Hebrew ידם in 2 Sam 18.28, yet makes no attempt to explain why John does not then render this αὐτοῦ τὴν πτέρναν.

[47] Cf. Roth, "Coding," 20 (otherwise, Brown, John 2, 554).

[48] Cf. Menken, "John 13:18," 66-67, 72-73.

"beguiled" by his betrayer.[49] For John, however, the idea that Judas beguiled Jesus cannot be reconciled with the Johannine portrait of Jesus' omniscience (see esp. John 13; cf. 6.64, 70-71; contrast 1.47-48; 2.24-25; 4.17-18; 5.6; 6.61; 18.4; 19.28). According to John, Jesus knew beforehand what Judas would do and embraced it because Jesus saw in it the fulfillment of Scripture.[50]

In summary, the evidence confirms that it is, in fact, John himself who has carefully shaped the form of this citation.[51] The evidence also suggests that John's citation is not his translation of a Hebrew version of Ps 41.10. Rather, John's possible reference in his citation to 2 Sam 20.21 OG suggests that the rest of his citation has also come from the OG. To what extent John means to recall the larger context of the psalm is uncertain.[52]

III.

In conclusion, Jesus' reference to the Old Testament in John 13.18 is a reference to Ps 41(40).10. What evidence there is for the influence of a specific textual tradition points in the direction of the OG. John feels free to substitute synonyms and draws on analogous contexts in order to adapt this citation to its present literary and theological context. John's citation serves to amplify his portrait of Judas as representative defector and instrument of the devil.

---

[49] Cf. the OG's rendering of the verb עקב in Gen 27.36, Jer 9.3, and Hos 12.4 with πτερνίζειν. Contrast the OG's rendering of the substantive עקבה in 2 Kgs 10.19 with πτερνισμός A similar understanding of this passage from the psalm appears in its Targum ("made himself great against me with wisdom") and in the Peshitta ("employed much deceit against me").

[50] Eric F. F. Bishop, "'He That Eateth Bread with Me Hath Lifted Up His Heel against Me.'–Jn xiii.18 (Ps xli.9)," *ExpTim* 70 (1958/1959): 331-33, points out that the lifting of the heel among today's Palestinian Arabs is an expression of contempt.

[51] Cf. Menken, "John 13.18," 73. Those who suggest that John edits the passage he cites in order to make it more "readable" to the Greek reader (Schnackenburg, *St. John* 3, 26; cf. Moo, *Passion Narratives*, 236 n. 7; Archer/Chirichigno, *OT Quotations*, xxii, 69) fail to adequately reckon with the role this citation plays in its present literary and theological context.

[52] According to Toy, *Quotations*, 89; Hoskyns, *Fourth Gospel*, 441; and Menken, "John 13.18," 73, the first clause of v. 10 is omitted by John in order to avoid the suggestion that Jesus trusted Judas (cf. John 2.24-25; 6.70-71). According to Brown, *John* 2, 571; and Menken, "John 13.18," 65, vv. 9 and 11 may have been read by John with reference to Jesus' resurrection (cf. John 13.19). For Bruce, *John*, 287, John does not recall v. 11 because it is inappropriate to the present occasion. Freed, *OT Quotations*, 91, on the other hand notes the compatibility of the context of the psalm and the Johannine context. Cf. also μακάριος/μακαριόω in vv. 2-3 and John 13.17.

Chapter 10

A SERVANT IS NOT GREATER
THAN HIS MASTER

The contents of Jesus' remarks in John 15.18-16.4a are reminiscent of similar remarks in the Synoptics (cf. Matt 10.17, 22; 24.9-12; Mark 13.9-13; Luke 10.16; 12.51-53; 21.12-19). The setting of John 15.18-16.4a, however, is distinctive.[1] In these verses, Jesus warns his disciples that the world will hate

---

[1] Scholars have frequently questioned whether John 15-17 appeared in John's original composition. One of the chief problems has been John 14.31. John 14.31 seems to indicate a change of scene rather than a formal pause in the dialogue, yet no change of scene takes place in the narrative until John 18.1. Scholars have therefore asserted that John 18.1 originally followed John 14.31 and have suggested a number of different explanations for the present form of the Fourth Gospel. Some scholars have attributed the present form of the Fourth Gospel to a sheer accident, i.e., the original sheets of the manuscript suffered a subsequent inadvertent disarrangement. Arguments of this type, however, have not been favorably received. The primary alternative arguments are these: (1) It was John himself who arranged his Gospel in this fashion using already existing materials at his disposal. (2) A later editor supplemented an original farewell discourse consisting of chapters 13-14 with chapters 15-17. The latter argument is the conclusion of most contemporary scholars. As for John 15.18-16.4a, several features are frequently held to be indicative of a later hand: (1) The reference in these verses to persecution seems to assume a situation different from that addressed elsewhere by John. (2) John 15.20 recalls John 13.16, but seems to use the saying in the service of a different agenda. (3) The quotation formula in John 15.25 is distinctive both in terms of its length and in terms of its form. I have certain reservations about many of these arguments. For the purposes of the present investigation, however, it suffices merely to note some of the problems. A detailed examination of these arguments is not warranted because John 15.25 (we shall see) provides no information pertinent to the concerns of the present investigation.

them (cf. 17.14).[2] But this is to be expected because the world has hated Jesus first (15.18; cf. 3.20; 7.7). Because Jesus' disciples belong to Jesus and not to the world, the world will hate them as it has hated Jesus (15.19-20).

The world has hated Jesus because it does not know the Father who sent Jesus (15.21). This hatred, therefore, is directed against the Father as well (15.23-24). But this too was to be expected. The antipathy of Jesus' enemies represents the fulfillment of Old Testament prophecy:[3] "(this has come to pass) to fulfill the word that is written in their Law,

ἐμίσησάν με δωρεάν" (15.25).

The Old Testament passage cited is not referred to elsewhere in the New Testament.[4] The formula used to introduce this citation is also uncommon. We have already seen that the ellipsis ἀλλ' ἵνα[5] and references to "fulfillment,"[6] to the "word,"[7] and "their Law"[8] are typical of John's formulas. The entire formula itself, however, is the lengthiest formula in the Fourth Gospel. It is, in fact, probably the lengthiest formula in the New Testament and appears in a comparable form nowhere else.[9]

---

[2] Cf. my remarks in chapter nine.

[3] See Jesus' reference to the OT in John 13.18 (cf. 6.45; 7.37-38; 8.17; 10.34; 17.12; 19.28). Contrast John 2.17; 12.38, 40.

[4] In b. Yoma 9b, Rabbi Johanan ben Torta offers as one of the causes for the destruction of the temple, "Because therein prevailed hatred without cause." J. Jocz, The Jewish People and Jesus Christ (London: SPCK, 1962), 43, suggests that this rabbi may have been influenced by a Hebrew Christian tradition echoing John 15.25. Jocz's theory, however, "goes considerably beyond the evidence" (Brown, John 2, 689). The Old Testament passage cited also seems to have held some currency in the pseudepigraphal literature. See further below.

[5] See my remarks in chapter nine. Bultmann, John, 551 n. 6, suggests that an unexpressed thought also links v. 24 with v. 25. He paraphrases this thought as follows: "such a reaction is indeed inconceivable, but . . ." (cited by Moo, Passion Narratives, 243 n. 1). Perhaps it would be better to take ἀλλά as copulative: "now" (see R 1185; Lenski, St. John, 1064-65; cf. John 8.26).

[6] See my remarks in chapter seven.

[7] See my remarks in chapter seven. Freed, OT Quotations, 94, notes that ὁ λόγος appears as the equivalent of ἡ γραφή in an OT citation indicating fulfillment in the NT only here and in John 12.38 (cf. Moo, Passion Narratives, 243 n. 2).

[8] See my remarks in chapter five. As was the case for John 10.34, "Law" is to be taken as a reference to the entire OT. Jesus does not with the use of the phrase "their Law" distance himself or his followers either from the OT or from the unfaithful. Rather, he uses this phrase "in order to rivet upon the Jews those scriptures in which they boast themselves so proudly, and then to prove those same scriptures prophetic of their apostasy" (Hoskyns, Fourth Gospel, 481).

[9] Freed, OT Quotations, 94; cf. Schnackenburg, St. John 3, 117.

The citation itself, on the other hand, is shorter than any other citation in the Fourth Gospel. The brevity of this citation has led to some understandable confusion concerning which Old Testament passage John 15.25 recalls.

I.

For the most part, scholars have only considered two Old Testament passages to be possible referents of John 15.25: Ps 35(34).19 and Ps 69(68).5. Now and then, various alternative referents have been considered (usually either Ps 109[108].3[10] or Ps 119[118].161[11]). But these alternatives have never been given any serious consideration.[12]

Scholars have had difficulty, however, in choosing between Ps 35(34) and Ps 69(68).[13] The reason for this difficulty has been that the same reading appears in both psalms ("those who hate me without a cause"). Occasionally, Ps 69(68).5 has been chosen as the more likely referent of John 15.25, usually because references to this psalm are prominent elsewhere both in the Fourth Gospel and in the rest of the New Testament.[14] But no other more immediate rationale for pre-

---

10 Cf. Morris, *John*, 682 (and idem, *Reflections on the Gospel of John*, vol. 3, *The True Vine: John 11-16* [Grand Rapids: Baker, 1988], 530); Schnackenburg, *St. John* 3, 117; Becker, *Johannes*, 491-92.

11 Cf. Freed, *OT Quotations*, 95; Pancaro, *Law*, 330; Schnackenburg, *St. John* 3, 117; Becker, *Johannes*, 491-92. See also Ps 120(119).7.

12 *Pss. Sol.* 7.1 (οἴ ἐμίσησαν ἡμᾶς δωρεάν) has also attracted some attention. But while it is possible that a NT writer might know this literature (contrast Noack, *Tradition*, 75; Schnackenburg, *St. John* 3, 423 n. 87), it is unlikely that he would draw on it and refer to it as "their Law" (Moo, *Passion Narratives*, 243 n.4; cf. Freed, *OT Quotations*, 95).

13 Those scholars who have preferred not to choose between these two psalms include Westcott, *St. John*, 224; Burney, *Aramaic Origin*, 121; Hoskyns, *Fourth Gospel*, 481; Schlatter, *Der Evangelist*, 309; Bultmann, *John*, 551 n. 7; Samuel Amsler, *L'Ancien Testament dans l'église: Essai d'herméneutique chrétienne*, Bibliothèque théologique (Neuchatel: Éditions Delachaux & Niestle, 1960), 124; Freed, *OT Quotations*, 94-95, 123; Morris, *John*, 682 (cf. idem, *Reflections*, 530); Pancaro, *Law*, 330; Schnackenburg, *St. John* 3, 117; Barrett, *St. John*, 28, 482; Newman/Nida, *Handbook*, 496; Becker, *Johannes*, 491-92; Fortna, *Fourth Gospel*, 313 n. 175; Kysar, *John*, 244; Carson, "John," 246; Humann, "OT Quotations," 33, 47-48; Jaak Seynaeve, "Les citations scripturaires en Jn., 19,36-37: Une preuve en faveur de la typologie de l'Agneau pascal?" *RAT* 1 (1977): 69. Haenchen, *John* 2, 138, argues that John 15.25 recalls *both* psalms and Ps 25(24).19.

14 Cf. Franke, *Alte Testament*, 283; Johnson, *Quotations*, 240-41, 245, 323; Bernard, *St. John*, 495; Dodd, *Scriptures*, 58 (and idem, *Historical Tradition*, 33, 38-39); Noack, *Tradition*, 75; Brown, *John* 2, 698; Hanson, *NT Interpretation*, 115, 158-59, 209 n. 7 (and idem, *Utterances*, 115); McCaffrey, *House*, 84; Bruce, *John*, 315; Beasley-Murray, *John*, 276. On the prominence of Ps 69(68), see my remarks in chapter two.

ferring Ps 69(68) has ever been offered.[15] Occasionally, it has also been suggested that the influence of a specific textual tradition is evident in John 15.25, the OG.[16] But the precise form of John 15.25 differs from every extant version of either Ps 35(34).19 or Ps 69 (68).5.[17] Consequently, some scholars have chosen to refer to John 15.25 as a "free reminiscence"[18] or a citation from memory.[19]

It is understandable that scholars have had difficulty in settling on a referent for John 15.25. Nothing in any of the extant versions of either Ps 35(34).19 or Ps 69(68).5 singles out one or the other psalm as a more likely referent of this citation. And those scholars who have argued that the influence of a particular textual tradition is evident in John 15.25 have failed to show why this is probable. The OG οἱ μισοῦντές με δωρεάν does not differ from the Hebrew חנם שׂנאי (=MT).

Unfortunately, an understanding of the purpose of this citation does little to resolve this problem. If anything, it renders the solution to this problem even more uncertain.

II.

We have already noted why some scholars have preferred to see Ps 69(68).5 as the more likely referent of John 15.25. There is, however, much about Ps 35(34).19 which identifies it as an equally possible referent. Ps 35(34) is "certainly in the vein of the 'Passion' psalms."[20] And the theme "without cause" seems particularly prominent in it (see esp. vv. 7 and 19).[21] Ps 35(34) also shares

---

[15] Evans, "Formulas," 80; and Archer/Chirichigno, OT Quotations, 69, are the only scholars I have been able to find who appear to opt in favor of Ps 35(34). Neither, however, explains why this option is to be preferred.

[16] Those scholars who have argued for the influence of both Ps 34.19 OG and Ps 68.5 OG include Goodwin, "Sources," 62-63; Braun, Jean 2, 13, 21; Longenecker, Exegesis, 73. Those who have argued for the influence of Ps 68.5 OG alone include Toy, Quotations, 90; O'Rourke, "OT Citations," 58; Lindars, John, 495; Reim, Studien, 43, 94; Moo, Passion Narratives, 243.

[17] Cf. Ps 35.19 Aq.: ἐχθραίνοντές με ἀναιτίως; Ps 69.5 Symm.: οἱ μισοῦντές με ἀναιτίως.

[18] See, e.g., Burney, Aramaic Origin, 121.

[19] See, e.g., Noack, Tradition, 75; Goodwin, "Sources," 62-63.

[20] Dodd, Historical Tradition, 38 (cited by Humann, "OT Quotations," 48).

[21] Cf. Humann, "OT Quotations," 48. Bultmann, John, 551 n. 8, rightly notes the significance of this term for John. Δωρεάν signifies not gratis (Matt 10,.8; Rom 3.24), nor frustra (Gal 2.21), but immerito (חנם; Tg. מגן סנאי = "meine Hasser aus nichtigem Grund"). Cf. Freed, OT Quotations, 95; Humann "OT Quotations," 37 n. 22. See also 2 Cor 11.7; 2 Thess 3.8; Rev 21.6; 22.17.

with the Fourth Gospel its portrait of those who, though esteemed as brothers (v. 14), are in fact unjust witnesses (v. 11) bent on persecution (v. 2; cf. v. 6; see esp. John 15.20). Returning evil for good (v. 12), they devour (v. 25; cf. John 2.17!) and destroy (v. 4).

It is, of course, possible that John 15.25 means to recall both psalm passages. It is not really necessary to make a final decision about this. In any case, a reference to either psalm would mean that the equivalent "they hated" was substituted for "those who hate" in order to adapt this citation to the context in which it now stands.[22]

In summary, various possible solutions present themselves. But no one solution emerges as the preferred solution. Whether a particular textual tradition is recalled is similarly uncertain. Any of the above solutions, however, would result in an essentially equivalent understanding of the purpose of this citation. The hatred of the Jews signals the fulfillment of Old Testament prophecy and the approaching consummation of Jesus' work in the world.

III.

In conclusion, it is not possible to ascertain precisely the Old Testament referent of John 15.25. The purpose of this citation, however, is apparent. John 15.25 asserts that the hatred of the Jews against Jesus was anticipated by Old Testament prophecy. Their hatred will bring to fruition that for which Jesus was sent into the world.

---

22 Cf. Noack, *Tradition*, 75; Braun, *Jean* 2, 13; Reim, *Studien*, 43; Hanson, *Utterances*, 115; Moo, *Passion Narratives*, 243; Archer/Chirichigno, *OT Quotations*, 69; Longenecker, *Exegesis*, 73 (who identifies John 15.25 as a pesher citation).

Chapter 11

HE LAID ASIDE HIS GARMENTS

The peculiar character of John's passion account, especially the unusual prominence in this account which John affords Jesus' royal status, is well-documented by scholars. Regrettably, space constraints preclude the possibility of discussing John's relationship to the Synoptics in any detail. For the purposes of the present investigation, it is sufficient to note that John's treatment of Jesus' passion bears no indication of his dependence upon the Synoptics.[1] There is among these Gospels a certain general similarity of structure. But beyond this, there is little resemblance between John's Gospel and the Synoptics. Indeed, what John's Gospel shares with the Synoptics "does not go beyond the minimum without which the story could hardly be told at all,"[2] except, of course, when John shares with the Synoptics a similar reference to the same Old Testament passage.

The next three chapters will examine John's three explicit citations of the Old Testament in his account of the suffering and death of Jesus. This chapter begins with the first of these citations in John 19.24.

Each of the Synoptic accounts of Jesus' passion mention that, when Jesus was crucified, the soldiers divided his clothing among them and that this

---

[1] For a detailed examination of this issue, see esp. Dodd, *Historical Tradition*, 121-36. See also Brown, *John 2*, 913-16; Till Arend Mohr, *Markus- und Johannespassion: Redaktions- und traditionsgeschichtliche Untersuchung der Markinischen und Johanneischen Passionstradition*, Abhandlungen zur Theologie des Alten und Neuen Testaments, Bd. 70 (Zürich: Theologischer Verlag, 1982), 313-64; Green, *Death*, 105-35.

[2] Dodd, *Historical Tradition*, 121.

involved the casting of lots (cf. Matt 27.35; Mark 15.24; Luke 23.34b). Only John, however, mentions that Jesus' garments were divided into four parts, one part for each soldier present (19.23a). Only John mentions that, because the soldiers did not want to tear Jesus' seamless tunic, they cast lots to see who would inherit it (19.23b-24a). And finally, only John offers the editorial observation (cf. 12.14-15, 38, 39-40; 19.28 [?], 36, 37) that all this took place to fulfill the Scripture,

> διεμερίσαντο τὰ ἱμάτιά μου ἑαυτοῖς
> καὶ ἐπὶ τὸν ἱματισμόν μου ἔβαλον κλῆρον   (19.24b).[3]

Outside of the New Testament, one encounters additional references to this same Old Testament passage.[4] But these references serve only to illustrate further the distinctive character of John's citation. John's quotation formula is similarly distinctive. His reference to the fulfillment of Scripture again participates in a scheme now well-established in the latter stages of his Gospel.[5] But the form of John's formula is unique to his Gospel (cf. 17.12; 19.36; contrast 13.18; 19.28).

John's distinctive citation has occasioned a considerable amount of discussion among scholars. Perhaps the least disputed issue among these scholars concerns John's referent.

I.

John's citation recalls Ps 22(21).19.[6] Indeed, John 19.24 reproduces without change the text of Ps 21.19 OG[7] (which itself follows rather closely the Hebrew of the MT). Two conflicting appraisals of this evidence have emerged: (1) Most scholars are agreed that the form of John's citation reflects the influence of the

---

    [3] A number of witnesses for Matt 27.35 (Δ Θ 0250 f[1.13] 1424 *al* it vg[cl] sy[h] mae; Eus) reflect the influence of John's Gospel and add the very same reference to this OT passage (but with a typically Matthaean formula).

    [4] Cf. *Barn.* 6; Justin, *Dial.* 97. See also *Gos. Pet.* 4.12; *Acts Pil.* 10.1b. For rabbinic references to this OT passage and additional references to it in the patristic literature, see further below.

    [5] See my remarks in chapter seven.

    [6] Dodd, *Historical Tradition*, 40, notes that "There is every reason to think that this psalm (which has yielded perhaps more testimonies than any other comparable scripture except Isa. lii.13-liii.13) was from the earliest days the great stand-by of Christian thinkers and teachers seeking an understanding of the sufferings and death of Christ (cf. idem, *Scriptures*, 97-98; Lindars, *NT Apologetic*, 89-93). On the rabbinic references to this psalm, see Str-B 2:574-80. Ps 22(21) is cited five different times in 1QH, but the passage cited by John is not one of the passages cited by 1QH (Longenecker, *Exegesis*, 156).

    [7] Few scholars, therefore, have described John's citation as a citation from memory. See, however, Goodwin, "Sources," 62.

OG.[8] (2) A few scholars, however, have argued that the OG does not deviate in any noticeable fashion from the Hebrew of the MT. For these scholars, then, it is not possible to establish whether John's citation recalls a Greek or Hebrew *Vorlage*.[9]

How are these conflicting appraisals to be evaluated? First, scholars have been much too anxious to find significance in the mere fact that John 19.24 reproduces without change the text of Ps 21.19 OG.[10] And second, scholars have neglected to note that the OG does not, in fact, correspond in every detail with the Hebrew *Vorlage* it appears to translate. The OG renders the Hebrew imperfects יְחַלְּקוּ and יַפִּילוּ with unexpected Greek aorists. That John's citation also exhibits these same aorists, then, is indicative of the influence of the OG.[11]

In the same vein, scholars have also been too quick to find significance in the Johannine *hapax legomenon* διεμερίσαντο.[12] The mere fact that John does not use this term elsewhere in his Gospel does not immediately suggest that he here recalls the OG. The expression διέδωκεν τοῖς ἀνακειμένοις in John 6.11, on the other hand, may well suggest that John would be more likely to render the Hebrew חלק pi'el with διαδίδωμι rather than διαμερίζομαι (cf. Gen 49.27 A OG).

In any case, the evidence does suggest that John's citation recalls Ps 21.19 OG. It remains to be seen, then, whether or not an understanding of John's intent in citing Ps 21 provides any additional support for this conclusion.

II.

We have already noted that John goes to great lengths in John 19.23-24 to elaborate on an event which receives only limited attention in the Synoptics. It is particularly noteworthy that John is the only Gospel writer who mentions Jesus'

---

8 Cf. Westcott, *St. John*, 275; Toy. *Quotations*, 90; Franke, *Alte Testament*, 283; Hühn, *Citate*, 94; Burney, *Aramaic Origin*, 122; Str-B 2:574; Bernard, *St. John*, 629; Goodwin, "Sources," 62; Noack, *Tradition*, 82; Lindars, *NT Apologetic*, 268 (and idem, *John*, 578); Dodd, *Historical Tradition*, 40; Bultmann, *John*, 670 n. 7; Braun, *Jean* 2, 9; Freed, *OT Quotations*, 100, 124, 126; O'Rourke, "Fulfillment," 437; Stendahl, *St. Matthew*, 131; Brown, *John* 2, 903; Reim, *Studien*, 47, 90, 93-94, 225, 229, 231; Longenecker, *Exegesis*, 137; Pancaro, *Law*, 340; Schnackenburg, *St. John* 3, 272-73; Newman/Nida, *Handbook*, 588; McCaffrey, *House*, 79, 83; Moo, *Passion Narratives*, 253, 256; Kysar, *John*, 288; Humann, "OT Quotations," 42; Menken, "Joh 12,15," 209.

9 Barrett, *St. John*, 28, 550; Archer/Chirichigno, *OT Quotations*, 65.

10 See esp. Burney, *Aramaic Origin*, 122.

11 Similarly, Freed, *OT Quotations*, 100, 124; Pancaro, *Law*, 340 n. 100; Moo, *Passion Narratives*, 253; Contrast O'Rourke, "Fulfillment," 437-38.

12 See, e.g., Moo, *Passion Narratives*, 253.

tunic. Indeed, Jesus' tunic seems to represent the central issue of concern in this scene. Scholars, therefore, have been quick to see in Jesus' woven, seamless tunic a special symbolic and theological significance. The nature of this significance, however, has been keenly debated.[13]

Two contrasting interpretations have emerged. One interpretation sees in Jesus' seamless tunic a symbol of his priestly status. A second interpretation sees in Jesus' tunic a symbol of the Church's unity. But only one of these interpretations possesses any exegetical merit.

Those scholars who see in Jesus' tunic a symbol of his sacerdotal dignity have been too quick to find significance in an isolated text from Josephus. In *Ant.* 3.161, the first-century historian describes the vestment of the high priest as a woven, seamless tunic. But scholars who find significance in this description are guilty of confusing two separate articles of clothing. The high priest's tunic was a cultic vestment worn on the outside over other vestments. The high priest's tunic, then, was quite unlike the undergarment described by John. This interpretation, therefore, is based on a mistaken correlation and is for this reason to be rejected.[14]

To this, one more thing must be added. There is also an internal reason for rejecting this interpretation. Scholars have failed to show that elsewhere in John's Gospel a theology of the priesthood of Jesus is to be found.[15] In sum, then, there is no exegetical basis for this interpretation.

By contrast, there does seem to be some warrant for seeing in Jesus' tunic a symbol of the Church's unity.[16] The theme of the Church's unity does appear to be present in this scene. The question is, how is this to be understood?

The answer to this question is not immediately evident. An intriguing possibility emerges, however, when one carefully examines the larger context of John's reference to Jesus' tunic. We have already noted that when Jesus washed the feet of his disciples in John 13, he did so in anticipation of his death on the

---

13 For what follows, see esp. Ignace de la Potterie, *The Hour of Jesus. The Passion and the Resurrection of Jesus according to John: Text and Spirit*, trans. Dom Gregory Murray (Middlegreen: St. Paul Publications, 1989), 124-32. See also his earlier efforts: "La tunique sans couture, symbole du Christ grand prêtre?" *Bib* 60 (1979): 255-69; and "La tunique 'non divisée' de Jésus, symbole de l'unité messianique," in *The New Testament Age: Essays in Honor of Bo Reicke*, vol. 1, ed. William C. Weinrich (Macon, Ga.: Mercer, 1984), 127-38.

14 Cf. Bernard, *St. John*, 630; Schnackenburg, *St. John* 3, 274 (cited by Moo, *Passion Narratives*, 255 n. 6); Beasley-Murray, *John*, 347; de la Potterie, *Hour*, 126.

15 Cf. Lindars, *John*, 578; Schnackenburg, *St. John* 3, 274; Moo, *Passion Narratives*, 255-56; Kysar, *John*, 287; de la Potterie, *Hour*, 114, 126.

16 This interpretation is ably defended in the treatment of the patristic references to John's text by Michel Aubineau, "La tunique sans couture du Christ: Exégèse patristique de Jean 19,23-24," in *Kyriakon: Festschrift Johannes Quasten*, vol. 1, eds. P. Granfield and J. A. Jungman (Münster, Westf.: Verlag Aschendorff, 1970), 100-27.

cross.[17] We also noted the possibility that the very laying down of Jesus' garments was for his disciples the promise of an eschatological cleansing. If this is the case, then John would have the reader see in Jesus' crucifixion, in the distribution of his garments among the soldiers, the graphic consummation of that which Jesus anticipated in John 13.[18] In his crucifixion, then, Jesus fulfills his promises by laying down his garments (i.e., his life) so that he might proffer life.[19] Not only this, one sees in the distribution of these garments that this life is given not only to the Jews (cf. 19.25-27) but also to the Gentiles.[20]

Indeed, the language John uses to describe the distribution of Jesus' garments consistently seems to affirm this interpretation. According to John, the Gentiles too will inherit a "part" ($\mu\acute{\epsilon}\rho o\varsigma$, 19.23; cf. 13.8!)[21] of that which Jesus lays down. To be sure, they will receive all that there is to receive (hence, John's statement $\kappa\alpha\grave{\iota}$ $\tau\grave{o}\nu$ $\chi\iota\tau\hat{\omega}\nu$, 19.23). In John's scheme of things, the Gentiles are to be "allotted" ($\lambda\alpha\gamma\chi\acute{\alpha}\nu\omega$, 19.24)[22] a full share in the eschatological cleansing which comes "from above" ($\grave{\epsilon}\kappa$ $\tau\hat{\omega}\nu$ $\ddot{\alpha}\nu\omega\theta\epsilon\nu$, 19.23; cf. 3.3, 7, 31; 8.23; 19.11).[23]

---

17 See my remarks in chapter nine. Cf. Acts Pil 10.1b.

18 Cf. Schnackenburg, St. John 3, 274.

19 Schnackenburg, St. John 3, 274, objects to seeing in Jesus' tunic a symbol for the Church's unity because "Jesus is deprived of his tunic" (emphasis his; cited by Beasley-Murray, John, 347). Schnackenburg sees in John 13.4 a parallel "laying down," but fails to interpret the laying down of Jesus' garments in terms of Jesus' promise to lay down his life. In other words, Schnackenburg fails to see that no one takes these things from Jesus. Jesus lays them down of his own accord (10.18). Contrast the irony of John 19.2, 5. Jesus does not come to put on a robe and crown and be king; he comes to be king in putting off his robe (in connection with this, Pilate's unconsciously prophetic exclamation $\grave{\iota}\delta o\grave{\upsilon}$ $\acute{o}$ $\ddot{\alpha}\nu\theta\rho\omega\pi o\varsigma$ may recall the only instance of the same exclamation in the OG, in 1 Sam 9.17; cf. v. 16: "thou shalt anoint him [Saul] to be ruler over my people Israel, and he shall save my people").

20 Augustine (Tract. in Joann. 118.4) asserts that the division of Jesus' garments into four parts refers to their distribution "throughout the world" (cf. Luke 22.17; Acts 2.3). The world John describes, however, is specifically the Gentile world. To this description, John adds later (19.25) a reference to four Jewish women (noting the problems of this text, yet asserting the significance of this contrast are Westcott, St. John, 275-76; Hoskyns, Fourth Gospel, 530; Morris, John, 811; Schnackenburg, St. John 3, 276-77; Barrett, St. John, 551). Altogether, then, John indicates that Jesus' cross has meaning for both Jews and Gentiles, men and women alike (see further below). Cf. Wis 18.24.

21 See also John 21.6.

22 In John 19.24, $\lambda\acute{\alpha}\chi\omega\mu\epsilon\nu$ followed by $\ddot{\epsilon}\beta\alpha\lambda o\nu$ $\kappa\lambda\hat{\eta}\rho o\nu$ represents a variation in style not uncommon in John's Gospel. Such variations, we have noted, can serve more than a merely stylistic function (see, e.g., my remarks in chapter six on John 12. 14-15: [$\epsilon\grave{\upsilon}\rho\grave{\omega}\nu$] $\grave{o}\nu\acute{\alpha}\rho\iota o\nu$ $\grave{\epsilon}\kappa\acute{\alpha}\theta\iota\sigma\epsilon\nu$ $\grave{\epsilon}\pi$' $\alpha\grave{\upsilon}\tau\acute{o}$ followed by $\kappa\alpha\theta\acute{\eta}\mu\epsilon\nu o\varsigma$ $\grave{\epsilon}\pi\grave{\iota}$ $\pi\hat{\omega}\lambda o\nu$ $\check{o}\nu o\upsilon$). When the soldiers "caste lots" for Jesus' tunic, then, they show that the Gentiles too will be "allotted a share" in Jesus (cf. 2 Pet 1.1; contrast Acts 1.17; see also 1 Sam 14.47 OG).

23 See esp. my remarks in chapter four.

This share, then, is "whole" (δι' ὅλου, 19.23) and, in turn, makes those who receive it "whole" (see 7.23; 13.10; contrast 9.34).[24]

John's view is perhaps especially perceptible in his statement that the soldiers did not want to "tear" their inheritance (19.24). Most translators speak here of "tearing." The term John uses, however, is σχίζω and is better rendered "to split," or better yet, "to divide." From this verb comes the noun σχίσμα ("schism").

This term appears elsewhere in John's Gospel in references to the division which the coming of Jesus provoked among the Jews (cf. 7.43; 9.16; 10.19).[25] It is against this backdrop that a related reference in John 21.11 is also to be understood. John 21.11 describes a net which gathers together a miraculous catch of fish, yet "was not torn" (οὐκ ἐσχίσθη). Few scholars would dispute that John 21.11 describes the indivisibility of that which Jesus gathers.[26] Overagainst the division, then, which Jesus provokes among those who reject him, John 19.24 describes an indivisible inheritance which, in turn, engenders a corresponding wholeness for those who receive Jesus.[27]

That it was John's intent to stimulate these associations is admittedly difficult to demonstrate. Still, the tunic of Jesus, its essence, its oneness, does seem to anticipate the future unity of the Church. Through Jesus, then, individuals are united not only to God but also to one another under God. This unity is anticipated earlier in John's Gospel by Caiaphas who unwittingly offers this prophecy: "It is expedient for you that one man should die for the people, and that the whole (ὅλος) nation should not perish" (11.50; cf. 18.14; contrast 4.53). John adds this editorial remark: "He did not say this of his own accord, but being high priest that year he prophesied that Jesus should die for the nation, and *not for the nation only*, but *to gather into one* (εἰς ἕν) the scattered children of God" (11.51-52). Thus, on the cross Jesus draws both Jew and Gentile to himself and makes them one (12.32; cf. 10.11, 14-18 [esp. v. 16], 27-29).[28]

---

[24] For Cyprian (*De unitate ecclesiae* 7), the soldiers draw lots for Jesus' tunic "to see which of them should put on Christ." And John's ἐκ τῶν ἄνωθεν designates that this blessing has its origin in God.

[25] Cf. Acts 14.4; 23.7. See also Luke 5.36.

[26] De la Potterie, *Hour*, 128, rightly points out that already in the OT the tearing of a garment was an established symbol for division. See, e.g., Ahijah's tearing of his garment to prefigure the division of Israel after the death of Solomon (1 Kgs 11.29-31).

[27] One should probably not, in this instance, draw a sharp contrast between Jesus' indivisible tunic and his other "divisible" garments. Jesus' tunic apparently serves a representative function in this scene and thus designates the mysterious character of an inheritance available to all Gentiles. Cf. Isa 61.1-11 OG, esp. v. 10.

[28] Contrast John 17.11, 21, 22, 23. Those scholars, therefore, who have made much of the connection between Jesus' tunic and that of the high priest overemphasize the significance of ἄραφος. The term appears in John 19.23 and in Josephus' description of the vestment of the

"A perspective is therefore opened towards the *future* of the Church (which at the cross does not yet exist but is there coming to birth)."[29] For John, it is only a matter of time before the reality that is born at the cross begins to take tangible shape in the lives of Jews and Gentiles.[30]

In summary, the scene depicted in John 19.23-24 is typically Johannine.[31] But an understanding of John's intent in citing the Old Testament in this context has not provided additional information concerning his source for his citation.[32]

---

high priest, but is absent elsewhere in the NT and in the OG. If John uses a term in his description of this scene to recall a specific person or OT theme consonant with the present literary and theological context, it is not likely that this term is ἄραφος. Cf., however, ὑφαντὸς with reference not only to the tunic of the high priest (cf. OG Exod 28.1-8, 28; 36.10, 11, 15, 30, 35) but also to the curtain of the tabernacle/temple (cf. OG Exod 26.1, 31; 35.35; 37.1-5, 20-21). Recall that at the beginning of his Gospel, John referred to Jesus' death in terms of the temple (see my remarks in chapter two). Contrast the Synoptic account of the rending of the temple curtain (cf. σχίζω in Matt 27.51; Mark 15.38 [contrast 1.10]; Luke 23.45). Note also λαγχάνω in Luke 1.9 (cf. Heb 10.19-20; see also 6.19). That it was John's intent, however, to stimulate these associations is also difficult to establish.

29 De la Potterie, *Hour*, 131 (emphasis his).

30 The scene that follows this one, then, seems to function as the natural complement to John 19.23-24, brimming again with theological import (note esp. the transition μὲν ... δὲ from the conclusion of v. 24 to the beginning of v. 25). In the mother of Jesus, one views the gathering of the Jews. Cf., e.g., de la Potterie, *Hour*, 144: "Mary constitutes precisely the transition, the passage, between the ancient and the new people of God. In this unique person the whole of the Old Covenant converges, but also, typologically, the New Israel arises, the Church." In the person of the beloved disciple, one views the selection of those who will stand in the stead of Jesus in the midst of the people Jesus has gathered (cf. Barrett, *St. John*, 552; Schnackenburg, *St. John* 3, 279).

31 There is, therefore, little reason to suspect that the difference between John and the Synoptics in the treatment of the psalm goes back to a different form of the tradition (thus esp. Dodd, *Historical Tradition*, 40, 122; cf. Anton Dauer, *Die Passionsgeschichte im Johannesevangelium: Eine traditionsgeschichtliche und theologische Untersuchung zu Joh 18,1-19,30*, Studien zum Alten und Neuen Testament, Bd. 30 [München: Kösel-Verlag, 1972], 182-85; Schnackenburg, *St. John* 3, 272; Becker, *Johannes*, 588-89; Reginald H. Fuller, "The Passion, Death and Resurrection of Jesus according to St. John," *CS* 25 [1986]: 51-63; Fortna, *Fourth Gospel*, 176-80).

32 We have already noted John's tendency to place genitives of personal pronouns before substantives and their articles (see my remarks in chapters eight and nine). Now the lack of such a tendency in the twofold use of μου in John 19.24 might initially suggest that John recalls the OG. Cf., however, John 19.23; see also 13.12 (John's tendency, then, seems to manifest itself especially in references to parts of the body). Also, it is frequently asserted that John's citation dispenses with the original synonymous parallelism of the OT passage cited (on the improbable suggestion that John thereby recalls the Targum, see Brown, *John* 2, 920; Moo, *Passion Narratives*, 256-57). It is unlikely, however, that John misunderstands the psalm or that he invents the scene he describes using as his point of departure the OT passage he cites. Instead, John starts with a historical fact and then sees "the two separate events already distinguished in the wording of the Psalm" (Pancaro, *Law*, 340-41). Note that while the direct objects in this psalm passage are synonyms, the verbs are not.

It seems probable that John knows more of the psalm he cites than just the passage he reproduces.[33] But it is difficult to see any evidence of this knowledge in the rest of his passion account.

III.

In conclusion, John's editorial reference to the Old Testament in John 19.24 recalls Ps 21.19 OG. John purposes with this citation to establish two propositions: (1) The parting of Jesus' garments, including the casting of lots for his tunic, was anticipated by Old Testament prophecy. (2) The reception of Jesus' garments by the soldiers who crucified Jesus anticipated the future unity of the Church.

---

[33] Aspects of the psalm congenial to John's purposes include the references in vv. 27-32 to the inclusion of the nations in God's salvation and to the "seed" which will proclaim this salvation to the yet unborn. Other aspects of this psalm are recalled elsewhere in the NT, but do not seem appropriate to John's purposes. Cf., e.g., v. 2 with Matt 27.46 and Mark 15.34; vv. 8-9 with Matt 27.39, 43, Mark 15.29, and Luke 23.35; v. 23 with Heb 2.12.

Chapter 12

THE DEATH OF JESUS (1)

John is the only New Testament writer who refers to the events immediately following the death of Jesus in John 19.31-37. At the conclusion of these verses, John offers the editorial observation (cf. 12.14-15, 38, 39-40; 19.24, 28 [?], 37) that the events which followed the death of Jesus represent a twofold fulfillment of Old Testament prophecy. John's last two explicit citations of the Old Testament in his account of the suffering and death of Jesus appear, then, as a compound citation in John 19.36-37 (cf. 12.13-15, 38-40). The focus of attention of the present chapter will be the first of these citations in John 19.36.

According to John, Jesus died on the day of Preparation. And because the Jews did not want the bodies of those crucified to remain on the cross during the Sabbath, the Jews asked Pilate to have the legs of these men broken so that they might die quickly and be taken away (19.31). So the soldiers did this (19.32). But when the soldiers came to Jesus, they found that he was already dead and did not, therefore, break his legs (19.33-34). This took place, John remarks, "that the Scripture might be fulfilled,"

ὀστοῦν οὐ συντριβήσεται αὐτοῦ (19.36).

No other New Testament writer recalls this Old Testament passage.[1] John's reference to the fulfillment of Scripture signals the end-point of an already well-established scheme involving the use of quotation formulas in this the climax of

---

[1] For references to this passage in the rabbinic literature, see Str-B 2:583.

his Gospel.[2] The form of this quotation formula is, once more, unique to John (cf. 17.12; 19.24; contrast 13.18; 19.28).[3] Scholars have struggled in their efforts to characterize John 19.36. Both John's intended referent and his intent in citing the Old Testament continue to be debated questions.

I.

The first problem involves identifying the Old Testament passage cited. Scholars have suggested four different possibilities: Exod 12.10 (OG), 46; Num 9.12; and Ps 34(33).21. The problem is that none of these passages correspond precisely to what one observes in John 19.36.[4]

The pertinent data may be summarized as follows: On the one hand, Exod 12.10 (OG), 46; and Num 9.12 all correspond word for word with John 19.36, with only two exceptions. John's citation exhibits (1) a verb form which does not appear in any of these Old Testament passages (i.e., συντριβήσεται)[5] and (2) the personal pronoun αὐτοῦ rather than the prepositional phrase ἀπ᾽ αὐτοῦ (בוֹ).[6] On the other hand, Ps 34(33).21 and John 19.36 share the same verb form, but differ in almost every other respect.

Scholars have responded to this data in a variety of ways. Some scholars have been reluctant to identify a specific Old Testament referent for John's

---

2 See my remarks in chapter seven.

3 Preceding ἵνα in John 19.36 is ἐγένετο γὰρ ταῦτα. These words recall the two events reported by John in vv. 31-35 for which there are in vv. 36-37 two corresponding citations (Bultmann, *John*, 677 n. 1; Brown, *John* 2, 937; Herbert Leroy, "'Kein Bein wird ihm gebrochen werden' [Jo 19,31-37]. Zur johanneischen Interpretation des Kreuzes," in *Eschatologie: Bibeltheologische und philosophische Studien zum Verhältnis von Erlösungswelt und Wirklichkeitsbewältigung. Festschrift für Engelbert Neuhäusler zur Emeritierung gewidmet von Kollegen, Freunden und Schülern*, hg. Rudolf Kilian, Klemens Funk, und Peter Fassl [St. Ottilien: EOS Verlag, 1981], 73; Becker, *Johannes*, 600).

4 Exactly that part of Exod 12.46 which parallels John's citation is missing in 8Q3 (de Waard, *Comparative Study*, 13 n. 3).

5 Cf. Exod 12.10 (OG): "he will not break" (οὐ συντρίψεται/Hebrew *Vorlage* lacking; some witnesses read οὐ συντρίψετε); 12.46: "you will not break" (οὐ συντρίψετε/תשברו ולא; some witnesses read οὐ συντρίψεται); Num 9.12: "they will not break" (οὐ συντρίψουσιν/ישברו לא; some witnesses read οὐ συντρίψεται). Scribal efforts to arrive at a common reading are evident. Yet John's citation corresponds to none of these readings. See further below.

6 There are still other lesser mss. which offer readings for each of these OT passages in which both συντριβήσεται appears and ἀπ᾽ is omitted. These witnesses, however, probably have been influenced by John's citation.

citation.[7] Usually, however, scholars have argued that John recalls an Old Testament passage from the Pentateuch, either Exod 12.10 (OG),[8] Exod 12.46,[9] or Num 9.12.[10] Still, a significant number of scholars have also argued that John recalls Ps 34(33).21.[11] And occasionally it has been suggested that John 19.36 represents a double (or even more complicated) reference to the Old Testament including a reference to both the Pentateuch and the Psalms.[12] Only rarely have scholars suggested that the accuracy of John's memory may be an important factor for this citation.[13]

How is one to evaluate these varying hypotheses? First, it is not likely that John's primary referent is Ps 34(33).21. John's citation and this psalm passage

---

7 Cf. Hühn, *Citate*, 94; Burney, *Aramaic Origin*, 122; Schlatter, *Der Evangelist*, 354; O'Rourke, "Fulfillment," 439; Bruce H. Grigsby, "The Cross as an Expiatory Sacrifice in the Fourth Gospel," *JSNT* 15 (1982): 58; Archer/ Chirichigno, *OT Quotations*, 17; Carson, "John," 246; Fortna, *Fourth Gospel*, 178, 270.

8 Cf. Freed, *OT Quotations*, 113, 125: "the most likely direct source" (cited by Brown, *John* 2, 937).

9 Cf. Westcott, *St. John*, 280; Bernard, *St. John*, 651; Edgar, "Context," 59; Saldarini, *Passover*, 78; Bruce, *John*, 377; Hanson, *NT Interpretation*, 158-59 (and idem, *Utterances*, 116-117); de la Potterie, *Hour*, 69. For Pancaro, *Law*, 344-50, esp. 350, John recalls either Exod 12.10 (OG) or 12.46.

10 Cf. Reim, *Studien*, 52-53, 90, 108, 176. Those arguing for a reference to the Pentateuch, but reluctant to choose between Exod 12.46 and Num 9.12 include George A. Barton, "'A Bone of Him Shall Not Be Broken,' John 19:36," *JBL* 49 (1930): 13-19; Morris, *John*, 823 (and idem, *Reflections*, 679); Moo, *Passion Narratives*, 315; Newman/Nida, *Handbook*, 596; Kysar, *John*, 292-93; Humann, "OT Quotations," 48-49.

11 Cf. Seynaeve, "Jn 19,36-37," 69-70; Toy, *Quotations*, 91-92; Dodd, *Scriptures*, 98-99 (and idem, *Historical Tradition*, 42-44, 131; *Interpretation*, 233-34, 424); Dauer, *Passionsgeschichte*, 140-41, 299; Longenecker, *Exegesis*, 135, 156 (an example of the pesher technique); Leroy, "Kein Bein;" Haenchen, *John* 2, 195; Robinson, *Priority*, 153, 281; Menken, "Joh 12,15," 194-95.

12 Cf. Johnson, *Quotations*, 246-47; Goodwin, "Sources," 70; Noack, *Tradition*, 78-79; Schnackenburg, *St. John* 1, 122; Braun, *Jean* 2, 19-20, 80; Freed, *OT Quotations*, 112-13, 125, 128 (a possibility); Mathias Rissi, "Die Hochzeit in Kana Joh 2,1-11," in *Oikonomia: Heilsgeschichte als Thema der Theologie. Oscar Cullmann zum 65. Geburtstag gewidmet*, hg. Felix Christ (Hamburg: Reich, 1967), 88; Longenecker, *Exegesis*, 135, 156 (a possibility); Brown, *John* 2, 953 (a possibility); J. Terence Forestell, *The Word of the Cross: Salvation as Revelation in the Fourth Gospel*, Analecta Biblica, vol. 57 (Rome: Biblical Institute Press, 1974), 90; Grigsby, "Cross," 58 (a possibility); Moo, *Passion Narratives*, 314-15; (a possibility); Jean-Noël Aletti, "Mort de Jésus et théorie du récit," *RSR* 73 (1985): 155; Humann, "OT Quotations," 33 (a possibility). According to Bultmann, *John*, 676-677, John's source had in view Ps 34(33).21, but John himself has shaped his citation in order to recall the Pentateuch. Cf. Lindars, *NT Apologetic*, 95-96, 268 (and idem, *John*, 590); Schnackenburg, *St. John* 3, 292; Barrett, *St. John*, 558; Becker, *Johannes*, 600-1; Fuller, "Passion," 57; Beasley-Murray, *John*, 355. Fortna, *Fourth Gospel*, 178 n. 412, however, judges Bultmann's proposal "interesting but unverifiable."

13 See, however, Noack, *Tradition*, 79; Freed, *OT Quotations*, 112-13, 125.

share the same verb form, "but in all other respects John's quotation is closer to the Exodus or Numbers passages" (note the singular ὀστοῦν the singular αὐτοῦ; and especially the word order).[14] It is, however, not possible to settle on a specific referent in the Pentateuch.

At this stage, it is also not possible to establish whether a specific textual tradition is recalled.[15] There are scholars who have argued that the influence of the OG is evident in the form of the verb which is shared by both John 19.36 and Ps 33.21 OG.[16] But a judgment on this matter is, again, not possible until one establishes John's intent in citing the Old Testament.

II.

In their efforts to characterize John's intent in citing the Old Testament in John 19.36, scholars have frequently looked to the larger context of John's account of Jesus' passion. Scholars have first attempted to establish whether or not John suggests elsewhere in this account that the death of Jesus represents the sacrifice of the eschatological Passover. If Jesus is the Paschal Lamb, scholars argue, then John cites the Pentateuch. If not, then John cites the psalm.

This type of argument, however, is most precarious. Formal considerations have already strongly suggested that John's citation recalls the Pentateuch. Now if this is the case, then John 19.36 is the only time in John's Gospel that John explicitly designates Jesus the Paschal Lamb. John's citation, then, may well represent *the* place in his Gospel where John would have the reader finally see that Jesus is without a doubt the Paschal Lamb.

---

14 Moo, *Passion Narratives*, 314-15; cf. Pancaro, *Law*, 345.

15 Reim, *Studien*, 52-53, 90, 108, 176, has argued that John's citation stands closest to the Hebrew of Num 9.12 MT (cf. Grigsby, "Cross," 58, 74; Moo, *Passion Narratives*, 316; contrast Longenecker, *Exegesis*, 137, for whom John's citation represents a paraphrastic variation of the OG which has been influenced by the Hebrew of the MT). According to Reim, the singular ὀστοῦν corresponds nicely to עֶצֶם (while Ps 33.21 OG exhibits the plural). The expression לֹא יִשְׁבְּרוּ "kann mit οὐ συντριβήσεται wiedergegeben werden" (p. 52). And αὐτοῦ represents a conceivable rendering of בוֹ. John's citation, however, could just as easily represent a rendering of the Hebrew of Exod 12.46 MT. Pancaro, *Law*, 345, on the other hand, has argued that John's citation represents a likely adaptation of Exod 12.10 (OG). Its verb (συντρίψεται) is already in the third person singular. All that is necessary is to change its voice. According to Pancaro, "the passive voice would come more natural to Jn, since the middle voice recedes in the Koiné and is substituted either by the active or by the passive forms." We have already noted, however, that Pancaro himself knows his argument to be less than conclusive. Hence, Pancaro identifies Exod 12.46 as another possible referent (p. 350). At this stage, then, the evidence does little to identify a likely referent.

16 See further below.

Even without the testimony of John 19.36, however, there is much in John's account of Jesus' passion which suggests that John understood Jesus to be the Paschal Lamb. In John 18.28, 19.14, and 19.31 (see also 19.42; cf. Matt 27.62; Mark 15.42; Luke 23.54), John refers to the Passover.[17] Jesus' death is to be associated with the slaughter of the paschal lambs in the temple courtyard, for Jesus dies on the day of Preparation for the Passover.[18]

In the midst of John's explicit references to the Passover, there is an additional feature of John's account which also represents a likely reference to Jesus' death as the sacrifice of the final Passover. In John 19.29, John mentions that Jesus was offered (cf. 16.2) a sponge filled with sour wine (cf. Ps 69[68].22) placed on "hyssop" (cf. Matt 27.48; Mark 15.36).[19] Now hyssop is in the Old Testament closely associated with the celebration of the Passover. In Exod 12.22, Moses instructs the elders of Israel to take a bunch of hyssop, dip it in the blood of the slaughtered paschal lamb, and touch it to the lintel of the two doorposts.[20] Hyssop was thus part of the annual paschal liturgy and was used to carry the blood of the paschal lamb. It is most unlikely, therefore, that John's reference to hyssop in his account of Jesus' death on the occasion of the preparation for the "great" Passover is nothing more than mere coincidence.[21] Rather, John seems particularly intent on identifying Jesus as the great Paschal Lamb.[22]

---

[17] Note that the third Passover in John's Gospel is the Passover of Jesus' death (cf. 2.13; 6.4).

[18] The Sabbath is called "great" in John 19.31 because it coincides with the first day of the Passover festival. For many scholars, John's reference in John 19.14 to "the sixth hour" also participates in this scheme. For these scholars, Jesus is taken away to be crucified at the very hour the slaughter of the paschal lambs began in the temple courtyard (see the helpful discussion of this issue by Brown, *John* 2, 882-83). It may be, however, that John only wishes to show that Jesus' "hour" has indeed come (Barrett, *St. John*, 545). Contrast the anticipatory character of Jesus' "anointing" on the sixth day prior to the Passover (the day the paschal lamb was traditionally selected) in John 12.1-8 (see my remarks in chapter six). Cf. John 2.6; 4.6.

[19] A considerable number of scholars (in spite of strong external evidence to the contrary) have argued that one should read ὑσσῷ rather than ὑσσώπῳ. The sponge would then be placed on a "spear." Brown, *John* 2, 909-10, however, notes that John uses λόγχη not ὑσσός for "spear" (19.34).

[20] Cf. the use of hyssop in Lev 14.4, 6, 49, 51, 52; Num 19.6, 18; Ps 51(50).7.

[21] Contrast Heb 9.19-22 (the only other instance of the use of "hyssop" in the NT).

[22] Note, then, the irony of John's reference to hyssop which bears the "bitter wine of death" (Brown, *John* 2, 930; cf. the "cup" in 18.11). In turn, Jesus as the Paschal Lamb offers the eschatological wine of life (19.34). John's reference, therefore, to Jesus as the Paschal Lamb recalls the Baptist's testimony concerning Jesus the "Lamb of God who takes away the sin of the world" (1.29) and declares that the taking away of sin has indeed come to pass (paying particular attention to this "inclusion" is Hoskyns, *Fourth Gospel*, 534). Scholars have, of course, argued that the slaughtering of the paschal lambs had no sacrificial significance in the OT. Pancaro, *Law*, 348, however, offers a number of important observations on this point. In Deut 16.1-5, the slaughtering of the paschal lambs is portrayed as a quasi-sacrificial act (taking

There is, therefore, no reason to doubt that John's reference to the Old Testament in John 19.36 recalls the Pentateuch. Indeed, John's reference to "hyssop" in John 19.29 may well suggest that both John 19.29 and 19.36 recall the same Old Testament context (i.e., Exod 12 rather than Num 9). Similarly, there is also no reason to treat John's citation as an "either/or" question (i.e., either John's citation recalls the Pentateuch or it recalls the psalm). We have already noted several instances in John's Gospel where John has incorporated into his Old Testament citations textual material from analogous Old Testament contexts. It is likely that John does so here as well.

The stipulations in the Pentateuch concerning the sacrifice of the paschal lamb and Ps 34(33) do not share much more than their mutual references to "bones" which will not be "broken" and their general references to a God who delivers those who trust in him. But John's conspicuous desire to portray the Son of God as the Paschal Lamb could easily have prompted him to associate his citation of the Pentateuch with the psalm's description of God's protection of the righteous. John 19.36, therefore, recalls the Pentateuch. John's selection of the verb συντριβήσεται, however, recalls Ps 34(33).21.

What is it that John purposes thereby to accomplish? John's use in his citation of the third person singular future passive reflects his intent "to make the passage appear as a prediction and refer specifically to Jesus."[23] John's αὐτοῦ reflects a similar intent. The substitution of the possessive pronoun αὐτοῦ for the prepositional phrase ἀπ' αὐτοῦ is a natural one when using αὐτοῦ of a person.[24]

---

place in the sanctuary). Exod 13.11-16, on the other hand, regards the paschal lamb as a substitution for the first-born of Israel. The first-born are not only redeemed by this substitution, they are spared death because of the blood of the lamb. In later Judaism, then, the slaughtering of the paschal lambs was considered a sacrificial rite (cf. Str-B 3:360). Finally, that the sacrificial death of Jesus, commemorated in the earliest celebrations of the Eucharist, was associated with the slaughtering of the paschal lambs is clear from 1 Cor 5.7 and 1 Pet 1.18-19. There is, therefore, no valid argument against seeing in John's Gospel these paschal associations. Other recent treatments of the expiatory death of Jesus in John's Gospel include Grigsby, "Cross;" Fuller, "Passion;" Fortna, Fourth Gospel, 265-83; R. Alan Culpepper, "The Death of Jesus: An Exegesis of John 19:28-37," FM 5 (1988): 64-70; F. J. Matera, "'On Behalf of Others,' 'Cleansing,' and 'Return.' Johannine Images for Jesus' Death," LS 13 (1988): 161-78; Max Turner, "Atonement and the Death of Jesus in John–Some Questions to Bultmann and Forestell," EvQ 62 (1990): 99-122.

23 Freed, OT Quotations, 113. Cf. Pancaro, Law, 345.

24 Freed, OT Quotations, 113 (quoted by Dauer, Passionsgeschichte, 140 n. 258). Similarly, Pancaro, Law, 345, who adds, "On the other hand, Jn could have fused the two members of Ps 34,21 into one so that ἐν ἐξ αὐτῶν (αὐτῶν referring to πάντα τὰ ὀστᾶ αὐτῶν) would have become ὀστοῦν and the αὐτῶν would have been changed to αὐτοῦ, in order to apply the text specifically to Jesus." Pancaro's suggestion, however, probably exceeds what is necessary in order to explain John's citation. John simply deletes ἀπ'.

But this is not all. The psalm passage "The Lord keeps all his bones; not one of them is broken" appears in an ancient Jewish prayer for the deceased. And Ezekiel's vision of the revivification of the dried up bones appears as a lesson from the prophets on the mid-festival Sabbath of the Passover. These observations together suggest that, even before John, "the inviolability of the bones of the Passover lamb was widely regarded as symbolizing the individual's hope of resurrection as well as the nation's of a glorious future."[25] That God did not allow Jesus' bones to be broken, then, may have suggested to John as well that Jesus' body would not remain in the grave. John's citation, therefore, "might well suggest to a Christian reader familiar with rabbinic exegesis a promise of the resurrection of Christ."[26]

In any case, John's citation, then, suggests that Jesus is both Paschal Lamb and one of the righteous described in Ps 34(33). As such, it may be that John's citation also serves one final purpose. Without John's reference to the psalm, the connection between his Old Testament citations in John 19.36 and 19.37 is difficult to define. With John's reference to the psalm, however, an effective bridge from one citation to the other is introduced.[27]

John's reference to the psalm finally also suggests that he does, in fact, recall a specific textual tradition. While the verb in John's citation agrees with Ps 33.21 OG, it is hardly a likely rendering of the Hebrew נשברה (=MT).[28] The verb form נשברה is either a third person singular feminine nif'al perfect or a singular feminine nif'al participle. Of the various places in the Old Testament where the former form is listed by Mandelkern,[29] Ps 34.21 is the only instance in which the OG appears to render this form with a future passive. Elsewhere, the OG renders

---

[25] David Daube, *The New Testament and Rabbinic Judaism* (University of London: The Athlone Press, 1956), 309.

[26] Dodd, *Historical Tradition*, 44 (see also p. 131). Cf. Brown, *John* 2, 953; Lindars, *NT Apologetic*, 96 (and idem, *John*, 590); Forestell, *Word*, 91-92; Seynaeve, "Jn 19,36-37," 70; Barrett, *St. John*, 556; Humann, "OT Quotations," 37 n. 23, 48 n. 61.

[27] Contrast Dauer, *Passionsgeschichte*, 140-41. Freed, *OT Quotations*, 113; and Pancaro, *Law*, 349-50, rightly point out that Ps 34(33) is not, properly speaking, a psalm of the "suffering righteous." Neither does the psalm seem to serve as a "testimonium" for the passion of Jesus elsewhere in the NT. Still, the psalm was familiar to NT writers (on its use in the NT, see Noack, *Tradition*, 79; Lindars, *NT Apologetic*, 95-98; Dodd, *Historical Tradition*, 43-44) and is congenial to John's theological agenda (cf. Forestell, *Word*, 90 n. 132). John's reference to the psalm, then, provides a smooth transition from his description of Jesus as the Paschal Lamb to his description of Jesus as "him whom they have pierced."

[28] On this point, see esp. Freed, *OT Quotations*, 112-13 (cited by O'Rourke, "Fulfillment," 439). Cf. Noack, *Tradition*, 78-79; Braun, *Jean* 2, 19-20, 80 (the work of the redactor); Pancaro, *Law*, 345; Leroy, "Kein Bein," 75.

[29] Solomon Mandelkern, *Veteris Testamenti concordantiae hebraicae atque chaldaicae*, 2d ed. (Berlin: Margolin, 1925).

this form with an aorist passive.[30] Of the instances where the latter form is listed, one is rendered with an aorist passive and the others are rendered with the perfect passive participle.[31] In view of this evidence, it is not likely that John's reference to the psalm represents a rendering of a Hebrew *Vorlage*. Instead, John's citation recalls Ps 33.21 OG.

In summary, both the Old Testament citation in John 19.36 and the scene which precedes it are typically Johannine.[32] In both, John describes Jesus' death as the death of the true Paschal Lamb. John's citation, therefore, recalls the Pentateuch. The specific passage within the Pentateuch John means to recall is probably either Exod 12.10 (OG) or 12.46 (perhaps both passages are recalled). An understanding of John's intent in citing the Old Testament in this instance has provided some evidence for the influence of a specific textual tradition. John's selection of the verb $\sigma\upsilon\nu\tau\rho\iota\beta\dot{\eta}\sigma\epsilon\tau\alpha\iota$ shows that he recalls Ps 33.21 OG. John's reference to this analogous passage (a reference to Jesus as one of the "righteous") prepares the reader for John's next citation (19.37) in which he will describe Jesus as the one "whom they have pierced." But John's choice of a verb can, at best, only be seen as limited evidence for the influence of the same textual tradition in the rest of his citation.

III.

In conclusion, John's editorial reference to the Old Testament in John 19.36 represents a likely reference either to Exod 12.10 (OG) or to Exod 12.46 (or to both). There is only limited evidence for the influence of a specific textual tradition in John's citation. This evidence appears in the form of the verb John chooses for his citation (which recalls the analogous passage Ps 33.21 OG). John purposes with this citation (1) to establish that Jesus died as the true Paschal Lamb in fulfillment of what was prophetically anticipated by the Old Testament and (2) to characterize Jesus as one of the righteous depicted in Ps 33 OG and thus pave the way for John's next citation.

---

[30] Cf. 1 Sam 22.49; Isa 24.10; Jer 14.17; Ezek 26.2; Dan 8.8. Two instances (Jer 48.4, 25) do not occur in the OG.

[31] Cf. Ps 51.19; Ezek 27.34; 30.22; 34.4, 16; Zech 11.16; Dan 8.22.

[32] There is, therefore, little reason to suspect that John simply parrots the tradition he inherits (cf. Reim, *Studien*, 54, 93, 108; Seynaeve, "Jn 19,36-37," 68, 76). Neither is there any reason to suspect that John invents the scene he describes using as his point of departure the OT passages he cites here and in John 19.37 (cf. Fortna, *Fourth Gospel*, 270).

Chapter 13

THE DEATH OF JESUS (2)

John's last citation of the Old Testament in his account of the suffering and death of Jesus appears as the second of the two juxtaposed citations in John 19.36-37 (cf. 12.13-15, 38-40). In this final citation, John offers the editorial observation (cf. 12.14-15, 38, 39-40; 19.24, 28 [?], 36) that the events which followed the death of Jesus represent the fulfillment of a second Old Testament prophecy (cf. 19.36).

According to John, the soldiers who broke the legs of the two others cruci-fied with Jesus that day (19.31-32) also intended to break Jesus' legs as well. But when they came to Jesus, they discovered that Jesus already appeared to be dead (19.33). In order to establish that Jesus had indeed expired, however, "one of the soldiers pierced his side with a spear" (19.34). Now this took place, John remarks, "that the Scripture might be fulfilled" (19.36),

ὄψονται εἰς ὃν ἐξεκέντησαν (19.37).

The actual formula which precedes John's citation is, of course, "And again another Scripture says" (19.37), a formula which does not occur anywhere else in the New Testament in precisely the same form.[1] We have already noted, how-ever, that in view of the close relationship and proximity of this citation to the one which immediately precedes it the introductory formula in John 19.36 is to

---

[1] Cf., however, Matt 4.7; Acts 13.35; Rom 15.9-12; 1 Cor 3.20; Heb 1.5-13; 2.13; 4.5; 5.6; 10.30. See also 2 Clem. 2.4 and similar examples in the rabbinic literature (Str-B 2:583; Schlatter, Der Evangelist, 355).

be applied to John's second citation as well.[2] That this was, in fact, John's intent is confirmed by his use in John 19.37 of πάλιν. John's final reference to the fulfillment of Scripture represents the end-point of an already well-established scheme involving the use of quotation formulas in this the climax of his Gospel.[3]

John's last explicit citation of the Old Testament may also represent "one of the most interesting examples of the use of a set but independent text form in the NT."[4] Similar yet distinct references to the same Old Testament passage appear in both Matt 24.30 and Rev 1.7. The same text form also seems to be known to Justin (cf. 1 *Apol.* 1.52; 52.12; *Dial.* 14.8; 32.2; 64.7; 118.1).[5] Of the three references to this Old Testament passage in the New Testament, however, only John 19.37 is an explicit citation.

Rev 1.7 reads, "and every eye will see him, every one who pierced him" (καὶ ὄψονται αὐτὸν πᾶς ὀφθαλμὸς καὶ οἵτινες αὐτὸν ἐξεκέντησαν). Rev 1.7 and John 19.37, then, share the verbs ὄψονται and ἐξεκέντησαν,[6] but they differ significantly otherwise. The Apocalypse also combines its reference to the Old Testament with other references to the Old Testament which do not appear in John's Gospel. For example, Rev 1.7 begins with the declaration, "Behold, he is coming with the clouds," an apparent reference to Dan 7.13.[7] Rev 1.7 concludes by identifying those who see this eschatological figure as "all the tribes of the earth" (πᾶσαι αἱ φυλαὶ τῆς γῆς), recalling Gen 12.3 (the phrase refers to those who inherit the blessing of Abraham).[8] The conclusion of Rev 1.7 also mentions that these tribes "will mourn on account of him" (κόψονται ἐπ' αὐτὸν). This last expression recalls the larger context of the same Old Testament passage from which both the Apocalypse and John's Gospel derived their references to those who "will see" the one whom "they have pierced." But this expression does not

---

[2] See my remarks in chapter seven.

[3] See my remarks in chapter seven.

[4] Max Wilcox, "Text form," in *It is Written: Scripture Citing Scripture. Essays in Honour of Barnabas Lindars*, eds. D. A. Carson and H. G. M. Williamson (Cambridge: Cambridge University Press, 1988), 201 (cf. Moo, *Passion Narratives*, 211).

[5] See also *Barn.* 7.9; *Did.* 16.7; Theodoret (in Goodwin, "Sources," 66).

[6] These two NT passages are, in fact, the only two instances of the use of the verb ἐκκεντέω in the NT.

[7] The form of this reference to Dan 7.13 is not that of the OG. Wilcox, "Text form," 201, suggests that the Apocalypse recalls either Theodotion or an Aramaic version of Daniel. This (we shall see) relates significantly to the issues that will be addressed below.

[8] Dodd, *Historical Tradition*, 132 n. 3. Perhaps Gen 28.14 and Ps 72(71).17 are also in view (Wilcox, "Text form," 202, who judges this phrase to be an example of "a stereotyped phrase, almost a piece of symbolic language, to cue in the idea that it is precisely those 'who bless themselves [or are blessed] through Abraham and his 'seed' who 'shall look upon him whom they pierced' and 'mourn for him as for an only son'").

appear in John's Gospel.[9] Altogether, then, it seems unlikely that either of these New Testament passages is dependent upon the other. Rather, both seem to recall the same prior text form. Each, however, utilizes this form independently in the service of a distinctive literary and theological agenda.[10]

Actually, Rev 1.7 seems to bear more in common with Matt 24.30 than it does with John 19.37. Matt 24.30, like Rev 1.7, describes an apocalyptic setting: "then will appear the sign of the Son of Man in heaven, and then all the tribes of the earth will mourn (κόψονται πᾶσαι αἱ φυλαὶ τῆς γῆς), and they will see (ὄψονται) the Son of Man coming on the clouds of heaven with power and great glory." Both in the Apocalypse and in Matthew's Gospel, the subject of the verbs κόψονται and ὄψονται is πᾶσαι αἱ φυλαὶ τῆς γῆς. And both New Testament passages also specify the object of these verbs to be the Son of Man figure described in Dan 7.13.

The preceding observations suggest the existence of "a careful piece of exegesis which seems to form a coherent pattern behind all three NT passages examined."[11] Still, John 19.37 is easily the most distinctive of these three passages, both in terms of its function and in terms of its form. What follows will illustrate further the singularity of John's citation.

I.

John 19.37 recalls Zech 12.10. Unlike every other explicit citation of the Old Testament in John's Gospel, however, John 19.37 does not appear to represent a reference to the OG. Zech 12.10 OG reads as follows: καὶ ἐπιβλέψονται πρός με ἀνθ᾽ ὧν κατωρχήσαντο.[12] Scholars, therefore, are generally unanimous in their judgment that John does not recall Zech 12.10 OG.

---

9 See further below.

10 See further below.

11 Wilcox, "Text form," 202 (cf. Moo, *Passion Narratives*, 212).. This same tradition underlies the references in Justin. Wilcox refers to a similar haggadic development which may well represent an even earlier exegetical tradition. In *b. Sukka* 52a, the Old Testament passage cited by John is linked with the idea of the (suffering) Messiah ben Joseph (cf. Str-B 2:273-99; 583-84; Schlatter, *Der Evangelist*, 355). In a "Targum Yerushalmi" fragment (appearing as a marginal gloss in Codex Reuchlinianus) a similar haggadic exposition appears in even greater detail and contains references to the Messiah's conflict with Gog and Gog's killing of him outside the gates of Jerusalem. Whether or not this haggadic development has influenced the NT, however, is unclear.

12 The OG apparently has read רקדו "they danced" (in triumph; i.e., "they mocked") for דקרו "they pierced" (on the motive for this, see further below). This is the only instance of the use of the verb κατορχέω in the OG.

John's citation does, on the other hand, seem to many scholars a possible rendering of the Hebrew one finds in Zech 12.10 MT (את אלי אלי והביטו אשר־דקרו).[13] For this reason, many have argued that especially (and finally) here John shows that he also knows at least a portion of the Hebrew Old Testament textual traditions.[14] Other scholars, however, have argued that John's citation need not represent a reference to a Hebrew *Vorlage*. Some, for example, have suggested that, instead, John employs a Greek tradition shared with Theodotion (καὶ ἐπιβλέψονται πρὸς μὲ εἰς ὃν ἐξεκέντησαν).[15] According to others, the form of John's reference to the Old Testament is of Christian origin.[16]

---

[13] The (for the Jews) theologically difficult אלי in Zech 12.10 evidently prompted numerous conjectural emendations. Among these emendations, one is particularly close to the form of John's citation (אל־אשר). Still, "the MT reading should probably be retained as *lectio difficilior*" (Moo, *Passion Narratives*, 211 n. 4, who offers additional references to the secondary literature). And hypotheses suggesting John's dependence upon such an emended version of Zech 12.10, while possible, are no more plausible than those which suggest that John recalls the Hebrew of the MT. Cf. Toy, *Quotations*, 93; Burney, *Aramaic Origin*, 123; Heinrich Schlier, "ἐκκεντέω," *TDNT* 2:447; Braun, *Jean* 2, 9; O'Rourke, "Fulfillment," 440; Freed, *OT Quotations*, 110, 114; Pancaro, *Law*, 350 n. 150; Brown, *John* 2, 938; Humann, "OT Quotations," 41. See further below.

[14] Cf. Johnson, *Quotations*, 27, 78-82; Westcott, *St. John*, xiv; Toy, *Quotations*, 92-94; Burney, *Aramaic Origin*,123; Bernard, *St. John*, 652 (a possibility); Schlier, "ἐκκεντέω," 447; Hoskyns, *Fourth Gospel*, 536; Dodd, *Scriptures*, 65 (and idem, *Historical Tradition*, 44-45); Noack, *Tradition*, 84; Braun, *Jean* 2, 20; O'Rourke, "Fulfillment," 440, 442; Morris, *John*, 823 n. 105; Forestell, *Word*, 89; Pancaro, *Law*, 350, Barrett, *St. John*, 28, 558-59 (a possibility); Archer/Chirichigno, *OT Quotations*, xxvi, 163; Hanson, *Utterances*, 117 (a possibility); Wilcox, "Text form," 201 (a possibility); Humann, "OT Quotations," 40-42; de la Potterie, *Hour*, 176-77 (apparently).

[15] Several mss. representing the Lucianic recension offer the same much more literal rendering of the Hebrew of the MT (καὶ ἐπιβλέψονται πρὸς μὲ εἰς ὃν ἐξεκέντησαν). The reading in these mss. either stems from an earlier Greek tradition shared with Theodotion (contrast Aq.: . . . σὺν ᾧ ἐξεκέντησαν; Symm.: . . . ἔμπροσθεν ἐπεξεκέντησαν) or reflects Christian influence. In either case, scholars argue that John 19.37 recalls a similar non-OG version of Zech 12.10 current during the time of John. Cf. Toy, *Quotations*, 93; Hühn, *Citate*, 94-95; Bernard, *St. John*, 652; Goodwin, "Sources," 66; Noack, *Tradition*, 79; Dodd, *Historical Tradition*, 44-45 (a possibility); Braun, *Jean* 2, 9 (a possibility); Freed, *OT Quotations*, 115, 125 (a possibility); Stendahl, *St. Matthew*, 179, 214; Brown, *John* 2, 938; Sidney Jellicoe, *The Septuagint and Modern Study* (Oxford: Oxford University Press, 1968; reprint, Ann Arbor, Mi.: Eisenbrauns, 1978), 87; Morris, *John*, 823 n. 105 (a possibility); Longenecker, *Exegesis*, 137 (a possibility); Barrett, *St. John*, 558-59 (a possibility); Leroy, "Kein Bein," 75; Hanson, *Utterances*, 117 (a possibility); Moo, *Passion Narratives*, 210-11; Wilcox, "Text form," 201 (a possibility).

[16] Freed, *OT Quotations*, 114, 125-26, suggests that John 19.37 may recall a Hebrew *Vorlage*, but that its present form originated with John himself (or with the writer of the Apocalypse, if another person). Cf. Toy, *Quotations*, 93 ("based on a translation and exegesis of the Hebrew that cannot be maintained"); Braun, *Jean* 2, 20 (cited *ad sensum*); O'Rourke, "Fulfillment," 440 (a pesher citation); Longenecker, *Exegesis*, 137 (a possible "*ad hoc*

Interestingly, John's ability to accurately recall from memory the Old Testament passage he cites has not been an issue in most scholars' attempts to characterize John 19.37.

The task of evaluating these varying hypotheses is a difficult one. The textual history of this Old Testament passage is decidedly complex. On the one hand, John's εἰς ὃν ἐξεκέντησαν seems a possible contraction either of a Greek *Vorlage* (cf. Theodotion) or of the Hebrew of the MT.[17] John's ὄψονται, on the other hand, seems independent of every extant version of Zech 12.10.[18] A preliminary examination of the textual evidence, therefore, does little to identify a particular Old Testament textual tradition as John's most likely referent. Indeed, the complexity of the textual history of this Old Testament passage has suggested to some scholars yet another possible solution to this problem. Some scholars have even considered the possibility that John had access to an edited (i.e., corrected) version of the OG (perhaps containing marginal emendations).[19]

But at this stage, no one solution emerges as the more likely one. Unfortunately, an examination of John's intent in citing this Old Testament passage does little to alleviate this problem.

---

creation"); Schnackenburg, *St. John* 3, 293 ("an intentional alteration to fit the text Christologically"); Humann, "OT Quotations," 41 n. 32 (who cites Freed). Freed (pp. 115, 125, 128) also considers the possibility that John's citation comes from prior Christian apologetic, perhaps a testimony collection. Cf. my remarks above with Dodd, *Scriptures*, 65 (and idem, *Historical Tradition*, 45); Lindars, *NT Apologetic*, 122-27 (and idem, *John*, 590); Schnackenburg, *St. John* 1, 122 (and idem, *St. John* 3, 463 n. 96; *Johannes* 4, 168-71); Reim, *Studien*, 54-56, 93, 108; Seynaeve, "Jn 19,36-37," 71, 76; Fuller, "Passion," 57; Fortna, *Fourth Gospel*, 178 n. 411. Kysar, *John*, 289, finds himself unable to decide whether John renders a Hebrew *Vorlage* or recalls Christian tradition.

17 The omission of πρός με in cod. 130 is probably due to its assimilation to the NT (Schnackenburg, *Johannes* 4, 167). Alfred Rahlfs, "Über Theodotion-Lesarten im Neuen Testament und Aquila-Lesarten bei Justin," *ZNW* 20 (1921): 182-99, in particular has contested the alleged connection between John and Theodotion. According to Ralphs, ἐκκεντέω is a natural rendering of דקר and both John and Theodotion are dependent upon a Hebrew *Vorlage*. Other scholars who have called this connection into question include Burney, *Aramaic Origin*, 123 (cited by Freed, *OT Quotations*, 109-10, 114); Schlier, ἐκκεντέω," 447; O'Rourke, "Fulfillment," 440 n. 29; Schnackenburg, *St. John* 3, 293 (and idem, *Johannes* 4, 167-68).

18 The verb ὁράω is used for נבט only three times in the OG (cf. Num 12.8; Job 6.19; Isa 38.11). The agreement between John's citation and the Peshitta is probably due to the latter's assimilation to the NT (Moo, *Passion Narratives*, 211). Burney, *Aramaic Origin*, 123, similarly defines the Christian marginal variant in cod. 240.

19 Bultmann, *John*, 677 n. 2.

II.

Scholars have debated over several issues in their efforts to characterize John's intent in citing Zech 12.10. The first of these issues has to do with the subject of ὄψονται. Who are "they?" Initially, the soldiers appearing in John 19.31-34 seem to be the ones who "look upon" him (cf. 19.33) whom they have pierced (cf. 19.34). But we have already noted that these soldiers act at the instigation of the Jews.[20] Is it the Jews, then, who look upon Jesus whom they themselves have pierced? (cf. 1.11; 8.28; 19.16, 31). Does, perhaps, John's reference in John 19.35 to ὁ ἑωρακὼς represent yet another possible referent of ὄψονται?

The issue is a difficult one to resolve with any certainty. But the preceding context of John's citation would seem to indicate that John is not intent on identifying those who committed the physical act of piercing Jesus' side (only one of the soldiers, in fact, pierces Jesus in John 19.34). Rather, John seems intent on identifying those ultimately responsible for Jesus' death. In the broadest possible sense, of course, John understands the entire world to be responsible for this piercing (cf. 1.29). If this is what John has in mind in John 19.37, then all of the possible referents identified above are intended in John's "they." Such a solution is attractive, but its likelihood is, again, admittedly difficult to demonstrate.[21]

This brings us to a second issue of significance in scholars' efforts to characterize John's intent in citing Zech 12.10. Specifically, what has prompted John to choose for his citation the verb ὁράω? We have already noted that ὄψονται appears also in the parallel references to this same Old Testament

---

[20] See my remarks in chapter twelve.

[21] If this is, in fact, what John has in mind, it may well also be that John finds it possible to refer to the fulfillment of Zech 12.10–(in which Zechariah states that the inhabitants of Jerusalem are those who "look")–because he understands the Jews to be included in the group designated "they" (see esp. Schnackenburg, *St. John* 3, 293-94 [and idem, *Johannes* 4, 171-73]; cf. Westcott, *St. John*, 280; Bernard, *St. John*, 652; Bultmann, *John*, 677 n. 3; Pancaro, *Law*, 351-52; Brown, *John* 2, 954-55; Seynaeve, "Jn 19,36-37," 73-76; Morris, *Reflections*, 679; Humann, "OT Quotations," 37; de la Potterie, *Hour*, 177; contrast the verbs for "seeing" in John 19.4, 5, 6, 14). The content of this Old Testament context suggests also that God "will pour out on the house of David and the inhabitants of Jerusalem a spirit of compassion and supplication, so that, when they look on him whom they have pierced, they shall mourn for him." Thus, those who mourn in this spirit of compassion and supplication for the one whom they have pierced, in spite of the crime they have committed, will be beneficiaries of the grace of God: "On that day there shall be a fountain opened for the house of David and the inhabitants of Jerusalem to cleanse them from sin and uncleanness" (13.1 MT; cf. 14.8-11; contrast John 19.34). John, however, does not seem intent on recalling this larger context (contrast Rev 1.7).

passage elsewhere in the New Testament (cf. Matt 24.30; Rev 1.7). But ὄψονται does not seem to recall any extant version of Zech 12.10.[22]

We have considered the possibility that ὄψονται is of Christian origin and that John's citation betrays his knowledge of this earlier tradition. This is conceivable. But even if this is the case, we have also consistently noted John's rather precise familiarity with the Old Testament contexts which his citations recall. It is unlikely, therefore, that he utilizes this verb form without having in mind its relationship to a specifically Old Testament *Vorlage* or that the choice of this verb is unrelated to John's own literary and theological agenda.

What, then, does John have in mind? Does John recall again an analogous context? Several interesting possible contexts present themselves.[23] Perhaps the most interesting of these possibilities is offered by Isaiah, where the prophecy of an eschatological "seeing" of God by his own people is especially prominent.[24] Still, it may be best to argue that John simply regarded ὄψονται as a suitable synonym for the verb he found in his Old Testament *Vorlage* (הביטו/ἐπι-

---

[22] Scholars' attempts to find in John's selection of this verb form either a misreading of the OG's κόψονται (Freed, *OT Quotations*, 115) or an example of "word play" similar to what one observes at Qumran (Moo, *Passion Narratives*, 211 n. 6) fail to convince (O'Rourke, "Fulfillment," 440 n. 29).

[23] In Mic 7.8-10, for example, one encounters a similar description of one who falls at the hands of enemies, but will eventually prevail. In v. 10, it is stated that his enemies "will see" and will recognize their "shame" (cf. v. 16: "The nations shall see and be ashamed"). This prophecy closes in vv. 18-20 with a very similar indication that God will cancel the iniquities of the remnant of Israel. Cf. Num 21.8-9 (the OT referent of John 3.14-15), where ὁράω and ἐπιβλέπω are used interchangeably in references to those who "look upon" the elevated serpent in the wilderness and "live." See also 1 Kgs 16.7, where ὁράω + εἰς (one of only two instances of this combination in the OG; cf. Eccl 12.5) and ἐπιβλέπω + εἰς are used interchangeably in an OT context in which God's ability to "see" the Lord's anointed is contrasted with that of the world.

[24] See, e.g., Isa 6.5; 29.18 (cf. vv. 22-24); 33.10-11, 17, 20, 22 (cf. Ἰδοὺ . . . ὁ ἄνθρωπος in vv. 1-2 with John 19.5); 35.2, 4-5; 40.9-10, 26; 42.6-7, 16. See esp. Isa 52.6-10. Isa 52.6-10, like Zech 12.10, anticipates a time when God will again reign in the midst of his formerly rebellious people. At that time, the Lord will be present in their midst and will preach to them glad tidings of peace and salvation. At that time, the people of God will rejoice, for "eyes shall look to (ὄψονται πρὸς) eyes" (52.8; cf. Zech 12.10: ἐπιβλέψονται πρὸς μὲ) when the Lord comes, is merciful, and delivers Jerusalem. Isa 52.8, then, anticipates in a fashion analogous to Zech 12.10 a time when the Jews will "see" God and undergo a change of heart. A reference to Isaiah would, of course, significantly complement what we have already noted concerning John's previous references to such passages as OG Isa 6.9-10; 42.18-20; 44.18; and 53.1 in John 12.38-40 (and would suggest that here too John recalls the same textual tradition). Cf. Isa 52.10 OG: "the Lord shall reveal his holy arm in the sight of all the nations; and all the ends of the earth shall see (ὄψονται) the salvation that comes from our God." See also v. 15: "for they to whom no report was brought concerning him, shall see (ὄψονται); and they who have not heard, shall consider." Contrast Rev 1.7: "every eye will see him."

βλέψονται).[25] It is unlikely that John would have found this element of his *Vorlage* suited to his purposes.[26]

This raises, then, one final question. Why does John choose for his citation the expression εἰς ὅν, an apparent contraction of his *Vorlage*?[27] The answer to this question is probably a simple one. But it is not likely that John's motive is similar to that evinced by the text of the OG.[28] Instead, John drops his *Vorlage*'s first person singular reference to God because this would not fit well in the New Testament context of John's citation. In the context of John's passion, a third person singular reference is called for.[29]

In summary, the overall form of John 19.37 is unique to John's Gospel, uniquely serves John's literary and theological purposes, and is, therefore, probably John's own creation. Still, John's citation bears much in common with parallel references to Zech 12.10 elsewhere in the New Testament (Matt 24.30; Rev 1.7).[30] It is conceivable, therefore, that John betrays with his citation a knowledge of a careful piece of exegesis which forms a coherent pattern behind each of these New Testament references to Zech 12.10. At the same time, however, it is unlikely that John does not also recall a specific Old Testament *Vorlage*.[31] The expression ὄψονται εἰς ὅν in John 19.37 is notably independent of both Matt 24.30 and Rev 1.7 and suggests, therefore, that John independently recalls some specific version of Zech 12.10.[32]

---

[25] The verbs ὁράω and ἐπιβλέπω are used interchangeably in Zech 4.10 (cf. 4.2; 10.4, 7).

[26] Ἐπιβλέπω appears only three times in the NT (cf. Luke 1.48; 9.38; James 2.3). Cf. Seynaeve, "Jn 19,36-37," 73; Humann, "OT Quotations," 40-41.

[27] John 19.37 is the only passage in John's Gospel in which the preposition εἰς is paired with ὁράω. Cf. βλέπω + εἰς in John 13.22. See also εἰς ὅν in John 5.45; 6.29; 18.1.

[28] See further below.

[29] Note the third person singular references in Zech 12.10 which immediately follow the portion of this Old Testament passage cited by John.

[30] On the use of Zechariah in the NT, see Dodd, *Scriptures*, 64-67; Lindars, *NT Apologetic*, 110-34; Moo, *Passion Narratives*, 173-224.

[31] We have noted that John also seems aware of the content of the OT context from which his citation comes. Whether or not John intends with his citation to evoke this entire OT context, however, is difficult to establish. Cf. Brown, *John* 2, 955; Schnackenburg, *St. John* 3, 292; Seynaeve, "Jn 19,36-37," 72; McCaffrey, *House*, 242-43; de la Potterie, *Hour*, 177-78.

[32] That John refers to Zech 12.10 in the context of the suffering and death of Jesus rather than in an apocalyptic setting similar to that of either Matt 24.30 or Rev 1.7 is similarly indicative of an independent treatment of Zech 12.10. The setting of John's citation is, of course, "in keeping with John's emphasis on 'realized eschatology'" (Moo, *Passion Narratives*, 214). John's ἐξεκέντησαν, on the other hand, when compared with νύσσω in John 19.34 represents another "example of John's love for slight variation" (Morris, *John*, 818 n. 86; cited by Humann, "OT Quotations," 41, for whom the choice of each verb "is best attributed to John"). Cf. my remarks in chapters six and eleven.

It is difficult, however, to identify which version of Zech 12.10 it is that John recalls. An understanding of John's purpose in citing this Old Testament passage has done little to solve this problem. Still, John's consistent use of the OG in citations of the Old Testament elsewhere in his Gospel would suggest that here too John recalls a Greek version of Zech 12.10 rather than a Hebrew one. Does John, then, recall a Greek tradition shared with Theodotion? This is possible. But it is also conceivable that John has access to an edited (i.e., corrected) version of the OG (perhaps John recalls a marginal reading from the OG).

In any case, John apparently finds the OG itself unsatisfactory because it seems to consciously avoid any suggestion that God himself might be "pierced."[33] This, however, is exactly what John is intent on asserting. In the person of Jesus, John means to say, God himself is pierced.[34] And so for the first time in this examination of John's explicit citations of the Old Testament, John goes against the OG. This does not necessarily mean that John shows thereby that he knows of an Old Testament textual tradition other than the OG. But if this is so, then this textual tradition may well be the one shared with Theodotion.[35]

III.

In conclusion, John's editorial reference to the Old Testament in John 19.37 recalls Zech 12.10. It is uncertain whether a specific Old Testament textual tradition is also thereby recalled. But John's consistent use of the OG in his explicit citations of the Old Testament elsewhere in his Gospel suggests that in John 19.37 as well he recalls a Greek *Vorlage* rather than a Hebrew one (either a corrected version of the OG or a tradition shared with Theodotion). John cites Zech 12.10 for two reasons: (1) to identify those ultimately responsible for the death of Jesus; and (2) to assert that the piercing of Jesus was anticipated by Old Testament prophecy.

---

33 See esp. Hoskyns, *Fourth Gospel*, 535.

34 Cf. Johnson, *Quotations*, 78-82; Brown, *John* 2, 955-56; Humann, "OT Quotations," 41-42.

35 Due to my own linguistic limitations, I have been regretfully unable to refer in this final chapter to the recent article published by Ignace de la Potterie, "'Volgeranno lo sguardo a colui che hanno trafitto.' Sangue di cristo e oblatività," *CivCatt* 137 (1986): 105-18.

Concluding Observations

This investigation of the interrelationship of form and function in the explicit Old Testament citations in the Gospel of John lends itself now to several unique concluding observations. Significant also are some of the correlative implications of this investigation for the larger issue of the overall role of the Old Testament in John's Gospel.

First, there is in John's citations tangible evidence for the use of one and only one textual tradition, the OG.[1] Indeed, John exhibits an exceedingly accurate knowledge of this particular textual tradition. We have noted that John's Gospel was produced in "a culture of high residual orality."[2] John, therefore, may well cite the Old Testament from memory. If this is the case, then John's ability to recall the passages he cites is indeed impressive.

That John recalls the passages he cites with exceptional accuracy does not mean, however, that John simply parrots the textual tradition which he recalls. Rather, John exhibits a notable willingness to deliberately deviate from the form of his *Vorlage*. For example, John frequently shortens the Old Testament passages he cites. Occasionally, John also feels free to substitute appropriate synonyms for certain terms in the passages he recalls. In the majority of cases, however, in which John substitutes a different term or expression for one in his

---

[1] We noted in chapter thirteen that John goes against the reading of the OG in John 19.37, but it is unclear whether or not this can be taken as evidence for his knowledge of an alternate textual tradition. There is little reason, therefore, to suspect that John recalls an alternate textual tradition in the case of John 2.17 (which we noted in chapter two seems initially a possible referent to either a Greek or a Hebrew *Vorlage*).

[2] See my remarks in my introduction.

Vorlage, John introduces into his citations textual materials external to the passages he actually cites.

John's citations, therefore, frequently contain textual materials not derived from the Old Testament passage cited. But these materials too come from the Old Greek, and in one of two ways: (1) Some materials come from the immediate context of the Old Testament passage cited (the Gospel of John evinces a consistently high regard for such contexts). (2) And other materials come from analogous contexts.[3] In both cases, one observes an exegetical procedure already well-established in first-century Judaism.[4]

Thus, the form of the explicit Old Testament citations in the Gospel of John is best explained in terms of John's purposeful editing of passages which John recalls from the Old Greek.[5] John's citations are products of his editorial activity which reflect his authorial intent. John has carefully adapted his citations to their eventual literary and theological context. As such, John's citations consistently complement both the immediate Gospel contexts in which they appear and the context of John's Gospel as a whole. This demonstrable reciprocity of form and

---

[3] That John, then, does not inadvertently or arbitrarily alter the form of his citations suggests he holds the textual tradition which he recalls in significantly high regard. In most instances, John appears to deviate from the form of his *Vorlage* not because he finds his *Vorlage* corrupt, but because he finds the form of his *Vorlage* not well-suited to his purposes. Still, John does deviate from the textual tradition he recalls and in John 19.37 he even exhibits an apparent willingness to go against the OG. It is, likely therefore, that John does recognize the OG to be a translation and that he then also finds his *Vorlage* in need of occasional correction. It is of great significance, however, that John's normal pattern for introducing such corrections does not involve resorting to an alternate textual tradition (John 19.37 represents, of course, the only possible exception to John's normal pattern). See further below.

[4] John's appropriation techniques, therefore, significantly parallel those evident elsewhere in contemporary Jewish literature. This does not mean, however, that there is nothing which distinguishes John's procedure from that of the Jews. In the case of John, "the underlying hermeneutical axioms are distinctively Christian. These relate not only to christology and the way the OT is read as a prefigurement of Jesus Christ, but even to the eschatological stance of the evangelist" (Carson, "John," 257). Unique to Christianity is the proclamation of the present and complete fulfillment of the Scripture. Such a stance is particularly strong in John's Gospel where realized or inaugurated eschatology prevails.

[5] Some scholars might argue that, instead, John recalls the not now extant Hebrew *Vorlage* of the OG. It is unlikely, however, that John recalls such a Hebrew *Vorlage*. John's citations too frequently reproduce the exact form of the OG when John's own style would suggest a different rendering of an equivalent Hebrew *Vorlage* (John presumably does not, in these instances, alter his *Vorlage* because such alterations would not significantly facilitate his purposes). Indeed, it is difficult to otherwise explain the form of John's repeated references both to the immediate OT contexts from which his citations have come and to the many analogous contexts he recalls. The form of John's many attempts to relate his literary and theological agenda to that of the Old Testament Wisdom literature also suggests a broad familiarity with the form of the OG.

function, in turn, confirms that it is indeed John himself who is ultimately responsible for the form of these citations.[6]

Is the OG, then, the only textual tradition John knows? The overall character of John's language in the remainder of his Gospel suggests otherwise. The influence of the OG on the rest of John's Gospel is not as pervasive as one might suspect. John does not, for example, like Luke exhibit an overall tendency in his Gospel to imitate the OG.[7] Indeed, there is much about the language of John's Gospel which seems to suggest, instead, a Semitic background for John.[8]

John's language has, in fact, spawned a prominent debate over the possibility of an Aramaic origin for John's Gospel.[9] Scholars have shown convincingly that John's Gospel was not originally composed in Aramaic. John's Gospel was written in Greek from the start. Still, this debate has served to illustrate the Semitic character (or at least Semitic coloring) of John's Gospel.

There is, therefore, in John's language evidence which seems to suggest that John thought in Aramaic, but wrote in Greek.[10] That he knew Hebrew as well is also suggested. These observations, in turn, suggest that John knew of the

---

[6] It is, of course, probable that many of the citations appearing in John's Gospel appeared also in the tradition which his Gospel recalls. But John's own ability to dialogue with the OT contexts from which these citations have come (and with other complementary OT contexts) has manifestly contributed to the adaptation of these citations to their eventual place in John's Gospel. John's citations, therefore, are now so thoroughly adapted both to their immediate Gospel contexts and to the context of John's Gospel as a whole that it is questionable whether there is value in speaking of their so-called pre-johannine form. John's citations, therefore, are uniquely his own. There is also, therefore, similarly little warrant for suggesting that an editor has adapted the form of John's citations so that they now recall the OG. Too often, elements of these citations which are especially indicative of the influence of the OG significantly complement the literary and theological contexts in which they appear. Such elements, then, are indicative not of an editor's hand, but of John's hand.

[7] Schnackenburg, St. John 1, 108.

[8] "Semitisms" are constructions common to Hebrew and Aramaic, but are not native to the Greek language. The influence of the OG does not constitute an adequate explanation for their appearance.

[9] On the nature of this debate, see esp. Schnackenburg, St. John 1, 105-11. Cf. the recent treatment of this data by Jack P. Lewis, "The Semitic Background of the Gospel of John," in Johannine Studies: Essays in Honor of Frank Pack, ed. James E. Priest (Malibu, Ca.: Pepperdine University Press, 1989), 97-110, esp. 107-10.

[10] The Semitic character or coloring of John's language "will make one hesitate to question his Jewish origin, while the correct Greek, which is impressive in its own way, forces one to suppose that he lived for a long time in a Hellenistic environment" (Schnackenburg, St. John 1, 110). See esp. Barrett, St. John, 11: "Perhaps it is safest to say that in language as well as in thought John treads, perhaps not unconsciously, in the boundary between the Hellenic and the Semitic; he avoids the worst kind of Semitism, but retains precisely that slow and impressive feature of Aramaic which was calculated to produce the effect of solemn, religious Greek, and may perhaps have influenced already the liturgical language of the church."

Aramaic and Hebrew Scriptures of the Jews. Why, then, does he not refer in his citations to either of these textual traditions? The reason for this is probably to be found not in the background of John, but in the background of his Gospel's intended audience. The OG is the Old Testament of the Johannine community. John naturally draws on the Bible of this audience when he cites the Old Testament.[11]

Why, then, does John cite the Old Testament? It is likely that his motive is the same as that for the rest of his references to the Old Testament. In one way or another, John's references to the Old Testament consistently touch on the identity of Jesus and assert that the details of Jesus' life and especially his death on the cross fulfill Scripture.[12] For John, therefore, the past, the Old Testament with its observances and all its institutions, is not negated; it is confirmed and completed.[13]

---

[11] The Greek OT was the most widely circulated form of the OT in apostolic times and furnished the vehicle for the earliest preaching and teaching of the Christian church in the Hellenistic world (see my remarks in my Introduction). The selection of such a vehicle (and of the Greek language for the composition of the NT) was, of course, a natural one in view of the eventual literary and cultural milieu of the expanding church. Such a selection need not have involved any antipathy for the Jews, for their language, or for their Scriptures. Rather, earliest Christianity's recourse to a Greek OT, in all likelihood, was governed principally by its desire to accommodate its message to the audience it intended to evangelize. Thus, in time the OG became the Bible of the Johannine community. Does this mean that John's references in his Gospel to the OG reflect a similar missionary zeal? John's recourse to the OG may well reflect now only the internal issues of an already existing, cosmopolitan Christian community in a Hellenistic environment. John may be familiar with the Aramaic and Hebrew Scriptures of the Jews, with their efforts to arrive at a fixed consonantal Hebrew text, or even with their efforts to revise the OG in the direction of such a normalized Hebrew text. But because the Bible of his community (and, therefore, its liturgy) is the OG, John does not exhibit in his Gospel any interest in any of these alternate textual traditions. When John cites the OT, he naturally confines himself to the OT of his community.

[12] On the role of John 19.28-30 in this scheme, see my remarks in chapter seven.

[13] Is to speak of the fulfillment of the γραφή and of the νόμος (or of the λόγος written in the Law) one and the same thing for John? Pancaro, *Law*, 326-29, shows that this does seem to be the case. The connection of the root γραφ- with the νόμος in John 1.45; 8.17; 10.34; and 15.25 appears significant. A comparison of John 7.23 with 10.35 (cf. also 10.34 with 10.35) and of John 7.38 and 7.42 with 12.34 suggests further that νόμος and γραφή are used by John interchangeably. "The νόμος is the νόμος of Moses (1,17; 7,19.23); the γραφαί are the γραφαί of Moses (1,45; 5,39.46.47). Insofar as νόμος stands for the Scriptures or a part thereof, γραφή, γραφαί and νόμος are synonymous. To this extent it is clear that, by fulfilling the Scripture(s), Jesus fulfills the Law" (p. 327). Why, then, in John's Gospel are γραφή, γραφαί, and γράμματα never qualified by either ὑμῶν or αὐτῶν, while νόμος frequently is? (cf. 7.51; 8.17; 10.34; 15.25; 18.31). Γραφή is, in fact, never qualified in this way in the NT (to qualify γραφή thus would introduce a reference to its author). John, we noted, qualifies νόμος in this manner in order to emphasize that the verity of Jesus' position is easily substantiated from the Jews' own sacred Scriptures. John thus accentuates the irony of their blindness (see my

This does not mean, however, that John's references to the Old Testament speak only of Jesus. Included in the aforementioned "details" of Jesus' life which fulfill Scripture are the responses Jesus elicits both from his disciples (1.23; 6.45) and from his adversaries (2.17; 12.38-40; 13.18; 15.25; 19.24, 37). References to the Old Testament by these two parties serve two complementary functions: (1) They expose each party's failure to understand and their corresponding misappropriation of Old Testament passages (2.17; 6.31). (2) And they contrast each party's failure to understand with the perspective of Jesus and with the post-resurrection perspective of Jesus' followers (2.22; 12.16; 14.20, 23-26; 15.20, 26; 16.4, 13).[14] Still, even the failure of each party to understand (cf. also 6.45; 10.34; 12.15; 13.18) serves, finally, to illustrate both the identity of Jesus and Jesus' fulfilling of the purposes of God. Chiefly, then, John's references to the Old Testament proclaim how the person and work of Jesus, especially the death of Jesus, are to be understood.[15]

John's Old Testament citations are admittedly few in number. John obviously makes no attempt with his citations to exhaust the connections that could have been made between the person and work of Jesus and the Old Testament. Still, we have noted that whenever John refers to a particular passage from the Old Testament, it is always the entire Old Testament, the body of God's revelation given through Moses and passed on from generation to generation, which is also in view.[16] Thus, John employs Old Testament citations as discrete, concrete illustrations of his Gospel's larger scheme to convey John's conviction

---

remarks in chapter five). Why does John never directly speak of Jesus fulfilling the Law? (the verbs $\pi\lambda\eta\rho\delta\omega$, $o\dot{v}$ ... $\lambda\dot{v}\omega$, and $\tau\epsilon\lambda\epsilon\iota\delta\omega$ never appear with $\nu\delta\mu\sigma s$ as either subject or object; contrast Matt 5.17). The reason for this is not that John's use of $\nu\delta\mu\sigma s$ in his Gospel holds for him some "negative connotation" (pp. 327-28, 514-34). John avoids referring to Jesus' fulfillment of the Law not in order to distinguish between his use of $\nu\delta\mu\sigma s$ and his use of $\gamma\rho\alpha\phi\dot{\eta}$. Rather, John avoids such references in order to specify that when he uses $\nu\delta\mu\sigma s$ he means this to be understood as $\gamma\rho\alpha\phi\dot{\eta}$. John thus distinguishes between his use of $\nu\delta\mu\sigma s$ and that of the Jews for whom the Law was both written and oral. In keeping with the apologetic of the early Christian church, John distinguishes between the written Law (the OT) and the oral traditions of the Jews which he rejects as the doctrines of men. For John, then, Jesus fulfills only one aspect of the $\nu\delta\mu\sigma s$ of the Jews, the $\gamma\rho\alpha\phi\dot{\eta}$.

14 In chapter one, we noted that the Baptist in John 1.23 embodies beforehand this perspective.

15 This is why "It is difficult to discern any principle of discrimination that associates certain kinds of OT texts with certain speakers. What stands out is not which party in the FG appeals to the OT, but what is accomplished in each instance. The OT citations in one way or another point to Jesus, identifying him, justifying the responses he elicits, grounding the details of his life and death in the Scriptures" (Carson, "John," 246).

16 Cf. Pancaro, Law, 515, 517. For John, then, "the part represents the whole, the whole is present in its parts" (p. 515).

that the entire Old Testament testifies to Jesus (5.39, 45-46). Jesus, therefore, has fulfilled all of Scripture and is himself its ultimate significance.[17]

---

[17] During the final stages of the preparation of this dissertation, I discovered that Evans, "Isa 6:9-10," had been revised and published as *To See and Not Perceive: Isaiah 6.9-10 in Early Jewish and Christian Interpretation*, Journal for the Study of the Old Testament Supplement Series, vol. 64 (Sheffield: JSOT Press, 1989). Because this discovery came so late in the preparation of my own dissertation, I have retained my references to Evans' original work.

Bibliography

Abbott, Edwin A. *Johannine Grammar*. London: A. & C. Black, 1906.

Achtemeier, Paul J. "*Omne verbum sonat*: The New Testament and the Oral Environment of Late Western Antiquity." *Journal of Biblical Literature* 109 (1990): 3-27.

Ackerman, James S. "The Rabbinic Interpretation of Psalm 82 and the Gospel of John: John 10:34." *Harvard Theological Review* 59 (1966): 186-91.

Aker, Benny C. "The Merits of the Fathers: An Interpretation of John 8:31-59." Ph.D. diss., Saint Louis University, 1984.

Aletti, Jean-Noël. "Le discours sur le pain de vie (Jean 6): Problèmes de composition et fonction des citations de l'Ancien Testament." *Recherches de science religieuse* 62 (1974): 169-97.

―――. "Mort de Jésus et théorie du récit." *Recherches de science religieuse* 73 (1985): 147-60.

Amsler, Samuel. *L'Ancien Testament dans l'église: Essai d'herméneutique chrétienne*. Bibliothèque théologique. Neuchatel: Éditions Delachaux & Niestle, 1960.

Anderson, A. A. *The Book of Psalms*. 2 vols. New Century Bible. London: Oliphants, 1972.

Archer, Gleason L., and Gregory Chirichigno. *Old Testament Quotations in the New Testament: A Complete Survey*. Chicago: Moody, 1983.

Ashton, J. "The Transformation of Wisdom. A Study of the Prologue of John's Gospel." *New Testament Studies* 32 (1986): 161-86.

Aubineau, Michel. "La tunique sans couture du Christ: Exégèse patristique de Jean 19,23-24." In *Kyriakon: Festschrift Johannes Quasten*, vol. 1, 100-27. Edited by P.Granfield and J. A. Jungman. Münster, Westf.: Verlag Aschendorff, 1970.

Baldensperger, Wilhelm. *Der Prolog des vierten Evangeliums: Sein polemisch-apologetischer Zweck*. Tübingen: Mohr- Siebeck, 1898.

Bammel, Ernst. "The Baptist in Early Christian Tradition." *New Testament Studies* 18 (1971/1972): 95-128.

Barrett, Charles K. *The Gospel According to St. John: An Introduction with Commentary and Notes on the Greek Text.* 2d ed. Philadelphia: Westminster, 1978.

————. "The Old Testament in the Fourth Gospel." *Journal of Theological Studies* 48 (1947): 155-69.

Barthelemy, Dominique. *Les devanciers d'Aquila: Première publication intégrale du texte des fragments du Dodécaprophéton.* Supplements to Vetus Testamentum, vol. 10. Leiden: E. J. Brill, 1963.

Barton, George A. "'A Bone of Him Shall Not Be Broken,' John 19:36." *Journal of Biblical Literature* 49 (1930): 13-19.

Bassler, Jouette M. "A Man For All Seasons: David in Rabbinic and New Testament Literature." *Interpretation* 40 (1986): 156-69.

Beasley-Murray, George R. *John.* Word Biblical Commentary, vol. 36. Waco, Tex.: Word Books, 1987.

Becker, Jürgen. *Das Evangelium des Johannes.* Bd. 1, *Kapitel 1-10.* 2. Aufl. Ökumenischer Taschenbuchkommentar zum Neuen Testament, Bd. 4/1. Gütersloh: Gerd Mohn, 1985. Bd. 2, *Kapitel 11-21.* 2. Aufl. Ökumenischer Taschenbuchkommentar zum Neuen Testament, Bd. 4/2. Gütersloh: Gerd Mohn, 1984.

————. "Ich bin die Auferstehung und das Leben. Eine Skizze der johanneischen Christologie." *Theologische Zeitschrift* 39 (1983): 138-51.

Bergmeier, Roland. *Glaube als Gabe nach Johannes: Religions- und theologiegeschichtliche Studien zum prädestinatianischen Dualismus im vierten Evangelium.* Beiträge zur Wissenschaft vom Alten und Neuen Testament, 6. Folge, Bd. 12. Stuttgart: W. Kohlhammer, 1980.

Bernard, John H. *A Critical and Exegetical Commentary on the Gospel According to St. John.* 2 vols. International Critical Commentary. Edinburgh: T. & T. Clark, 1929.

Beutler, J. *Martyria: Traditionsgeschichtliche Untersuchungen zum Zeugnisthema bei Johannes.* Frankfurter Theologische Studien, Bd. 10. Frankfurt am Main: J. Knecht, 1972.

Bishop, Eric F. F. "'He That Eateth Bread with Me Hath Lifted Up His Heal against Me.'–Jn xiii.18 (Ps xli.9)." *Expository Times* 70 (1958/1959): 331-33.

Bittner, Wolfgang J. *Jesu Zeichen im Johannesevangelium: Die Messias-Erkenntnis im Johannesevangelium vor ihrem jüdischen Hintergrund.* Wissenschaftliche Untersuchungen zum Neuen Testament, 2. Reihe, Bd. 26. Tübingen: Mohr-Siebeck, 1987.

Blank, Josef. *Krisis: Untersuchungen zur johanneischen Christologie und Eschatologie.* Freiburg im Breisgau: Lambertus-Verlag, 1964.

Boice, James M. *Witness and Revelation in the Gospel of John.* Grand Rapids: Zondervan, 1970.

Boismard, Marie-Émile. "Jésus, le Prophète par excellence, d'après Jean 10,24-39." In *Neues Testament und Kirche. Für Rudolf Schnackenburg*, 160-71. Herausgegeben von J. Gnilka. Freiburg: Herder, 1974.

————. *Moïse ou Jesus: Essai de christologie johannique.* Bibliotheca Ephemeridum Theologicarum Lovaniensium, vol. 84. Leuven: University Press, 1988.

Boismard, Marie-Émile, and A. Lamouille. *Synopse des quatres évangiles en français avec paralleles des apocryphes et des Peres.* Tome 3, *L'Évangile de Jean.* 2e édition. Paris: Éditions du Cerf, 1987.

Borgen, Peder. *Bread from Heaven: An Exegetical Study of the Writings of Philo.* Supplements to Novum Testamentum, vol. 10. Leiden: E. J. Brill, 1965.

————. "Bread from Heaven. Aspects of Debates on Expository Method and Form." In his *Philo, John and Paul: New Perspectives on Judaism and Early Christianity,* 131-45. Brown Judaic Studies, nr. 131. Atlanta: Scholars Press, 1987.

Braun, François-Marie. "L'expulsion des vendeurs du Temple (Mt. xxi,12-17, 23-27; Mc. xi,15-19, 27-33; Lc. xix,45-xx,8; Jo. ii,13-22)." *Revue biblique* 38 (1929): 178-200.

————. *Jean le théologien.* Tome 2, *Les grandes traditions d'Israel et l'accord des Écritures, selon le Quatrième Évangile.* Études bibliques. Paris: Gabalda, 1964.

Brodie, Louis T. "Jesus as the New Elisha: Cracking the Code." *Expository Times* 93 (1981): 39-42.

Broer, Ingo. "Noch einmal: Zur religionsgeschichtlichen 'Ableitung' von Jo 2,1-11." *Studien zum Neuen Testament und seiner Umwelt* 8 (1983): 103-23.

Brooke, George J. *Exegesis at Qumran: 4QFlorilegium in Its Jewish Context.* Journal for the Study of the Old Testament Supplement Series, vol. 29. Sheffield: JSOT Press, 1985.

Brooks, J. A. "The Influence of Malachi Upon the New Testament." *Southwestern Journal of Theology* 30 (1987): 28-31.

Brown, Raymond E. *The Gospel According to John.* Vol. 1, (i-xii): *Introduction, Translation, and Notes.* 2d ed. Anchor Bible, vol. 29. Garden City, N.Y.: Doubleday, 1985. Vol. 2, (xiii-xxi): *Introduction, Translation, and Notes.* Anchor Bible, vol. 29A. Garden City, N.Y.: Doubleday, 1970.

Brown, Raymond E., D. W. Johnson, and Kevin G. O'Connell. "Texts and Versions." In *The New Jerome Biblical Commentary,* 1083-1112. Edited by Raymond E. Brown, Joseph A. Fitzmyer, and Roland E. Murphy. With a Foreword by Carlo Maria Cardinal Martini. Englewood Cliffs, N.J.: Prentice Hall, 1990.

Bruce, F. F. *The Gospel of John: Introduction, Exposition and Notes.* Grand Rapids: Eerdmans, 1983.

Bühner, Jan-A. *Der Gesandte und sein Weg im vierten Evangelium: Die kultur- und religionsgeschichtlichen Grundlagen der johanneischen Sendungschristologie sowie ihre traditionsgeschichtliche Entwicklung.* Wissenschaftliche Untersuchungen zum Neuen Testament, 2. Reihe, Bd. 2. Tübingen: Mohr-Siebeck, 1977.

Bullock, C. Hassell. "Ezekiel: Bridge between the Testaments." *Journal of the Evangelical Theological Society* 25 (1982): 23-31.

Bultmann, Rudolf. "Der Religionsgeschichtliche Hintergrund des Prologs zum Johannesevangelium." In *Exegetica: Aufsätze zur Erforschung des Neuen Testaments*, 10-35. Herausgegeben von Erich Dinkler. Tübingen: Mohr- Siebeck, 1967.

―――. *The Gospel of John: A Commentary*. Translated by G. R. Beasley-Murray. Edited by R. W. N. Hoare and J. K. Riches. With an Introduction by W. Schmithals. Philadelphia: Westminster, 1971.

Burge, Gary M. *The Anointed Community: The Holy Spirit in the Johannine Tradition*. Grand Rapids: Eerdmans, 1987.

Burney, Charles F. *The Aramaic Origin of the Fourth Gospel*. Oxford: Clarendon Press, 1922.

Buse, Ivor. "The Cleansing of the Temple in the Synoptics and in John." *Expository Times* 70 (1958/1959): 22-24.

Campbell, R. J. "Evidence for the Historicity of the Fourth Gospel in John 2:13-22." In *Studia Evangelica*. Vol. 7, *Papers Presented to the Fifth International Congress on Biblical Studies Held at Oxford, 1973*, 101-20. Edited by E. A. Livingstone. Texte und Untersuchungen zur Geschichte der altchristlichen Literatur, Bd. 112. Berlin: Akademie-Verlag, 1982.

Carey, G. L. "Lamb of God and Atonement Theories." *Tyndale Bulletin* 32 (1981): 97-122.

Carson, Don A. *Divine Sovereignty and Human Responsibility: Biblical Perspectives in Tension*. New Foundations Theological Library. Atlanta: John Knox Press, 1981.

―――. "John and the Johannine Epistles." In *It is Writtten: Scripture Citing Scripture. Essays in Honour of Barnabas Lindars*, 245-64. Edited by D. A. Carson and H. G. M. Williamson. Cambridge: Cambridge University Press, 1988.

Carson, Don A., and H. G. M. Williamson, eds. *It is Written: Scripture Citing Scripture. Essays in Honour of Barnabas Lindars*. Cambridge: Cambridge University Press, 1988.

Chesnutt, Randall D. "Bread of Life in *Joseph and Aseneth* and in John 6." In *Johannine Studies: Essays in Honor of Frank Pack*, 1-16. Edited by James E. Priest. Malibu, Ca.: Pepperdine University Press, 1989.

Clark, D. K. "Signs and Wisdom in John." *Catholic Biblical Quarterly* 45 (1983): 201-9.

Cullmann, Oscar. "Ο ΟΠΙΣΩ ΜΟΥ ΕΡΧΟΜΕΝΟΣ." In *In honorem Antonii Fridrichsen sexagenarii*, 26-32. Coniectanea Neotestamentica, vol. 11. Lund: C. W. K. Gleerup, 1947.

Culpepper, R. Alan. *Anatomy of the Fourth Gospel: A Study in Literary Design*. With a Foreword by Frank Kermode. Foundations and Facets: New Testament. Philadelphia: Fortress, 1983.

―――. "The Death of Jesus: An Exegesis of John 19.28- 37." *Faith and Mission* 5 (1988): 64-70.

Dahl, Nils A. "The Johannine Church and History." In *Current Issues in New Testament Interpretation: Essays in Honor of Otto A. Piper*, 124-42. Edited by W. Klassen. New York: Harper & Brothers, 1962.

Daube, David. *The New Testament and Rabbinic Judaism.* University of London: The Athlone Press, 1956.

Dauer, Anton. *Die Passionsgeschichte im Johannesevangelium: Eine traditionsgeschichtliche und theologische Untersuchung zu Joh 18,1-19,30.* Studien zum Alten und Neuen Testament, Bd. 30. München: Kösel-Verlag, 1972.

Derrett, J. Duncan M. "Law in the New Testament: The Palm Sunday Colt." *Novum Testamentum* 13 (1971): 241-58.

———. "The Zeal of the House and the Cleansing of the Temple." *Downside Review* 95 (1977): 79-94.

Dibelius, Martin. *Die urchristliche Überlieferung von Johannes dem Taüfer.* Forschungen zur Religion und Literatur des Alten und Neuen Testaments, Bd. 15. Göttingen: Vandenhoeck & Ruprecht, 1911.

Dodd, Charles H. *According to the Scriptures: The Substructure of New Testament Theology.* London: Nisbet, 1952.

———. *Historical Tradition in the Fourth Gospel.* Cambridge: Cambridge University Press, 1963.

———. *The Interpretation of the Fourth Gospel.* Cambridge: Cambridge University Press, 1953.

Domeris, William R. "The Holy One of God as a Title for Jesus." *Neotestamentica* 19 (1985): 9-17.

———. "The Office of the Holy One." *Journal of Theology for Southern Africa* 54 (1986): 35-38.

Edgar, S. L. "Respect for Context in Quotations from the Old Testament." *New Testament Studies* 9 (1962/1963): 55-62.

Ellis, E. Earle. *Paul's Use of the Old Testament.* Grand Rapids: Baker, 1957.

Emerton, John A. "Melchizedek and the Gods: Fresh Evidence for the Jewish Background of John X.34-36." *Journal of Theological Studies,* n.s. 17 (1966): 399-401.

———. "Some New Testament Notes." *Journal of Theological Studies,* n.s. 11 (1960): 329-32.

Eppstein, Victor. "The Historicity of the Gospel Account of the Cleansing of the Temple." *Zeitschrift für die neutestamentliche Wissenschaft* 55 (1964): 42-58.

Evans, Craig A. "The Function of Isaiah 6:9-10 in Mark and John. *Novum Testamentum* 24 (1982): 124-38.

———. "Isaiah 6:9-10 in Early Jewish and Christian Interpretation." Ph.D. diss., Claremont Graduate School, 1983.

———. "Isaiah 6:9-10 in Rabbinic and Patristic Writings." *Vigiliae christianae* 36 (1982): 275-81.

———. "Jerome's Translation of Isaiah 6:9-10." *Vigiliae christianae* 38 (1984): 202-4.

———. "Jesus' Action in the Temple: Cleansing or Portent of Destruction?" *Catholic Biblical Quarterly* 51 (1989): 237-70.

———. "On the Quotation Formulas in the Fourth Gospel." *Biblische Zeitschrift* 26 (1982): 79-83.

———. "The Text of Isaiah 6:9-10." *Zeitschrift für die alttestamentliche Wissenschaft* 94 (1982): 415-18.

———. *To See and Not Perceive: Isaiah 6.9-10 in Early Jewish and Christian Interpretation*. Journal for the Study of the Old Testament Supplement Series, vol. 64. Sheffield: JSOT Press, 1989.

Farmer, William R. "The Palm Branches in John 12:13." *Journal of Theological Studies*, n.s. 3 (1952): 62-66.

Faure, Alexander. "Die alttestamentlichen Zitate im 4. Evangelium und die Quellenscheidungshypothese." *Zeitschrift für die neutestamentliche Wissenschaft* 21 (1922): 99-121.

Feuillet, André. *Johannine Studies*. Translated by Thomas E. Crane. Staten Island, N.Y.: Alba House, 1965.

———. *Le prologue du quatrième Évangile*. Paris: Brouwer, 1968.

Finkel, Abraham. *The Pharisees and the Teacher of Nazareth: A Study of their Background, their Halachic and Midrashic Teachings, the Similarities and Differences*. Arbeiten zur Geschichte des antiken Judentums und des Urchristentums, Bd. 4. Leiden: E. J. Brill, 1964.

Fischer, Günter. *Die himmlischen Wohnungen: Untersuchungen zu Joh 14,2f*. Europäische Hochschulschriften, 23. Reihe, Theologie, Bd. 38. Bern: H. Lang, 1975.

Fitzmyer, Joseph A. "The Use of Explicit Old Testament Quotations in Qumran Literature and in the New Testament." *New Testament Studies* 7 (1960/1961): 297- 333.

Forestell, J. Terence. *The Word of the Cross: Salvation as Revelation in the Fourth Gospel*. Analecta Biblica, vol. 57. Rome: Biblical Institute Press, 1974.

Fortna, Robert T. *The Fourth Gospel and Its Predecessor: From Narrative Source to Present Gospel*. Philadelphia: Fortress, 1988.

Franke, August H. *Das Alte Testament bei Johannes: Ein Beitrag zur Erklärung und Beurtheilung der johanneischen Schriften*. Göttingen: Vandenhoeck & Ruprecht, 1885.

Freed, Edwin D. "*Egō Eimi* in John 1:20 and 4:25." *Catholic Biblical Quarterly* 41 (1979): 288-91.

———. "The Entry into Jerusalem in the Gospel of John." *Journal of Biblical Literature* 80 (1961): 329-38.

———. *Old Testament Quotations in the Gospel of John*. Supplements to Novum Testamentum, vol. 11. Leiden: E. J. Brill, 1965.

Fujita, Neil S. *A Crack in the Jar: What Ancient Jewish Documents Tell Us About the New Testament*. New York: Paulist, 1986.

Fuller, Reginald H. "The Passion, Death and Resurrection of Jesus according to St. John." *Chicago Studies* 25 (1986): 51-63.

Gaeta, Giancarlo. "Battesimo come testimonianza. Le pericopi sul Battista nell'evangelo di Giovanni." *Christianesimo nella storia* 1 (1980): 279-314.

Gärtner, Bertil. *John 6 and the Jewish Passover.* Coniectanea neotestamentica, vol. 17. Lund: C. W. K. Gleerup, 1959.

Gaston, Lloyd. *No Stone on Another: Studies in the Significance of the Fall of Jerusalem in the Synoptic Gospels.* Supplements to Novum Testamentum, vol. 23. Leiden: E. J. Brill, 1970.

Geiger, Georg. "Aufruf an Ruckkehrende: Zum Sinn des Zitats von Ps 78,24b in Joh 6,31." *Biblica* 65 (1984): 449- 64.

Gese, Hartmut. *Essays on Biblical Theology.* Translated by K. Crim. Minneapolis: Augsburg, 1981.

Glasson, T. Francis. *Moses in the Fourth Gospel.* Studies in Biblical Theology, vol. 40. Naperville: Allenson, 1963.

Gnilka, Joachim. *Die Verstockung Israels: Isaias 6,9-10 in der Theologie der Synoptiker.* Studien zum Alten und Neuen Testament, Bd. 3. München: Kösel-Verlag, 1961.

Goguel, Maurice. *Au seuil de l'evangile: Jean Baptiste.* Paris: C. Payot, 1928.

Goodwin Charles. "How Did John Treat His Sources?" *Journal of Biblical Literature* 73 (1954): 61-75.

Green, Joel B. *The Death of Jesus: Tradition and Interpretation in the Passion Narrative.* Wissenschaftliche Untersuchungen zum Neuen Testament, 2. Reihe, Bd. 33. Tübingen: Mohr-Siebeck, 1988.

Greenspoon, L. "The Use and Abuse of the Term 'LXX' and Related Terminology in Recent Scholarship." *Bulletin of the International Organization for Septuagint and Cognate Studies* 20 (1987): 21-29.

Grese, William C. "'Unless One is Born Again:' The Use of a Heavenly Journey in John 3." *Journal of Biblical Literature* 107 (1988): 677-93.

Grigsby, Bruce H. "The Cross as an Expiatory Sacrifice in the Fourth Gospel." *Journal for the Study of the New Testament* 15 (1982): 51-80.

Grundmann, Walter. *Der Zeuge der Weisheit: Grundzüge der Christologie des Johannesevangeliums.* Mit einer Einführung herausgegeben von W. Wiefel. Berlin: Evangelische Verlaganstalt, 1985.

Guilding, Aileen. *The Fourth Gospel and Jewish Worship: A Study of the Relation of St. John's Gospel to the Ancient Jewish Lectionary System.* Oxford: Clarendon Press, 1960.

Haag, H. "'Son of God' in the Language and Thinking of the Old Testament." *Concilium* 153 (1982): 31-36.

Haenchen, Ernst. *John.* Vol. 1, *1: A Commentary on the Gospel of John Chapters 1-6.* Translated by R. W. Funk. Edited by R. W. Funk with U. Busse. Hermeneia– A Critical and Historical Commentary on the Bible. Philadelphia: Fortress, 1984. Vol. 2, *2: A Commentary on the Gospel of John Chapters 7-21.* Translated by R. W. Funk. Edited by R. W. Funk with U. Busse. Hermeneia–A Critical and Historical Commentary on the Bible. Philadelphia: Fortress, 1984.

Hahn, Ferdinand. *Christologische Hoheitstitel: Ihre Geschichte im frühen Christentum.* Forschungen zur Religion und Literatur des Alten und Neuen Testaments, Bd. 83. Göttingen: Vandenhoeck & Ruprecht, 1963.

Hanson, Anthony T. "John's Citation of Psalm LXXXII: John X.33-36." *New Testament Studies* 11 (1964/1965): 158- 62.

———. "John's Citation of Psalm LXXXII Reconsidered." *New Testament Studies* 13 (1966/1967): 363-67.

———. *The Living Utterances of God: The New Testament Exegesis of the Old.* London: Darton, Longman and Todd, 1983.

———. *The New Testament Interpretation of Scripture.* London: SPCK, 1980.

Hartman, Lars. "'He Spoke of the Temple of His Body' (Jn 2:13-22)." *Svensk exegetisk årsbok* 54 (1989): 70-79.

Harvey, A. E. *Jesus on Trial: A Study in the Fourth Gospel.* Atlanta: John Knox, 1977.

Hill, John Spencer. "Τὰ βαΐα τῶν φοινίκων (John 12:13): Pleonasm or Prolepsis?" *Journal of Biblical Literature* 101 (1982): 133-35.

Hindley, J. C. "Witness in the Fourth Gospel." *Scottish Journal of Theology* 18 (1965): 319-37.

Hollenbach, Bruce. "Lest They Should Turn and Be Forgiven: Irony." *The Bible Translator* 34 (1983): 312-21.

Holst, R. A. "The Relation of John, Chapter Twelve, to the So-Called Johannine Book of Glory." Ph.D. diss., Princeton Theological Seminary, 1974.

Homcy, Stephen L. "'You are Gods'? Spirituality and a Difficult Text." *Journal of the Evangelical Theological Society* 32 (1989): 485-91.

Hoskyns, Edwyn C. *The Fourth Gospel.* 2d ed. Edited by F. N. Davey. London: Faber and Faber, 1947.

Hühn, Eugen. *Die messianischen Weissagungen des israelitisch- jüdischen Volkes bis zu den Targumim historisch- kritisch untersucht und erläutert.* 2. Teil, *Die alttestamentlichen Citate und Reminiscenzen im Neuen Testament.* Tübingen: Mohr-Siebeck, 1900.

Humann, Roger J. "The Function and Form of the Explicit Old Testament Quotations in the Gospel of John." *Lutheran Theological Review* 1 (1988/1989): 31-54.

Jellicoe, Sidney. *The Septuagint and Modern Study.* Oxford: Oxford University Press, 1968; reprint, Ann Arbor, Mi.: Eisenbrauns, 1978.

Jeremias, Joachim. "Zwei Miszellen: 1. Antik-jüdische Munzdeutungen. 2. Zur Geschichtlichkeit der Tempelreinigung." *New Testament Studies* 23 (1976/1977): 177-80.

Jocz, J. *The Jewish People and Jesus Christ.* London: SPCK, 1962.

Johnson, Franklin. *The Quotations of the New Testament from the Old Testament in the Light of General Literature.* Philadelphia: American Baptist Publication Society, 1895.

Jonge, Marinus de. "Jewish Expectations about the 'Messiah' according to the Fourth Gospel." *New Testament Studies* 19 (1972/1973): 246-70.

Jonge, Marinus de, and Adam S. van der Woude. "11QMelchizedek and the New Testament." *New Testament Studies* 12 (1965/1966): 301-26.

Jungkuntz, Richard. "An Approach to the Exegesis of John 10:34-36." *Concordia Theological Monthly* 35 (1964): 556-65.

Kingsbury, Jack Dean. "The Gospel in Four Editions." *Interpretation* 33 (1979): 363-75.

Koenig, Jean. *L'Herméneutique analogique du Judaïsme antique d'après les témoins textuels d'Isaïe.* Supplements to Vetus Testamentum, vol. 33. Leiden: E. J. Brill, 1982.

Koester, Craig R. *The Dwelling of God: The Tabernacle in the Old Testament, Intertestamental Jewish Literature, and the New Testament.* The Catholic Biblical Quarterly Monograph Series, vol. 22. Washington, D.C.: Catholic Biblical Association, 1989.

Kotila, Markku. *Umstrittener Zeuge: Studien zur Stellung des Gesetzes in der johanneischen Theologiegeschichte.* Annales Academiae Scientiarum Fennicae, Dissertationes Humanarum Litterarum, Bd. 48. Helsinki: Suomalainen Tiedeakatemia, 1988.

Küschelm, Roman. "Verstockung als Gericht: Eine Untersuchung zu Joh 12,35-43; Lk 13,34-35; 19,41-44." *Bibel und Liturgie* 57 (1984): 234-43.

Kysar, Robert. *The Fourth Evangelist and His Gospel: An Examination of Contemporary Scholarship.* Minneapolis: Augsburg, 1975.

————. "The Fourth Gospel. A Report on Recent Research." In *Aufstieg und Niedergang der römischen Welt: Geschichte und Kultur Roms im Spiegel der neueren Forschung,* 2. Principat, Bd. 25/3, 2389- 2480. Herausgegeben von Wolfgang Haase. New York: de Gruyter, 1984.

————. "The Gospel of John in Current Research." *Religious Studies Review* 9 (1983): 314-23.

————. *John.* Augsburg Commentary on the New Testament. Minneapolis: Augsburg, 1986.

Lacocque, André. "The Narrative Code of the Fourth Gospel: Response to Wolfgang Roth's Paper." *Biblical Research* 32 (1987): 30-41.

Lacomara, Aelred. "Deuteronomy and the Farewell Discourse (Jn 13:31-16:33)." *Catholic Biblical Quarterly* 36 (1974): 65-84.

Lagrange, Marie-Joseph. *L'évangile selon saint Jean.* 7th ed. Études bibliques. Paris: Gabalda, 1948.

Lenski, R. C. H. *The Interpretation of St. John's Gospel.* Minneapolis: Augsburg, 1943.

Leroy, Herbert. "'Kein Bein wird ihm gebrochen werden' (Jo 19,31-37). Zur johanneischen Interpretation des Kreuzes." In *Eschatologie: Bibeltheologische und philosophische Studien zum Verhältnis von Erlösungswelt und Wirklichkeitsbewältigung. Festschrift für Engelbert Neuhäusler zur Emeritierung gewidmet von Kollegen, Freunden und Schülern,* 73-81. Herausgegeben von Rudolf Kilian, Klemens Funk, und Peter Fassl. St. Ottilien: EOS Verlag, 1981.

Lewis, Jack P. "The Semitic Background of the Gospel of John." In *Johannine Studies: Essays in Honor of Frank Pack,* 97-110. Edited by James E. Priest. Malibu, Ca.: Pepperdine University Press, 1989.

Lieu, J. M. "Blindness in the Johannine Tradition." *New Testament Studies* 34 (1988): 83-95.

Lindars, Barnabas. *Behind the Fourth Gospel*. London: SPCK, 1971.

————. *The Gospel of John*. New Century Bible Commentary. London: Marshall, Morgan, & Scott, 1972; reprint, Grand Rapids: Eerdmans, 1987.

————. *New Testament Apologetic: The Doctrinal Significance of the Old Testament Quotations*. Philadelphia: Westminster, 1961.

Loader, W. R. G. "The Central Structure of Johannine Christology." *New Testament Studies* 30 (1984): 188- 216.

Longenecker, Richard N. *Biblical Exegesis in the Apostolic Period*. Grand Rapids: Eerdmans, 1975.

Losie, Lynn A. "The Cleansing of the Temple: A History of a Gospel Tradition in Light of Its Background in the Old Testament and in Early Judaism." Ph.D. diss., Fuller Theological Seminary, 1984.

Macdonald, John. *The Theology of the Samaritans*. New Testament Library. London: SCM Press, 1965.

Malina, B. J. *The Palestinian Manna Tradition: The Manna Tradition in the Palestinian Targums and Its Relationship to the New Testament Writings*. Arbeiten zur Geschichte des späteren Judentums und des Urchristentums, vol. 7. Leiden: E. J. Brill, 1968.

Malmede, Hans H. *Die Lichtsymbolik im Neuen Testament*. Studies in Oriental Religions, vol. 15. Wiesbaden: Otto Harrassowitz, 1986.

Mandelkern, Solomon. *Veteris Testamenti concordantiae hebraicae atque chaldaicae*. 2d ed. Berlin: Margolin, 1925.

Marshall, I. Howard. "An Assessment of Recent Developments." In *It is Written: Scripture Citing Scripture. Essays in Honour of Barnabas Lindars*, 1- 21. Edited by D. A. Carson and H. G. M. Williamson. Cambridge: Cambridge University Press, 1988.

Martyn, J. Louis. *The Gospel of John in Christian History: Essays for Interpreters*. Theological Inquiries: Studies in Contemporary Biblical and Theological Problems. New York: Paulist, 1979.

März, Claus-Peter. *"Siehe, Dein König kommt zu Dir...." Eine traditionsgeschichtliche Untersuchung zur Einzugsperikope*. Erfurter theologische Studien, Bd. 43. Leipzig: St. Benno-Verlag, 1980.

Matera, F. J. "'On Behalf of Others,' 'Cleansing,' and 'Return.' Johannine Images for Jesus' Death." *Louvain Studies* 13 (1988): 161-78.

Mathews, Kenneth A. "John, Jesus and the Essenes: Trouble at the Temple." *Criswell Theological Review* 3 (1988): 101-26.

Matsunaga, Kikuo. "The 'Theos' Christology as the Ultimate Confession of the Fourth Gospel." *Annual of the Japanese Biblical Institute* 7 (1981): 124-45.

Mayer, A. "Elijah and Elisha in John's Sign Source." *Expository Times* 99 (1988): 171-73.

McCaffrey, James. *The House with Many Rooms: The Temple Theme of Jn. 14,2-3.* Analecta Biblica, vol. 114. Rome: Editrice Pontificio Istituto Biblico, 1988.

Meeks, Wayne A. "Moses as God and King." In *Religions in Antiquity: Essays in Memory of E. R. Goodenough*, 354- 71. Edited by J. Neusner. Studies in the History of Religion, vol. 14. Leiden: E. J. Brill, 1968.

————. *The Prophet-King: Moses Traditions and the Johannine Christology.* Supplements to Novum Testamentum, vol. 14. Leiden: E. J. Brill, 1967.

Mendner, Siegfried. "Die Tempelreinigung." *Zeitschrift für die neutestamentliche Wissenschaft* 47 (1956): 93-112.

Menken, M. J. J. "Die Form des Zitates aus Jes 6,10 in Joh 12,40." *Biblische Zeitschrift* 32 (1988): 189-209.

————. "The Old Testament Quotation in John 6,45: Source and Redaction." *Ephemerides theologicae lovanienses* 64 (1988): 164-72.

————. "The Provenance and Meaning of the Old Testament Quotation in John 6:31." *Novum Testamentum* 30 (1988): 39-56.

————. "The Quotation from Isa 40,3 in John 1,23." *Biblica* 66 (1985): 190-205.

————. "Die Redaktion des Zitates aus Sach 9,9 in Joh 12,15." *Zeitschrift fur die neutestamentliche Wissenschaft* 25 (1989): 193-209.

————. "Some Remarks on the Course of the Dialogue: John 6,25-34." *Bijdragen* 48 (1987): 139-49.

————. "The Translation of Psalm 41.10 in John 13.18." *Journal for the Study of the New Testament* 40 (1990): 61-79.

Merode, Marie de. "L'accueil triomphal de Jésus selon Jean 11-12." *Revue théologique de Louvain* 13 (1982): 49- 62.

Metzger, Bruce M. "The Formulas Introducing Quotations of Scripture in the NT and the Mishna." *Journal of Biblical Literature* 70 (1951): 297-307.

————. *A Textual Commentary on the Greek New Testament.* London: United Bible Societies, 1971.

Michel, Otto. "Der aufsteigende und herabsteigende Gesandte." In *The New Testament Age: Essays in Honor of Bo Reicke*, vol. 2, 335-61. Edited by William C. Weinrich. Macon, Ga.: Mercer, 1984.

Moeller, H. R. "Wisdom Motifs and John's Gospel." *Bulletin of the Evangelical Theological Society* 6 (1963): 93- 98.

Mohr, Till Arend. *Markus- und Johannespassion: Redaktions- und traditionsgeschichtliche Untersuchung der Markinischen und Johahheischen Passionstradition.* Abhandlungen zur Theologie des Alten und Neuen Testaments, Bd. 70. Zürich: Theologischer Verlag, 1982.

Moloney, Francis J. "The Structure and Message of John 13:1-38." *Australian Biblical Review* 34 (1986): 1-16.

Moo, Douglas J. *The Old Testament in the Gospel Passion Narratives.* Sheffield: Almond Press, 1983.

Morris, Leon. *The Gospel according to John: The English Text with Introduction, Exposition and Notes*. The New International Commentary on the New Testament. Grand Rapids: Eerdmans, 1971.

————. *Reflections on the Gospel of John*. Vol. 1, *The Word Was Made Flesh: John 1-5*. Grand Rapids: Baker, 1986. Vol. 2, *The Bread of Life: John 6-10*. Grand Rapids: Baker, 1987. Vol. 3, *The True Vine: John 11 16*. Grand Rapids: Baker, 1988. Vol. 4, *Crucified and Risen: John 17-21*. Grand Rapids: Baker, 1988.

Mulder, Martin Jan, ed. *Mikra: Text, Translation, Reading and Interpretation of the Hebrew Bible in Ancient Judaism and Early Christianity*. Compendia Rerum Iudaicarum ad Novum Testamentum, section 2, The Literature of the Jewish People in the Period of the Second Temple and the Talmud, vol. 1. Philadelphia: Fortress, 1988.

Nereparampil, Lucius. *Destroy This Temple*. Bangalore: Dharmaram, 1978.

Neusner, Jacob. "Money-Changers in the Temple: The Mishnah's Explanation." *New Testament Studies* 35 (1989): 287-90.

Newman, Barclay M., and Eugene A. Nida. *A Translator's Handbook on the Gospel of John*. Helps for Translators. London: United Bible Societies, 1980.

Neyrey, Jerome H. *An Ideology of Revolt: John's Christology in Social-Science Perspective*. Philadelphia: Fortress, 1988.

————. "'I Said: You are Gods:' Psalm 82:6 and John 10." *Journal of Biblical Literature* 108 (1989): 647-63.

Noack, Bent. *Zur johanneischen Tradition: Beiträge zur Kritik an der Literarkritischen Analyse des vierten Evangeliums*. Teologiske Skrifter, Bd. 3. Copenhagen: Rosenkilde og Bagger, 1954.

Odeberg, Hugo. *The Fourth Gospel: Interpreted in Its Relation to Contemporaneous Religious Currents in Palestine and the Hellenistic-Oriental World*. Amsterdam: B. R. Grüner, 1968.

O'Grady, John G. "Recent Developments in Johannine Studies." *Biblical Theology Bulletin* 12 (1982): 54- 58.

Olsson, Birger. *Structure and Meaning in the Fourth Gospel: A Text-Linguistic Analysis of John 2:1-11 and 4:1-42*. Translated by Jean Gray. Coniectanea Biblica: New Testament Series, vol. 6. Lund: C. W. K. Gleerup, 1974.

O'Rourke, John J. "Explicit Old Testament Citations in the Gospels." *Studia Montis Regii* 7 (1964): 37-60.

————. "John's Fulfillment Texts." *Sciences ecclésiastiques* 19 (1967): 433-43.

Ottley, Richard R. *The Book of Isaiah according to the Septuagint*. Vol. 1, *Introduction and Translation with a Parallel Version from the Hebrew*. London: C. J. Clay, 1904. Vol. 2, *Text and Notes*. Cambridge: Cambridge University Press, 1906.

————. *A Handbook to the Septuagint*. New York: E. P. Dutton, 1919.

Painter, John. "Christology and the Fourth Gospel. A Study of the Prologue." *Australian Biblical Review* 31 (1983): 45-62.

————. "Christology and the History of the Johannine Community in the Prologue of the Fourth Gospel." *New Testament Studies* 30 (1984): 460-74.

———. "Eschatological Faith in the Gospel of John." In *Reconciliation and Hope: New Testament Essays on Atonement and Eschatology Presented to L. L. Morris on His 60th Birthday*, 36-52. Edited by J. Banks. Exeter: Paternoster Press, 1974.

Pancaro, Severino. *The Law in the Fourth Gospel: The Torah and the Gospel, Moses and Jesus, Judaism and Christianity according to John*. Supplements to Novum Testamentum, vol. 42. Leiden: E. J. Brill, 1975.

Perdue, Leo G. *Wisdom and Cult: A Critical Analysis of the Views of Cult in the Wisdom Literatures of Israel and the Ancient Near East*. Society of Biblical Literature Dissertation Series, vol. 30. Missoula: Scholars Press, 1977.

Pesch, Rudolf, and Reinhard Kratz. *So liest man synoptisch: Anleitung und Kommentar zum Studium der synoptischen Evangelien*. Bd. 6, *Passionsgeschichte: Erster Teil*. Frankfurt am Main: Verlag Josef Knecht, 1979.

Peterson, Erik. "Die Einholung des Kyrios." *Zeitschrift für die systematische Theologie* 7 (1930): 682-702.

Phillips, W. Gary. "An Apologetic Study of John 10:34-36." *Bibliotheca Sacra* 146 (1989): 405-19.

Pinto, Basil de. "Word and Wisdom in St. John." *Scripture* 19 (1967): 19-27.

Pinto, Evarist. *Jesus the Son and Giver Life in the Fourth Gospel*. Rome: Pontificia Universitas Urbaniana, 1981.

Potterie, Ignace de la. *The Hour of Jesus. The Passion and Resurrection of Jesus according to John: Text and Spirit*. Translated by Dom Gregory Murray. Middlegreen: St. Paul Publications, 1989.

———. "La tunique 'non divisée' de Jésus, symbole de l'unité messianique." In *The New Testament Age: Essays in Honor of Bo Reicke*, vol. 1, 127-38. Edited by William C. Weinrich. Macon, Ga.: Mercer, 1984.

———. "La tunique sans couture, symbole du Christ grand prêtre?" *Biblica* 60 (1979): 255-69.

———. "'Volgeranno lo sguardo a colui che hanno trafitto.' Sangue di cristo e oblatività." *Civiltà Cattolica* 137 (1986): 105-18.

Rahlfs, Alfred, ed. *Septuaginta: Id est Vetus Testamentum graece iuxta LXX interpretes*. 2 vols. in 1. Stuttgart: Deutsche Bibelgesellschaft, 1979.

———. "Über Theodotion-Lesarten im Neuen Testament und Aquila-Lesarten bei Justin." *Zeitschrift für die neutestamentliche Wissenschaft* 20 (1921): 182-99.

Räisänen, Heikki. *The Idea of Divine Hardening: A Comparative Study of the Notion of Divine Hardening, Leading Astray and Inciting to Evil in the Bible and Qur'ān*. Publications of the Finnish Exegetical Society, vol. 25. Helsinki: Finnische Exegetische Gesellschaft, 1976.

Reim, Günter. "Jesus as God in the Fourth Gospel: The Old Testament Background." *New Testament Studies* 30 (1984): 158-60.

———. *Studien zum alttestamentlichen Hintergrund des Johannesevangeliums*. Society for New Testament Studies Monograph Series, vol. 22. New York: Cambridge University Press, 1974.

Reinhartz, Adele. "Jesus as Prophet: Predictive Prolepses in the Fourth Gospel." *Journal for the Study of the New Testament* 36 (1989): 3-16.

Richter, Georg. "Die alttestamentlichen Zitate in der Rede vom Himmelsbrot Joh 6,26-51a." In *Schriftauslegung: Beiträge zur Hermeneutik des Neuen Testaments und im Neuen Testament*, 193-279. Herausgegeben von Josef Ernst. München: F. Schöningh, 1972.

——. "'Bist du Elias?' (Joh 1,21)." *Biblische Zeitschrift*, n.F. 6 (1962): 79-92, 238-56 and 7 (1963): 63-80.

Rissi, Mathias. "Der Aufbau des vierten Evangeliums." *New Testament Studies* 29 (1983): 48-54.

——. "Die Hochzeit in Kana Joh 2,1-11." In *Oikonomia: Heilsgeschichte als Thema der Theologie. Oscar Cullmann zum 65. Geburtstag gewidmet*, 76-92. Herausgegeben von Felix Christ. Hamburg: Reich, 1967.

——. "Die Logoslieder im Prolog des vierten Evangeliums." *Theologische Zeitschrift* 31 (1975): 321-36.

——. "Voll grosser Fische, hundertdreiundfünfzig, Joh. 21,1-14." *Theologische Zeitschrift* 35 (1979): 73-89.

Roberge, Michel. "La composition de Jean 6,22-59 dans l'exégèse récente." *Laval Théologique et Philosophique* 40 (1984): 91-123.

——. "Le discours sur le pain de vie (Jean 6,22-59): Problèmes d'interprétation." *Laval Théologique et Philosophique* 38 (1982): 265-99.

Robinson, J. A. T. "Elijah, John and Jesus. An Essay in Detection." *New Testament Studies* 4 (1957/1958): 263-81.

——. *The Priority of John*. Edited by J. F. Coakley. London: SCM Press, 1985.

——. "The Significance of the Footwashing." In *Neotestamentica et Patristica: Eine Freundesgabe, Herrn Professor Dr. Oscar Cullmann zu seinem 60. Geburtstag überreicht*, 144-47. Edited by W. C. van Unnik. Supplements to Novum Testamentum, vol. 6. Leiden: E. J. Brill, 1962.

Roth, Cecil. "The Cleansing of the Temple and Zechariah xiv 21." *Novum Testamentum* 4 (1960): 174-81.

Roth, Wolfgang. "Scriptural Coding in the Fourth Gospel." *Biblical Research* 32 (1987): 6-29.

Sahlin, Harald. *Zur Typologie des Johannesevangeliums*. Uppsala universitetsarskrift, Bd. 1950/4. Uppsala: Lundequistska Bokhandeln, 1950.

Saito, Tadashi. *Die Mosevorstellung im Neuen Testament*. Europäische Hochschulschriften, 23. Reihe, Theologie, Bd.100. Bern: Peter Lang, 1977.

Saldarini, Anthony. *Jesus and Passover*. New York: Paulist, 1984.

Sandelin, Karl-Gustav. *Wisdom as Nourisher: A Study of an Old Testament Theme, Its Development within Early Judaism and Its Impact on Early Christianity*. Acta Academiae Aboensis, Ser. A, Humaniora, vol. 64, nr. 3. Åbo: Åbo Akademi, 1987.

Sanders, E. P. "Jesus and the Temple." In his *Jesus and Judaism*, 61-76. Philadelphia: Fortress, 1985.

Sayers, Dorothy L. *The Man Born to be King*. New York: Harper, 1943.

Schenke, Ludger. *Die wunderbare Brotvermehrung: Die neutestamentlichen Erzählungen und ihre Bedeutung*. Würzburg: Echter Verlag, 1983.

Schlatter, Adolf. *Der Evangelist Johannes: Wie er spricht, denkt, und glaubt. Ein Kommentar zum vierten Evangelium*. 2d ed. Stuttgart: Calwer Verlag, 1948.

Schnackenburg, Rudolf. *The Gospel according to St. John*. Vol. 1, *Introduction and Commentary on Chapters 1-4*. Translated by K. Smith. Freiburg: Herder, 1968; reprint, New York: Crossroad, 1982. Vol. 2, *Commentary on Chapters 5-12*. Translated by C. Hastings, F. McDonagh, D. Smith, and R. Foley. New York: Search Press, 1979; reprint, New York: Crossroad, 1987. Vol. 3, *Commentary on Chapters 13- 21*. Translated by D. Smith and G. A. Kon. New York: Search Press, 1982; reprint, New York: Crossroad, 1987.

————. *Das Johannesevangelium*. 4. Teil, *Ergänzende Auslegungen und Exkurse*. Herders theologischer Kommentar zum Neuen Testament, Bd. 4. Freiburg: Herder, 1984.

Schoonenberg, P. "A Sapiential Reading of John's Prologue: Some Reflections on Views of Reginald Fuller and James Dunn." *Theology Digest* 33 (1986): 403-21.

Schweizer, Eduard. *Ego Eimi.... Die religionsgeschicht- liche Herkunft und theologische Bedeutung der johanneischen Bildreden, zugleich ein Beitrag zur Quellenfrage des vierten Evangeliums*. Forschungen zur Religion und Literatur des Alten und Neuen Testaments, Bd. 56. Göttingen: Vandenhoeck & Ruprecht, 1939.

Scobie, C. H. H. *John the Baptist*. London: SCM Press, 1964.

Septuaginta: *Vetus Testamentum graece auctoritate Societatis Gottingensis editum*. Göttingen: Vandenhoeck & Ruprecht, 1931-.

Seynaeve, Jaak. "Les citations scripturaires en Jn., 19,36- 37: Une preuve en faveur de la typologie de l'Agneau pascal?" *Revue Africaine de Théologie* 1 (1977): 67- 76.

Sheppard, Gerald T. *Wisdom as a Hermeneutical Construct: A Study in the Sapientializing of the Old Testament*. Beiheft zur Zeitschrift für die alttestamentliche Wissenschaft, Bd. 151. New York: de Gruyter, 1980.

Smend, F. "Die Behandlung alttestamentlicher Zitate als Ausgangspunkt der Quellenscheidung im 4. Evangelium." *Zeitschrift für die neutestamentliche Wissenschaft* 24 (1925): 147-50.

Smith, Dwight Moody. "John 12,12ff. and the Question of John's Use of the Synoptics." *Journal of Biblical Literature* 82 (1963): 58-64.

————. "The Setting and Shape of a Johannine Narrative Source." *Journal of Biblical Literature* 95 (1976): 231-41.

Smits, C. *Oud-Testamentische Citaten in het Nieuwe Testament*. Bd. 2, *Handelingen van de Apostelen Evangelie van Johannes, Apocalyps en Katholieke Brieven*. Collectanea Franciscana Neerlandica, Bd. 8/2. Bois-le-Duc: L. C. G. Malmberg, 1955.

Spicq, Ceslaus. "Le Siracide et la structure littéraire du Prologue de saint Jean." In *Memorial Lagrange: Cinquantenaire de l'école biblique et archéologique française* de Jérusalem (15 novembre 1890 - 15 novembre 1940), 183-95. Paris: Gabalda, 1940.

———. "Τρώγειν: Est-il synonyme de φαγεῖν et d'ἐσθίειν dans le Nouveau Testament?" New Testament Studies 26 (1979/1980): 414-19.

Sproston, Wendy E. "'Is Not This Jesus, the Son of Joseph . . . ?' (John 6.42): Johannine Christology as a Challenge to Faith." Journal for the Study of the New Testament 24 (1985): 77-97.

———. "'The Scripture' in John 17:12." In Scripture: Meaning and Method. Essays Presented to Anthony Tyrrell Hanson for His Seventieth Birthday, 24-36. Edited by Barry P. Thompson. Hull: Hull University Press, 1987.

Stendahl, Krister. The School of St. Matthew and Its Use of the Old Testament. Copenhagen, 1954; reprint, Philadelphia: Fortress, 1968.

Summers, Ray. Behold the Lamb: An Exposition of the Theological Themes in the Gospel of John. Nashville: Broadman, 1979.

Sundberg, A. C. Jr. "On Testimonies." Novum Testamentum 3 (1959): 268-81.

Temple, William. Readings in St. John's Gospel. London: Macmillan, 1939.

Theological Dictionary of the New Testament. Edited by Gerhard Kittel and Gerhard Friedrich. 10 vols. Grand Rapids: Eerdmans, 1987-1990. s.v. "ὁδός," by Wilhelm Michaelis. 5:42-96. s.v. "ἐκκεντέω," by Heinrich Schlier. 2:446-47.

Tomson, P. J. "The Names Israel and Jew in Ancient Judaism and in the New Testament." Bijdragen 47 (1986): 12- 40, 266-89.

Tov, Emanuel. "The Septuagint." In Mikra: Text, Translation, Reading and Interpretation of the Hebrew Bible in Ancient Judaism and Early Christianity, 161- 88. Compendia Rerum Iudaicarum ad Novum Testamentum, section 2, The Literature of the Jewish People in the Period of the Second Temple and the Talmud, vol. 1. Philadelphia: Fortress, 1988.

Toy, Crawford H. Quotations in the New Testament. New York: Scribners, 1884.

Trocmé, Etienne. "L'expulsion des marchands du Temple (Mt 21:12-17)." New Testament Studies 15 (1968/1969): 1- 22.

Tsuchido, Kiyoshi. "Tradition and Redaction in John 12.1- 43." New Testament Studies 30 (1984): 609-19.

Turner, Max. "Atonement and the Death of Jesus in John– Some Questions to Bultmann and Forestell." Evangelical Quarterly 62 (1990): 99-122.

Tyler, Ronald L. "The Source and Function of Isaiah 6:9-10 in John 12.40." In Johannine Studies: Essays in Honor of Frank Pack, 205-20. Edited by James E. Priest. Malibu, Ca.: Pepperdine University Press, 1989.

Visser't Hooft, W. A. "Triumphalism in the Gospels." Scottish Journal of Theology 38 (1985): 491-504.

Voelz, James W. "The Discourse on the Bread of Life in John 6: Is It Eucharistic?" Concordia Journal 15 (1989): 29-37.

———. "The Language of the New Testament." In Aufstieg und Niedergang der römischen Welt: Geschichte und kultur Roms im Spiegel der neueren Forschung, 2.

Principat, Bd. 25/2, 893-977. Herausgegeben von Wolfgang Haase. New York: de Gruyter, 1984.

Waard, J. de. *A Comparative Study of the Old Testament in the Dead Sea Scrolls and in the New Testament*. Studies on the Texts of the Desert of Judah, vol. 4. Leiden: E. J. Brill, 1965.

Wagner, Josef. *Auferstehung und Leben: Joh 11,1-12,19 als Spiegel johanneischer Redaktions- und Theologie- geschichte*. Biblische Untersuchungen, Bd. 19 Regensburg: Verlag Friedrich Pustet, 1988.

Wahlde, Urban C. von. "Faith and Works in Jn VI 28-29. Exegesis or Eisegesis?" *Novum Testamentum* 22 (1980): 304-15.

———. "The Johannine 'Jews:' A Critical Survey." *New Testament Studies* 28 (1982): 33-60.

———. "Literary Structure and Theological Argument in Three Discourses with the Jews in the Fourth Gospel." *Journal of Biblical Literature* 103 (1984): 575-84.

Walton, M. *Witness in Biblical Scholarship: A Survey of Recent Studies 1956-1980*. Interuniversitair Instituut voor Missiologie en Oecumenica, Bd. 15. Leiden: IIMO, 1986.

Weinrich, William C. *Spirit and Martyrdom: A Study of the Work of the Holy Spirit in Contexts of Persecution and Martyrdom in the New Testament and Early Christian Literature*. Washington, D.C.: University Press, 1981.

Weiss, Herold. "Footwashing in the Johannine Community." *Novum Testamentum* 21 (1979): 298-325.

Westcott, B. F. *The Gospel according to St. John: The Authorized Version with Introduction and Notes*. London, 1880; reprint, Grand Rapids: Eerdmans, 1981.

Whale, Peter. "The Lamb of John: Some Myths About the Vocabulary of the Johannine Literature." *Journal of Biblical Literature* 106 (1987): 289-95.

Wieser, Thomas. "The Way of Life." *Ecumenical Review* 34 (1982): 221-27.

Wilcox, Max. "The Composition of John 13:21-30." In *Neotestimentica et Semitica: Studies in Honour of Matthew Black*, 143-56. Edited by E. Earle Ellis and Max Wilcox. Edinburgh: T. & T. Clark, 1969.

———. "Text form." In *It is Written: Scripture Citing Scripture. Essays in Honour of Barnabas Lindars*, 193- 204. Edited by D. A. Carson and H. G. M. Williamson. Cambridge: Cambridge University Press, 1988.

Willett, Michael E. "Wisdom Christology in the Fourth Gospel." Ph.D. diss., Southern Baptist Theological Seminary, 1985.

Williams, Ronald J. *Hebrew Syntax: An Outline*. 2d ed. Toronto: University of Toronto Press, 1976.

Wink, Walter. *John the Baptist in the Gospel Tradition*. Society for New Testament Studies Monograph Series, vol. 7. London: Cambridge University Press, 1968.

Witherington, Ben III. "The Waters of Birth: John 3.5 and 1 John 5.6-8." *New Testament Studies* 35 (1989): 155-60.

Wyller, Egil A. "In Solomon's Porch: A Henological Analysis of the Architectonic of the Fourth Gospel." *Studia theologica* 42 (1988): 151-67.

Zeller, Dieter. "Elijah und Elischa im Frühjudentum." *Bibel und Kirche* 41 (1986): 154-60.